MANAGEMENT POLICIES
FOR COMMERCIAL BANKS

PRENTICE-HALL INTERNATIONAL, INC.
London · Tokyo · Sydney · Paris
PRENTICE-HALL OF CANADA, LTD.
PRENTICE-HALL DE MEXICO, S.A.

MANAGEMENT POLICIES
FOR COMMERCIAL BANKS

Howard D. Crosse
Vice-President
Federal Reserve Bank of New York

PRENTICE-HALL, INC.
ENGLEWOOD CLIFFS, N. J.

© 1962

PRENTICE-HALL, INC.

ENGLEWOOD CLIFFS, N. J.

*HG
1601
.C774*

Current printing (last digit):

12 11 10 9 8 7 6 5 4 3

LIBRARY OF CONGRESS
CATALOG CARD No. 62–16654

PRINTED IN THE UNITED STATES OF AMERICA

54899—C

FOREWORD

Management Policies For Commercial Banks by Howard D.
Crosse, Vice President of the Federal Reserve Bank of New York,
meets a long-felt need of the commercial banker as well as the
teacher and student of banking. A great merit of the book is that it
brings together in one volume a large number of topics which are
usually treated in separate works. Its value is enhanced by the fact
that the author has a thorough theoretical background combined
with practical knowledge based on years of experience.

The book deals not only with practical problems of great interest
to the banker, but also with broader questions, such as commercial
bank functions, the banking structure, and the relation of the bank
to the community. Some chapters are of particular current interest
at a time when the banks have to adjust themselves to changed
conditions, notably the rapid increase in time and savings deposits.

Chapter V, dealing with Earnings, and Chapters VII and VIII,
dealing with bank liquidity, are of particular importance. Because
of steadily rising costs, all banks are troubled by a profit squeeze
and are seeking ways to overcome it. Liquidity is a long-standing
problem which still confronts many banks. These chapters offer
practical guidance that will help overcome these problems. The
solutions suggested are based on vast experience with all classes
of banks, large as well as small.

Also of great interest is the discussion of capital adequacy, another topic which has received a great deal of attention from
bankers, students of banking, and the supervisory authorities.

It is not often that a busy executive of a Federal Reserve Bank
finds the time to write a book embodying the fruits of years of

study and investigation. *Management Policies For Commercial Banks* is a valuable contribution to the literature on United States banking and will be welcomed by all concerned with this subject.

Marcus Nadler
Professor of Finance
New York University

PREFACE

The management policies of the more than 13,000 commercial banks in the United States are the responsibility of their directors. Relatively few bank directors, however, are professionally trained in banking but, to perform their directorial duties effectively, they should have some knowledge of the basic principles which underlie commercial bank policy formation. At the same time there are thousands of students in banking schools and universities who want to know what makes our uniquely diversified banking system function. Some of these, in time, will themselves become senior bank officers or bank directors.

This book attempts to examine the whole spectrum of commercial bank policy formation and to relate practice to theory in all those various aspects which make each individual bank the unique institution that it is. The early chapters establish a background of understanding of the function of commercial banks, the banking structure, bank organization and banking risks to which specific policies can be meaningfully related. Subsequent chapters develop the formulation of policy in specific areas in such a way as to minimize risk while performing the essential banking functions most effectively. The specific techniques of banking, which are the province of executive management rather than the policymaker, have been covered only to the extent necessary to make their direction meaningful.

Most of the views expressed in this book are derived from the author's thirty years of experience as bank examiner, operating officer, and bank supervisor with the Federal Reserve Bank of New York. They are entirely personal views, however, and in no way reflect any official position of the Federal Reserve System. The form of presentation is derived from the author's experience in presenting similar material to students of banking and to bank directors in various banking schools and seminars and as Lecturer in Banking at the Graduate School of Business, Columbia University, for the past four years.

Acknowledgment is due to Dr. Marcus Nadler of New York University who has been my friend and mentor throughout all my thirty years in banking and without whose prodding this book would not have been written. I am also deeply grateful to Mr. R. B. Wiltse, retired Vice President of the Federal Reserve Bank of New York, whose sound advice and graceful editing have contributed substantially to the book as they did during the ten fruitful years when, as my "boss," he encouraged me to pursue the studies that led to its writing.

Thanks go also to Miss Mae Greene, my patient secretary, and to many other members of the staff of the Bank Examinations Department of the Federal Reserve Bank of New York, who have helped materially with typing, charts, and footnotes, and also to Dr. William H. Baughn, Dean of the College of Business and Public Administration, University of Missouri, who read the manuscript. Special acknowledgment is due my artist-wife who designed the book's jacket.

H.D.C.

CONTENTS

I

COMMERCIAL BANKING FUNCTIONS

INTRODUCTION

A clear and concise understanding of the role of commercial banking in the economy is obviously a prime prerequisite for the formulation of bank policy.   Often the banker's concept of that role shapes the nature and character of his bank.   The deposit-minded banker may overstress conservatism and liquidity; the loan-minded banker may underemphasize safety.   These attitudes often reflect the nature of the locality in which a bank operates; conservatism is frequently the mark of the stable, long-settled comunity, whereas more aggressive banking is found where growth is rapid and the need for credit greatest.

Actually, commercial banks perform a number of interrelated functions, all of which are vital and form a part of a balanced view of banking policy.   Commercial banks bring into being the most important ingredient of the money supply—demand deposits— through the creation of credit in the form of loans and investments. Banks are the custodians of the community's money as well as the suppliers of its liquidity.   For those bank customers who seldom borrow, the depository function may be the most important.   Commercial banks also provide flexibility and mobility to the money supply by maintaining the interchangeability of currency and bank deposits, and by providing the mechanism through which money payments can be most speedily and efficiently carried out.   Commercial banks participate with other institutions in the process of accumulating and investing real savings and perform a number of other incidental functions.

1

As creators and custodians of the money supply the concern of commercial banks with the liquidity of the economy is of course fundamental.

CREDIT CREATION

It is the ability of the comercial banks to create money in the form of demand deposits by making loans and investments that distinguishes them from all other financial institutions.[1] This is a seeming magic which is often difficult for the layman to understand and which occasionally even baffles bankers. For the individual bank, as contrasted with the banking system as a whole, cannot expect that the deposits it creates will remain with it. The money it can lend and invest is, at any moment, its excess of cash and bank balances over required reserves and minimum cash requirements. The individual bank must stand ready to pay out the deposits it creates when it makes new loans and to pay for the securities it buys upon delivery.

In practice, out of the vast aggregate of financial transactions the individual bank gains and loses funds in the course of each day's business. From its net gains it can increase its loans and investments; if it has net losses it must collect loans or sell investments. As one of the theoretical aggregate of "all banks" it competes for its share of the deposits which the banking system as a whole may create when additional reserves are supplied by the Federal Reserve System.

A bank does not create credit [2] in a vacuum; it creates it in order to supply the funds that are needed by the community it serves and the nation of which it is a part. Bank loans and investments

---

[1] For a complete explanation of deposit creation, see *The Federal Reserve System; Its Purposes and Functions*, Board of Governors of the Federal Reserve System (Washington, D. C., 1947), chap. II.

[2] Chapin and Hassett define credit as "the measure of the ability of an individual or a business enterprise or government authority to obtain present values (money, goods, or services) while deferring payment, usually in the form of money, to a definite future time." The creation of credit by a commercial bank is the other side of this coin. It is the recognition of the borrower's credit-worthiness and need. Albert F. Chapin and George E. Hassett, Jr., *Credit and Collection Principles and Practice* (7th ed.; New York: McGraw-Hill Book Company, Inc., 1960), p. 4.

may finance production, distribution, investment, consumption and the needs of government. Credit enables goods to move through the channels of trade, young couples to acquire homes, factories to be built, workers to buy automobiles, the nation to finance its defense, and many other useful or profitable purposes. Without credit, business as we know it would be almost impossibly impeded and our level of living would never have been attained.

Bank credit supplies money where it is needed and when it is needed, and the repayment of bank credit removes money from circulation when the specific need for it has passed. When the economist speaks of a "balanced" economy he envisions an over-all balance between production and consumption. With respect to both the businessman and the individual, however, such a balance usually involves a time lag. The farmer puts six months' effort and investment of seed and fertilizer into a crop before he can harvest and sell it. The manufacturer must assemble, pay for, and put to use plant, materials, and labor before he can produce a saleable product. The individual who wants to buy a car or who must meet unexpected medical expenses may not have the money on hand, but is able to make his purchase or pay his bills out of future income. In supplying credit to farmers, manufacturers, and individuals, the commercial bank bridges the time lag between production and consumption and thus helps to bring the financial affairs of the economy into balance.

This is another way of saying that commercial banks supply liquidity to the economy. Through their ability to lend and invest they can provide money immediately in consideration of assets or efforts which have a future money value. This is not to say that they convert assets into money—a common fallacy; a sound extension of credit is one that will be repaid in the normal course of business from the liquidation of the transaction financed, or from income generated by it or otherwise normally available to the borrower. Sound bank credit, as will be elaborated upon in a later discussion of lending policy, is temporary; it calls for repayment, not forced liquidation.

The granting of credit takes many specialized forms. In larger banks separate departments are generally established to specialize in certain forms of lending. The foreign departments of some large banks, for example, are almost separate institutions in themselves.

In smaller banks, farm lending, or consumer credit is frequently departmentalized.

THE DEPOSITORY FUNCTION

It is easy to say, as the layman does, that a bank "is a place to keep your money." So it is, but to put it thus is an oversimplification. Commercial banks hold different kinds of deposits and hold them in a variety of forms. There are also other places to "keep your money," ranging from the cookie jar to a mutual investment fund.

The most useful way of examining the depository function of the commercial banking system is to look at the purposes for which money is deposited. Again the layman's concept is likely to be misleading; "for convenience" he says, or "for safety." These are partial truths which shed but little light on the functional role of banks as depositories.

Demand deposits in commercial banks constitute the major portion of the money supply.[3] A primary function of money is its use as a means of payment. Consequently, one of the most important reasons for becoming a bank depositor is to use the payment facilities of the commercial banking system. Demand deposits also frequently consist of funds kept with a bank to support credit requirements or to compensate the bank for a wide variety of banking services. All such funds can be designated collectively as "working balances." Whether held by individuals or corporations, they are funds needed in the transaction of daily business and cannot even be temporarily invested. They are funds which must be kept in the most liquid of all forms—money.

Money has another primary function; that of providing a reservoir of purchasing power for the future. It shares this attribute with a number of other assets which can normally be readily exchanged for money at short notice and with minimum risk of loss. Such assets include short-term government securities, commercial paper, bankers acceptances, and, for individuals, funds held (generally in

---

[3] Usually defined as currency outside banks plus demand deposits adjusted (Federal Reserve Bulletins). The volume of demand deposits, however, is not an accurate measure of their importance as money because of their relatively rapid turnover (velocity).

fairly substantial amounts) in the form of savings deposits or savings and loan share accounts. Such assets are held for reasons of liquidity (known or anticipated future expenditures) and, in contrast with working balances and real savings, may be designated as investment funds or liquidity reserves. Such funds generally seek the highest available interest return consistent with ready or specific availability at minimum risk.

Finally, funds may be deposited in commercial banks for true savings purposes. Such funds are generally accumulated by individuals over relatively long periods of time for nonspecific purposes such as the proverbial "rainy day," retirement, or unknown personal emergencies. These funds have greater stability than "investment funds," and the latter, in turn, are less volatile than "working balances." True savings are more likely to be deposited in banks for the sake of convenience than for the sake of interest return and are therefore less sensitive to interest rate differentials between different savings media and savings institutions.

It is important to recognize that form does not necessarily follow function in bank deposits. A considerable number of depositors still keep their liquidity reserves, and, in the case of individuals, even their savings, in the form of idle demand deposits. The former reluctance of New York City banks to accept time deposits from domestic corporations, for example, stemmed from their appraisal of the degree to which such corporations still kept a portion of their liquidity reserves in non-interest-bearing demand deposits. Conversely, some individuals may try to keep their working balances in savings accounts, although commercial banks discourage this practice because it results in abnormally high, and costly account activity.

Essentially, demand deposits are likely to represent working balances; time deposits (other than savings deposits) [4] usually consist of the liquidity reserves of corporations, including municipalities and foreign banks, and of individuals when banks offer higher rates

---

[4] *Regulation Q of the Board of Governors of the Federal Reserve System* distinguishes between "time certificates of deposit" with fixed maturity and "time deposits open account" subject to stated notice of withdrawal. It provides further that "savings deposits" may be held only for individuals and certain nonprofit organizations engaged in charitable, educational and similar activities.

on longer-term certificates of deposit. Savings deposits are likely
to represent an admixture of true savings and of the investment
funds or liquidity reserves of individuals.

Because commercial banks are the primary source of commercial
and industrial loans, and because they operate the payments, or
check collection system, they have little competition for the deposits
that represent purely working balances. This is the bread-and-
butter business of the commercial banking system. For investment
funds and savings deposits the competition is very keen [5] and has
grown keener with the postwar rise in the level of interest rates.
This fact has vital implications for bank policy and practice.

When banks could pay interest on demand deposits [6] it was customary for corporations and others to keep their liquidity reserves
as well as their working balances in the form of demand deposits,
although, in 1928 and 1929 when market rates reached abnormally
high levels, large amounts of such funds were placed, through the
banks, in the "call loan" market. During the long depression of
the 1930s, through the Second World War, interest rates were kept
so low that it did not pay depositors to transfer their liquidity reserves from demand deposits to other short-term investment media.
This was a period of very high bank liquidity. When short-term
interest rates began to rise after 1947 the cost of money, and therefore the cost of keeping money idle, rose commensurately. As a
result, both individuals and corporations tended to convert that portion of their demand deposits which they did not need for working
balance purposes into earning assets. The holding of such assets
has risen steadily since, imposing an increasing squeeze on bank
liquidity. Between 1946 and 1958, while the money supply was
increasing by just under 20 per cent, holdings of other liquid assets
increased by 78 per cent.[7] The impact of this drastic shift of liquid

---

[5] *Cf.* Jules I. Bogen, *The Competitive Position of Commercial Banks,* New
York University, Graduate School of Business Administration, Banking Research
Study.

[6] The payment of interest on demand deposits was prohibited by the Banking
Act of 1933.

[7] John G. Gurley "Liquidity and Financial Institutions in the Postwar Period,"
Joint Economic Committee; in *Employment, Growth and Price Levels, Study
Paper No. 14,* 86th Cong. 1st sess., 1960. (Washington, D.C.: Government
Printing Office, 1960), p. 5.

assets from the banking system to the nonbanking sector of the economy will be discussed later. Its effect has been to reduce the volume of deposits in the banking system and to make the remaining balances more volatile.

THE PAYMENTS MECHANISM

The commercial banking system not only creates the principal means of payment (demand deposits) and serves as the custodian of this supply of money, but it provides the means by which payments can be simply and expeditiously made. This is the collection system through which checks, primarily, but also notes, drafts, coupons, and money transfers by letter and telegraph are made each day in tremendous and ever-increasing volume. It has been estimated that over 90 per cent of the payments made in the economy each year are made by check.[8]

Checks serve as money, although they are not legal tender, because they can be collected quickly and cheaply through the banking system. The collection of checks and other forms of payment orders is largely a routine banking function. The law with respect to negotiable instruments has been well standardized and the procedures of collection, as almost uniformly followed, are set forth in detail in the regulations of the Federal Reserve System. Nevertheless, if one includes the payment and receipt of funds through the teller's "window," more man-days are spent by banks in the performance of the collection function than in any other. Available figures indicate that a third of bank operating costs, exclusive of interest paid, are the direct costs of their teller-transit-bookeeping operations.

From the viewpoint of bank policy, the operation of the collection system is primarily a service function. While banks may not pay interest on demand deposits, the Board of Governors of the Federal Reserve System, in administering the law, has taken the position generally that the failure to charge is not a payment. As a result banks have competed for demand deposits on the basis of

---

[8] *Report of the Joint Committee on Check Collection System.* (A study group established by the Federal Reserve System, The American Bankers Association, and the Association of Reserve City Bankers), June 15, 1954, p. 1.

services which they are willing to render the depositor; mostly in the form of handling his collection problems.[9] Where the size of the deposit is not large enough to support the related collection activity, banks generally impose service charges. If these charges are adequate, the operation of the collection function can be a source of additional income to the bank.

SAVINGS ACCUMULATION AND INVESTMENT

A function which the comercial bank shares with a number of other financial institutions is that of accumulating and investing savings funds. The savings process takes place when a holder of money elects to defer its spending for current consumption to some definite or indefinite future date. The saver exchanges his money for a claim on money subject to varying, but specific conditions. The liquidity of these claims on money range from savings deposits and savings and loan share accounts which are payable virtually on demand, under normal circumstances, through securities of various maturities, to equities with no fixed payment date, the "liquidity" of which depends upon their marketability.

Through the savings process purchasing-power is diverted from current consumption into the market for capital goods. As savings are invested in plant and equipment, in homes, or, through Government, in schools and roads and exploration of space, the productive capacity and therefore the real wealth of the economy is increased. In this vital process commercial banks play two roles; they themselves help to channel savings into productive uses and, through their short-term lending, they supplement or provide liquidity to other savings institutions and investment media.

The holding of savings deposits is not essential to the operation of a commercial bank. In fact, there are a few commercial banks that do not accept such deposits. It was because many commercial banks especially in large cities were not interested in "thrift deposits" that the mutual savings banks were originally organized as a kind of eleemosynary institution.

---

[9] One of the most recently developed services of this character is the so-called "locked-box" system in which the bank's depositor arranges for his customers' remittances to be mailed to a post office box under the bank's control. The bank collects the checks and accounts to its depositors for the accompanying bills or invoices.

While not essential, time and savings deposits have long been an important part of commercial banking. From the viewpoint of the individual bank both demand and time deposits bring in funds (reserves) which are equally available for lending and investing. In many small communities the local bank could not take care of the community's credit needs without the availability of savings funds.[10]

In 1913 the Federal Reserve Act recognized savings deposits only as a variety of time deposits for reserve purposes. It was not until 1927 that national banks were empowered to invest in residential mortgages of more than one year's maturity, and the holdings of such mortgages were directly related to the aggregate of their savings deposits. In 1926 the House Committee on Banking and Currency had found that "National banks have on deposit about $5 billion of savings deposits from 11,000,000 depositors."[11] And with varied success commercial banks have been in the savings deposit business ever since. In recent years time deposits of all insured commercial banks accounted for about one-third of all deposits, which is about the same percentage as they held in 1926. Savings deposits have not until recently been regularly separated from the total of "time deposits" in reported figures. In September 1961 they accounted for 76 per cent of the total of time deposits.[12]

TRUST SERVICES

The fiduciary field is a specialized function not directly related to ordinary commercial banking operations. Commercial bank trust departments, nevertheless, are by far the most important group of corporate fiduciaries in the country. Trust business is generally handled by a specialized and separate staff (except in the smaller banks) and the operations of the trust department are subject to a separate body of law and tradition.

Trust business, nevertheless, is an important adjunct to the activities of many of the country's larger commercial banks. As of a recent date it was estimated that there were 3,100 banks exercising

---

[10] Marcus Nadler, *The Banking Situation in New York State.* Study prepared for New York Bankers Association (1956), p. 287.

[11] House Report No. 83, 69th Cong., 1st sess., 1926, p. 6.

[12] Board of Governors of the Federal Reserve System, *Summary Report*, No. 161, Sept. 27, 1961, p. 3.

trust powers in the United States. These banks held in personal trust accounts assets estimated to aggregate in excess of $49 billion.[13] Because of wide differences in accounting practice, however, book value figures are not a good measure of the relative importance of trust business. A more accurate measure is income from trust activities. For all member banks (including those not exercising trust powers) income from trust activities amounts to about 5 per cent of gross operating income. For the large banks in New York City, where the nation's trust business is concentrated, income from trust departments represents more than 10 per cent of gross income.

For most small banks, however, the operation of a trust department is not profitable; such departments are run primarily as an additional service to the community or to enable the bank to offer a complete package of banking services.

OTHER SERVICES

Commercial banks render many miscellaneous services to the public. Some of these are profitable side lines and some are "loss-leaders" motivated by considerations of public relations. Most banks operate safe deposit facilities and hold securities and other valuables in safekeeping for their customers. Many banks act as agent for the collection of utility bills. Nearly all banks provide credit information to their business customers. A recent survey by Dun & Bradstreet [14] indicated that businessmen find the financial guidance and advice they receive from their banks to be one of the most important of banking services.

More recently a few banks have been exploring the possibilities of electronic data-processing equipment with a view to finding additional services which they might economically perform for their customers as well as themselves. Essentially there is little difference between the kind of records that banks keep and the kind of bookkeeping their customers do. The computers which banks will

---

[13] Joseph H. Wolfe, "Report of National Survey of Personal Trust Accounts," *The Trust Bulletin,* Vol. 39, No. 1, (New York: American Bankers Association, Trust Division, September 1959), p. 2.

[14] *Dun's Review and Modern Industry,* Vol. 73, No. 6, June 1959, "Business Men Size Up Their Banks," pp. 175–177.

be using in the future will have the capacity of maintaining not only bank records, but of doing the bookkeeping, billing, and inventory control accounting for their business customers. A few banks are already exploring this field.

A very important aspect of banking service is the form in which traditional bank credit and depository facilities are offered to the public. Whatever the virtues or deficiencies of check credit and charge account plans, they represent an effort on the part of banks to tailor their traditional credit-granting and depository functions to the needs or desires of their customers. Christmas clubs, special checking accounts, and bank money orders, similarly are new forms for old functions, adaptations, if one will, to the changing economic and social scene.

A prominent banker has called the miscellaneous services which banks render to their customers "the greatest give-away-program in history." It does not need to be so. Under the pressure of competition banks have provided services of all kinds in lieu of interest payments to attract and hold deposits. At some point banks will have to re-examine the cost of these services more closely and develop a market for them at fair prices.

All too often one hears the public relations officer of a bank make the statement that "all we have to sell is service." Actually what banks have to sell is credit, which is another name for liquidity or purchasing power. Service is not a product but a price; the cost of a bank's deposits which are, in turn, the raw material of its credit-creating business. Where services are truly sold, they are an adjunct to the true banking function.

II

THE BANKING STRUCTURE

INTRODUCTION

The concept of structure is often used in a static and formal sense as of building blocks placed one upon the other. More recently physicists have used the word to describe the dynamic relationship that exists between forces held together in some meaningful relationship, as one speaks of the structure of matter.[1]

In much the same manner the banking structure is more than the aggregate of banking institutions; it encompasses the forces of law and tradition that constitute the dynamic framework within which banking institutions function to provide the banking services required by the community. The banking structure includes the legal and historical development of the "dual banking system" of state and Federally chartered banks. It encompasses the "correspondent" relationships that have enabled banks to work together in ways in which the thousands of small local banks can serve their communities to a degree far beyond their individual powers. And finally, involved in the banking structure are the diverse ways in which banks themselves are organized as "unit" banks, branch banks, or as members of group banking organizations. These institutional forms and legal relationships have developed over the years in response to the changing needs of the economy, both national and re-

---

[1] "Scientists today picture the basic building block of the universe, the proton, as a mere bundle of forces." Robert Hofstadter, Report to the tenth international High Energy Physics Conference, University of Rochester, August 29, 1960. (Reported in the New York *Herald Tribune*, August 30, 1960).

gional, and in response to public attitudes reflected in political views which have sometimes been more emotional than logical.

In the broadest sense the banking structure encompasses the whole complex of financial intermediaries through which the liquid funds and savings of the public are channelled into the loans and investments that supply the credit base to the economy. This discussion, however, will be confined to a narrower concept; the structure of the commercial banking system. This structure is still in transition. Recent years have seen important new Federal legislation regulating bank holding companies and bank mergers. Two states, Missouri and Illinois, have had public referenda on the question of expanding branch banking, and in New York the legislature only recently enacted legislation redefining State policy and authorizing the formation of holding companies and some further branch powers under close supervision.

THE DUAL BANKING SYSTEM

A unique aspect of banking in the United States is the existence, side by side, of banks chartered by the Federal government and by the fifty states as well. The result, at first glance, is a seeming maze of banking law and tradition that is baffling indeed to the foreign visitor even if he comes from no farther away than neighboring Canada. The dual nature of American banking springs from the still unresolved conflict between Federal power and States' rights but, almost coincidentally, it results in a flexibility of the banking structure that has, on balance, helped promote a healthy adaptation to an expanding economy.

Historical Development. The first bank organized in the newly independent United States perfectly exemplified the "dual" banking concept. The Bank of North America was chartered by the Continental Congress in 1781 and was subsequently chartered by the Commonwealth of Pennsylvania as well. Secretary Alexander Hamilton found the dual nature of this bank to be an "ambiguous situation" [2] and reason enough to go forward with his cherished plan for a purely national bank, the Bank of the United States.

---

[2] "Report on a National Bank," December 13, 1790, in *Papers on Public Credit, Commerce and Finance,* ed. Samuel McKee, Jr. (New York: Columbia University Press, 1934).

State banking, however, remained virtually the sole form of banking until the Civil War. Both the first and second Banks of the United States foundered on the rocks of political opposition while state banking flourished. By 1834 there were 506 state banks, and in 1861, just before the advent of the National Banking System, there were 1,601.[3] It was not until the passage of the National Bank Act in 1863 that the dual banking system was finally and firmly established.

National chartering and supervision of banking was undertaken as a reform measure to correct the abuses of the note-issue privilege [4] which had persistently cropped up in state-chartered banking.[5] From the beginning of the National Banking System there has been a struggle, sometimes tacit and sometimes overt, between state-chartered banks and those chartered by the Federal government. While ostensibly a contest between states' rights and Federal power, it was often beneath the surface a struggle between plentiful money and easy credit on the one hand, and sound money and strictly supervised banking on the other. The tax on state bank notes, imposed by the Congress in 1866, nearly put the state banks out of business but the growth of deposit banking, in combination with more liberal state laws on the organization and operation of new banks, brought state banking back into prominence at the close of the nineteenth century. State-chartered banks today hold 85 per cent as many deposits as are held by national banks.

Significance of Dual Banking. The "dual" banking system is actually not as dual as its vociferous adherents [6] would like it to be. Most of the state-chartered banking institutions have come under Federal supervision of one kind or another. With the establishment of the Federal Reserve System in 1913, those state-chartered banks which became members of the System subjected themselvs volun-

---

[3] Comptroller of the Currency, *Annual Report for 1876* (Washington, D.C., December 2, 1876), p. 159.

[4] The privilege of issuing bank notes—a form of currency which often depreciated sharply in value.

[5] The need to develop a market for United States government securities contributed to the timing of this essentially reform legislation.

[6] Recent banking legislation in New York (Chapter 237 of the Laws of 1960) makes preservation of the dual banking system a matter of State policy. Like motherhood, dual banking is a concept to which all bank orators give abundant lip service. *Cf.* Proceedings National Association of Supervisors of State Banks, any year.

tarily to such supervision and to many of the legal restrictions imposed by the law on national banks. Most of the large state banks, particularly those in the principal financial centers, chose to become member banks. With the advent of the Federal Deposit Insurance Corporation in 1935 most of the remaining state-chartered banks accepted Federal supervision as a condition of deposit insurance. There remain in the country about 300 nonmember, noninsured banks of deposit with assets aggregating less than $2 billion not subject to Federal supervision.

The chief virtue of the dual banking system lies in its flexibility. While the diversity of banking law may seem confusing, uniformity often tends to foster rigidity. Banks which find the laws of one system or of one Federal supervisory authority too restrictive, or find one kind of supervision too arbitrary may change to another jurisdiction.[7]

The danger of the dual system lies in what might be called the "Gresham's Law" of bank supervision: the danger that excessively liberal state bank supervision may drive out or undermine strong supervision. Some evidence of this tendency can be found in the progressive liberalization of the national banking laws to permit national banks to "compete" more effectively with state-chartered banks. On the whole, the "competition" between the state- and Federally-chartered systems in recent years has encouraged adaptation to changing circumstances and has not degenerated into competition in looseness of supervision.

The ability of banks to convert readily from state to Federal charter and vice versa is, in the last analysis, a guarantee against arbitrary or unimaginative supervision. Even more important is the freedom of choice between various Federal bank supervisory agencies.[8] An insured commercial bank may be a national bank, a member state bank of the Federal Reserve System or a nonmember state bank subject to the supervision of the Federal Deposit

---

[7] Between 1945 and 1952 nine member banks in the Second Federal Reserve District alone left the system to establish out-of-town branches not permitted to member banks with capital under $500 million. This wholesale exodus contributed to the liberalization of the national banking law in 1952.

[8] In the 1930s the author examined several national banks in the process of their conversion to state member banks as the direct result of what they considered supervisory "persecution." Findings bore out the banks' contention that the classification of assets was unwarrantedly severe.

Insurance Corporation. There is little difference in the rules between national and state member banks. As between member and nonmember banks, however, the difference is substantial. The legal reserve requirements of the Federal Reserve System are more stringent than those of most of the states with the result that member banks must keep a larger proportion of their assets uninvested than do nonmember banks. The potential earnings on these uninvested assets represents the theoretical "cost " of membership.

In a dual banking system membership in the Federal Reserve System is a voluntary choice of bank management. The cost of membership is partially offset by certain free services, principally the use of the system's collection facilities, the discount privilege, and a degree of prestige, but in most cases membership is undertaken or maintained primarily in at least tacit recognition of the fact that the banking system could not function without a central bank and that membership in that central bank is a civic obligation rather than a money-making proposition. Member banks today control nearly 85 per cent of the total deposits held by insured banks.

CORRESPONDENT BANKING

Before the existence of the Federal Reserve System many of its functions were performed for the smaller banks by the larger banks in the principal financial centers. This earliest form of banking organization still vigorously survives. It is the system of correspondent banking. Without such a form of organization the thousands of unit banks could not have served the credit needs of a rapidly expanding economy.

The correspondent banking system is an entirely informal arrangement whereby the small banks in towns and villages maintain deposit balances with larger banks in nearby cities and look to them for a wide variety of services and assistance. The city banks, in turn, keep correspondent balances with the still larger banks in the principal money centers. Before the establishment of the Federal Reserve System, checks were collected entirely through this network of correspondent banks (often by devious and roundabout routing) and, more importantly, the correspondent system served as a means of mobilizing the supply of credit and channelling it to areas where and when it was needed. Thus correspondent banks provided liquidity and credit fluidity to a diverse economy. Country banks could deposit their idle funds with their correspondents which invested them in money-market loans (theoretically at least) and then, at times of peak demand for seasonal agricultural credit, the country banks would not only draw down their balances but borrow from their correspondents as well. The inadequacies of these arrangements, which did not include a central bank, were evident in recurring panics and finally led to the establishment of the Federal Reserve System. Nevertheless, without correspondent relationships, the credit needs of the country could hardly have been met at all.

Correspondent banks are still active in the collection of checks and still supply credit to the smaller banks in consideration of the balances which the latter maintain. In addition, correspondent banks perform many services which would otherwise be unobtainable by the smaller banks and their customers. They give investment advice, hold customers' securities in safekeeping, arrange for the purchase and sale of securities, provide foreign banking services, trade in Federal funds, participate in loans too large for the small banks to make on their own, give technical advice on operating problems, and help plan new bank buildings.

The larger correspondent banks, nearly all of which are members of the Federal Reserve System, indirectly channel the benefits of that system to those banks which are not members and, at the same time, provide some services even to member banks (such as giving investment advice) which would be inappropriate for the central bank to perform.

Interbank balances are the measure of the importance of correspondent bank activity. They still play an important although reduced role in the liability structures of the commercial banks in the larger money centers.[9]

---

[9] In 1896 correspondent balances represented 10% of total deposits in commercial banks. They rose to 13% in 1913 just before the organization of the Federal Reserve System, then declined gradually to 7.3% in 1928. Today they represent about 7.5% of total bank deposits. In the central reserve city banks of New York and Chicago, however, they account for approximately 13% (excluding foreign bank deposits). (Source: *All Bank Statistics* 1896–1955. Later figures from Federal Reserve Bulletins.)

Correspondent banking, like dual banking, enjoys a measure of emotional as well as logical support.[10]   Correspondent relationships are frequently justified on the grounds of loyalty or appreciation for past services with little or no close analysis by either party of the present-day economics of the relationship.   The large banks, seeking to maintain or enlarge their correspondent balances, have aggressively sought account activity often without regard to careful cost studies.   In so doing they have encouraged some clearly uneconomic practices, such as the centralization of check sorting in the larger centers.[11]   This practice has resulted not only in higher overall costs to the banking system for check collection but in some delay in presentation of items as well.

If a country member bank sends its checks for collection to its correspondent and adequately compensates that correspondent for the work performed, it is, in effect, paying for a service which is available without cost (or at the nominal cost of pre-sorting) from its Federal Reserve Bank.   Despite this fact, less than half of the member banks [12] use the collection facilities of the Reserve Banks directly.

Other correspondent services are more difficult to measure or evaluate.   They are undoubtedly valuable.   Loan participations,[13] business referral, more liberal credit accommodation than may be available from the Federal Reserve Banks in periods of credit restraint, a country bank's own need for liquidity; all of these factors enter into a careful consideration of which correspondents and what size balances a country bank should maintain, and what services can be profitably rendered in consideration thereof by the city

---

[10] *The American Banker* publishes an annual "Correspondent Bank Issue" in which the virtues of correspondent banking are perennially extolled.

[11] Most correspondent banks do not require the simple pre-sorting that is required by the Reserve Banks which eventually process many of the same checks in tremendous volume.   Sorting at the bank of deposit is usually easier and less costly, particularly now that banks of any size have mechanical proving and sorting equipment.

[12] *The Report of the Joint Committee on Check Collection System*, p. 34 indicates that in 1954 only 3,315 of the 6,992 eligible member banks were using any of the check collection facilities of their Federal Reserve Banks.   Only 1,678 were sending all of their items directly to the Reserve Banks.

[13] In recent years this has been a two-way street with country banks purchasing participations in brokers loans and selling participations in their larger commercial and mortgage credits.

banks. Despite the difficulty, competent management should attempt an appraisal of these factors. It is probable that many correspondent relationships are unprofitable to one or both of the participants.

THE BRANCH BANKING CONTROVERSY

Most of the banks in the United States have traditionally been unit banks; single-office institutions serving primarily their local communities. In point of number this is still the situation. As of December 1960, there were 13,480 banks in the United States, of which 11,025 were unit banks. The tide toward multiple-office banking, however, is running strong. The number of branch banking offices has increased from 4,613 in 1948 to 10,605 as of December 1960.[14] This increase has been the result both of the establishment of new branches in growing communities and of the absorption of previously independent banks by merger. The pros and cons of bank mergers and multiple-office banking are in the forefront of bank policy considerations today.

Historical Development. Branch banking has been a controversial subject since the earliest days of the Republic. Alexander Hamilton himself had grave doubts about it. In 1790 he said, "The situation of the United States naturally inspires a wish that the form of the institution [Bank of the United States] could admit of a purality of branches. But various considerations discourage from pursuing the idea." Then, as now, in Hamilton's words, "The complexity of such a plan would be apt to inspire doubts, . . ." [15] Despite these doubts both the first and second Banks of the United States were branch banking institutions.[16]

Early state banks were also branch banks in many instances. There were 406 state banks in 1834 and they operated 100 branches. On the eve of the Civil War there were 170 state bank branches in eleven states. The number of banks, however, had grown to over 1,500, indicating a clear trend toward unit banking.

Opposition to branch banking arose from two directions. Re-

---

[14] Federal Deposit Insurance Corporation, *Annual Report for 1960*, p. 128.

[15] "Report on a National Bank," *op. cit.*

[16] The Second Bank, organized in 1816, had established 19 offices in 14 states by October 1817.

mote branches (as well as remote banks) tended to facilitate some of the worst abuses of the note-issue privilege in the days of wild-cat banking, so that banking reform and early attempts at bank supervision often led to the abolishment of the branch banking privilege.[17] And secondly, the Jacksonian campaign against the Second Bank of the United States and the subsequent Populist campaigns for cheap money were in a real sense directed against the concentration of money power in large eastern banks, some of which were branch institutions. The resultant political furor helped to establish the emotional tone that is still evident in much of the popular and political opposition to branch banking.[18]

When the National Bank Act was passed in 1863 the question of branches was not even discussed. The Federal Reserve Act of 1913 extended the privilege of membership to state banks without prohibiting them from operating existing branches but did not accord to national banks, for which membership was compulsory, the right to establish new branches. Gradually over the years limited branch powers were granted to national banks and subsequently extended until, in 1952, national banks were in effect empowered to establish branches to the same degree as banks chartered by the respective states.

The history of banking in the United States, therefore, starts out with branch banking, swings in the direction of unit banks, and is now quite rapidly swinging back again. Opposition to branch banking, however, is still strong in some areas and state laws with respect to the establishment of branches vary widely. State-wide branching is prevalent in 14 states, limited area branching is prevalent in 16, and unit banking in 18, although, of the latter, 7 states permit very limited branching.[19]

---

[17] In 1844 the New York Legislature passed an act providing that no one should conduct the business of banking except at his place of residence. Similar legislation had previously been enacted in Rhode Island and Massachusetts.

[18] In a recent court case, *Old Kent Bank and Trust Company* vs. *William McC. Martin et al.,* Judge Washington, dissenting, said ". . . There has long been public hostility to the extension, by means of branches, of a bank's geographic area of operation. At one time branch banking was almost uniformly forbidden in the United States. Many persons feared, and still fear that, among other things, unrestrained branch operations would enable a few wealthy urban banks to extend their operations to a point where the independence and prosperity of the poorer banks . . . would be seriously jeopardized."

[19] Federal Deposit Insurance Corporation, *Annual Report for 1960.* Statistics as of Dec. 31, 1958.

A Current Appraisal. Against this background of diversity—this wide disparity in law and tradition—those who are responsible for managing banks must attempt a logical assessment of the virtues and deficiencies of unit banking. The issues are obviously not clear-cut and definitive; else they would long ago have been resolved. Nor is the available evidence, even when objectively weighed, entirely conclusive. It is nevertheless incumbent on bank management and the student of banking to put aside the prejudices of the past and the emotional or sentimental attachments to home-town banking, and appraise the banking structure, actual and prospective, in the light of economic reality and the expanding needs of a complex and dynamic economy.

One thing is clear; where branch banking is permitted by law, it has grown rapidly in recent years. Much of this growth has taken place through the absorption of smaller banks by the larger ones. In the ten years from 1950 through 1959, 1,503 commercial banks in the United States were absorbed in mergers.[20] The trend is even more dramatically illustrated in a state such as New York where branch banking is permitted within extensive "banking districts," each comprising a number of counties. From 1945 to 1960 forty per cent of the banks in New York State were absorbed in mergers.

Reasons for Merger Trend. Most authorities find no single reason for the trend toward merging. The Comptroller of the Currency in 1954 [21] cited seven reasons why the small banks sell out, and five reasons why the large banks seek to acquire others. In condensed form they were:

Reasons for selling:

1. The advancing age of management and failure to provide successor management.
2. Attractive terms (price) well above limited local markets.
3. Desire to provide more effective competition to larger neighboring banks.
4. Failure to keep up with aggressive competition.

---

[20] *Hearings* before Subcommittee No. 2 of the Committee on Banking and Currency of the House of Representatives, 86th Cong., 2d sess., on S. 1062, February 16–18, 1960, pp. 15–16.

[21] Comptroller of the Currency, *Annual Report for 1954* (Washington, D.C.: Government Printing Office, 1955), pp. 9–10.

5. Inability of small banks to meet borrowing needs of their customers.

6. Loss of business through acquisition of local concerns by national industries.

7. Greater fringe benefits and compensation paid to employees by larger banks.

Reasons for acquiring:

1. Need to increase volume of retail business.

2. Need or desire to better service existing business; to follow customers to the suburbs.

3. Desire to expand lending limits.

4. Normal urge to excel in growth.

5. Desire to improve earnings.

The comptroller did not believe that "rising costs and inferior earnings . . . have been a major contributing factor." [22]

An analysis of 208 bank mergers, made in 1955 by Alhadeff and Alhadeff,[23] led to the conclusion that inadequate management was *not* a primary factor, nor was high operating cost. The Alhadeffs make a useful distinction between the "initiating cause" of a merger and its "facilitating causes." Many of the reasons cited by the comptroller would, in these terms, be facilitating causes; the kind which ripen the plum for the picking by more able, aggressive, and expansion-minded bankers. The dynamics of branch expansion, according to the Alhadeffs, can be found in the desire of just such aggressive management to expand its field of operations. They concluded, in short, that expansion through merger and the establishment of additional branches is, in itself, a competitive practice.

However, banking costs have had more to do with the merger trend than were found by either the Alhadeffs or the comptroller. The failure to recognize their importance results from the fact that the costs which bring about bank mergers are not revealed in the statistics because they are prospective costs. Prospective costs are the costs which the small bank faces but has not actually met. They

---

[22] *Annual Report for 1954*, pp. 10–11.

[23] Charlotte P. Alhadeff and David A. Alhadeff, "Recent Bank Mergers," *Quarterly Journal of Economics*, LXIX, No. 4 (November 1955) 503–32.

include the salary cost of a suitable replacement for top management, the cost of fringe benefits that have never actually been provided for the employees, the cost of meeting the competition in savings interest rates, the cost of mechanization and modernization which have never been undertaken. These are costs which a successful bank must pay in a competitive situation if it is to provide the services offered by other banks, but they are costs which dismay the stockholders and directors of many small banks who have not faced up to the obsolescence of their management practices and their physical plant.

An important facilitating factor, which the comptroller touches upon but does not stress, is the failure of bank management in many cases to provide for successor ownership by developing a local market for the bank's stock at a fair price. As Nadler points out:

> At times the management of a smaller bank, which makes the market for its own shares, keeps the market price low, often substantially below actual or stated book value. The rest of the stockholders, dissatisfied with this situation, are naturally eager for a merger in order to obtain a higher price for their stock.[24]

Many small banks do not publish their earnings figures or in any way indicate to their shareholders the true value of their stock. Too often the older directors are reluctant to relinquish their positions and bring in some of the younger businessmen of the community as directors and stockholders. These are aspects of bank management which will be discussed at greater length in later chapters, but they are also contributing factors to the merger trend.

The most important initiating factor affecting the trend of mergers, however, lies deeper than the more superficial facilitating factors usually cited and goes beyond the aggressiveness of expansion-minded management. The merger trend in banking is part and parcel of the economic development of the nation. It is a response to the changing character of the communities which banks serve. The rise in automobile production, improved roads and the resultant mobility of the population, the growth of shopping centers and chain stores, and the merger trend in industry generally have had more to do with bank mergers than most of the banking factors discussed

---

[24] *The Banking Situation in New York State*, p. 56.

above. There is a great deal of evidence that the well-managed small or medium-sized unit bank can still operate successfully; can find successor management and ownership if it tries, but supermarket banking, like supermarket retailing, can give the public a far wider variety of banking services at lower cost.

Banking consolidation has been hampered by traditional attitudes and legislative restrictions, but the very businessmen who champion the small unit bank are beginning to complain of its failure to render them adequate service. Dun and Bradstreet's survey of what businessmen think of their banks indicated that the great dissatisfaction with such services was expressed by the small-town businessman who deals primarily with small banks.[25]

One has but to look at Main Street in any American community to note the change from local merchant to chain store, from small local manufacturer to the branch of a nationally known company to realize that, except where they specialize in serving particular banking needs, small and purely local banks are no longer completely adequate to the needs of expanding American businesses. The state-wide or nation-wide business enterprise is seeking and needs service from larger and more extensive banking organizations. This, however, is not to say that there is not room for the specialty bank which, like the specialty retailer, can cater most effectively to some select clientele.

An Evaluation of Branch Banking. In order to find out what actually happens when small banks are taken over by larger institutions and to evaluate branch banking as objectively as possible, a study was made of three large branch-banking organizations in New York State.[26] This study indicated the following potential advantages of branch banking:

1. It is more efficient to establish a "de novo" branch than to organize a new bank because established banks can absorb the losses incurred in the early years of the new operation and can provide complete customer service upon opening.

2. The expansion and diversification of industry and the population movement to the suburbs require additional banking services and larger credit lines which the limited resources and inexperienced

---

[25] *Dun's Review and Modern Industry, loc. cit.*

[26] Unpublished Study made under the author's supervision in the Bank Examinations Department of the Federal Reserve Bank of New York, 1956. Three "de novo" and eight acquired branches were investigated in detail.

personnel of many small local banks are unable to provide. Branch banks are able to service such accounts and can offer technical and financial advice through especially trained personnel.

3. The lending authority of branch managers can be, and usually is higher than that of the officers of the small unit banks they take over so that branches can provide a faster and more satisfactory loan service to borrowing customers.

4. Credit files are more likely to be complete in the branch banks, providing a sounder basis for making loan commitments and giving sound financial advice. Credit files in unit banks are usually inadequate as to history, operating figures, and other supporting financial data.

5. Branches can be operated more economically than unit banks because of pooled operations, specialization of function, and the more general use of mechanized equipment. Larger and more diversified loan and investment portfolios of branch banks furnish higher gross earnings. As a result, branch banks can usually afford to pay higher interest rates on time deposits.

6. Branch banks, through business development departments, can maintain close personal contacts with customers and thus create and maintain closer and more productive customer relationships. Few small banks regularly visit the customers' places of business.

7. Salaries of branch bank personnel have increased faster than the average for all banks. Higher individual salaries, particularly at the officer level, were offset in the branch banks by reduction in the number of personnel.

8. Branch banking systems usually provide pensions (frequently noncontributory) and have profit-sharing plans, hospitalization insurance, life insurance, reimbursement of tuition fees, and vacations of more than the usual two weeks' duration, whereas fringe benefits are virtually nonexistent in the smaller unit banks.

9. Personnel programs which include job evaluation and merit review are common in branch banks but not in unit banks.

10. Branch banking systems usually improve working conditions by renovating old quarters or by building new buildings when they acquire small banks by merger. Modern kitchen and cafeteria facilities, lounge rooms, soundproofing, and air conditioning are usually included when such renovations are made.

11. The capital stock of branch banking systems has a wider market at a higher price in relation to book value and earnings than the stock of small unit banks for which, frequently, no real market exists.

12. Branch bank organizations can attract new capital more readily because of the wider market for their stock and their ability to engage underwriters and develop a broad market through more effective stockholder relations.

Most of these potential advantages had been realized by the three large branch banking systems covered by this study, especially in comparison with the record of the unit banks which they had absorbed. It is usually the least progressive and least successful of the unit banks that are merged first. The cases studied, of course, represent a very small sampling.[27]

It should be emphasized also that these advantages of the branch banking systems are *potentials* that may not be fully realized in all cases. The successful operation of a branch banking system requires a high degree of management competence, good intra-bank communications, and intelligent cost control, all of which will be considered in later chapters. Suffice it to say here that, in the absence of sound management, branch banking can be self-defeating and subject itself to the criticisms so frequently heard. Among them are the charges that:

1. Branch officers lack flexibility and initiative. They operate solely "by the book."
2. Branches lose close personal contact with the community. Rotation of branch officers, which may be a sound personnel policy for the bank as a whole, results in the branch community doing business with "strangers."
3. Branch officers fail to rely on character and reputation in granting credit. Many local businesses resent filing elaborate credit information that a well-run bank should have in any event, but which small unit banks all too frequently dispense with.

Because of the difficulty which large branch banking organizations have in maintaining the "local touch" even when they serve the local community better than a former independent bank could possibly have done, well-run local banks do not find it excessively difficult to compete effectively for local business with the branches

---

[27] *Cf.* Irving Schweiger and John S. McGee, *Chicago Banking*, The Structure and Performance of Banks and Related Financial Institions in Chicago and Other Areas (Chicago: Graduate School of Business, University of Chicago Press, 1961). This study found that branch banks generally have higher loan-deposit ratios than unit banks, provide broader banking services including relatively more mortgage and consumer credit loans. Even small branch banks averaged a larger ratio of loans to assets than unit banks of much bigger size in comparable communities in the United States.

of larger banks. In a hearing before the Board of Governors of the Federal Reserve System in connection with the application of the First New York Corporation to form a bank holding company the author testified, after study, that the independent national banks in Westchester County which competed directly with branches of the dominant large branch bank in the county had increased their demand deposits in the ten-year period from 1947 through 1956 by 91.7 per cent, while directly competing offices of the large branch bank had increased their demand deposits by only 62.5 per cent. Since demand deposits are directly related to credit accommodation, they may be considered the most accurate single measure of a bank's ability to compete for local commercial banking business. G. Russell Clark, former New York State Superintendent of Banks, stated that studies made by his department and studies made by the Office of the Comptroller of the Currency indicated that the ability of the well-run local bank to compete with branches of larger banks or units of large holding company organizations was evident throughout New York State and the nation.[28]

The touchstone of success in banking, as in other endeavors, is not form or structure, but capable management. Where this is found in small or large banks they are outstandingly successful. In fact the most profitable bank in the Second Federal Reserve District is a unit bank with total resources of approximately $10 million.[29] The larger a bank becomes and the more far-flung its branch operations, the more difficult are its management problems. On the other hand, the larger banks have the resources, if they will, to attract and train a higher caliber of general management and especially trained staff specialists and so to provide a wider range of highly specialized banking services to the public.

GROUP BANKING

Group banking is a generic term used to describe the ownership or substantial control of two or more banks by the same interests. The term chain banking is generally used to designate such organi-

---

[28] Statement before the Joint Legislative Committee to Revise the Banking Law, Albany, New York, February 25, 1960.

[29] This bank had "net operating earnings" more than twice as high as the average for comparable banks, as the result of both higher income and reduced expenditures attributable to excellent management.

zations when the controlling interest is vested in an individual or group of individuals. The term bank holding company has come into general use to designate ownership or control by a corporation.[30] Both chain banking systems and bank holding companies originally came into being partly to circumvent branch banking prohibitions [31] and partly to extend the banking interests of aggressive groups over wide areas particularly in farm communities and the rapidly expanding states of the far west.[32] Chain banking is self-limiting because the large amounts of capital required are today only rarely available to individuals. The corporate form of control offers many advantages and many of the original chains were converted into branch banking or holding companies. Chain banks are of only local importance today.

Nadler and Bogen, in their study of *The Bank Holding Company*,[33] make a further distinction between the holding company which is a corporation or trust holding all or a large part of the capital stock of its commercial bank subsidiaries and the holding company which is, itself, a bank, usually a larger city bank, controlling the stock of other banks in its trade area either directly or through an affiliated company. The difference, however, is more of form than of substance and essentially the same principles apply to the operations of both kinds.

The distinctive feature of the bank holding company [34] lies in its ability to realize many of the benefits and render most of the services that are rendered by wide-spread branch banking organizations, while retaining the decentralization of management that can pre-

---

[30] The Bank Holding Company Act of 1956 defines a bank holding company as any company which owns or controls 25% or more of the voting shares of two or more banks or otherwise controls the election of a majority of their directors.

[31] It is interesting to note, however, that bank holding companies are strongest today in the states that *permit* branch banking.

[32] Board of Governors of the Federal Reserve System, *Banking Studies* (Baltimore: Waverly Press, 1941) p. 126.

[33] Marcus Nadler and Jules I. Bogen, *The Bank Holding Company* (New York: New York University, Graduate School of Business Administration, 1959).

[34] As of December 31, 1960, 47 bank holding companies had registered or been authorized pursuant to the Bank Holding Company Act of 1956. They controlled 426 banks operating 1,463 offices in 31 states. Source: Federal Reserve Bulletin, June 1961, p. 722.

serve the "local touch." Each banking unit of a holding company system is typically managed by a board of directors comprised of local citizens. These local directors retain a substantial measure of autonomy with respect to lending policies and local management problems. Without such a substantial grant of local autonomy the outstanding citizens and business leaders of the various communities could hardly be induced to serve as directors since, in most cases, they hold only a nominal stock interest in the bank or the holding company. Given enough local authority, they will look upon their directorships as a form of public service.

The relationship of the holding company to its subsidiary banks is largely that of an informed and helpful stockholder. Such a role combines many of the functions often rendered to country banks by their city correspondents with provision for effective group action in such fields as accounting, purchase of supplies, or investment analysis. The holding companies have, in short, developed as "staff organizations" [35] for their constituent banks.

Another substantial advantage of the holding company form of organization is that it provides for a certain amount of healthy competition among its units. This provides stimulus for experimentation and can lead to a diversity of approach that is less likely to be found in a branch organization where final management authority stems from one top-management team and a single board of directors.[36]

The holding company form of organization is not, of course, opposed to the branch banking form. Many of the individual units of holding company groups are themselves regional branch banks of substantial size. The holding company form also provides a medium for interstate banking where the state law permits.

---

[35] Nadler and Bogen, *op. cit.*

[36] Within the Marine Midland system, for example, eleven different management groups are working to outdo each other in results, knowing that these results can be, and will be compared on a comparable accounting basis. Furthermore, when a large New York City branch banking organization decided to inaugurate a charge-account credit plan, it had to make the decision for all of its offices. Far less was at stake when, several years earlier a unit of the Marine Midland system began the same experiment while the other units of the holding company group watched from the sidelines to see what its results might be.

DESIRABLE EXTENT OF BRANCH AND HOLDING COMPANY BANKING

Granting the potential advantage of multiple-office banking, the problem that faces bank management and the legislators is that of its appropriate extent. The problem is, in fact, two-fold. It must be considered *extensively, i.e.,* over what areas should multiple-office banking be permitted, and *intensively, i.e.,* to what extent should the traditional competition of many unit banks be eliminated. From the viewpoint of bank management, these questions can be considered in terms of operating efficiency and the ability of the bank to serve its customers effectively. From the viewpoint of public policy, the adequacy of banking competition has become the paramount issue.[37]

Area of Branch Expansion. Extensively, any purely geographical area is bound to be arbitrarily confining.[38] National corporations require nationwide banking services and, to an increasing extent, the larger banks provide such services through travelling officers who call on businesses in all parts of the country. Not even the largest bank, however, is big enough to accommodate alone any of the one hundred largest corporations in the nation. All of these use many banks and most of them use two or more even in New York City.[39]

---

[37] "There is no question that competition is desirable in banking, and that competitive factors should be considered in all aspects of the supervision and regulation of banks." Report of the Committee on Banking and Currency, House of Representatives, 86th Cong., 2d sess., 1960, on S.1062, a *Bill to Regulate Bank Mergers*, p. 3.

[38] In testifying before the Senate Banking and Currency Committee in 1931, Governor Harrison of the Federal Reserve Bank of New York said "There may be very much more reason why you should authorize branches within a hundred miles than within state limits. In the case of New York City, for instance, if you authorize a New York City bank to put a branch in White Plains, New York, and not in Newark, New Jersey, it would not seem a logical distinction to make." *Operations of National and Federal Reserve Banking Systems*, Hearings before a Subcommittee of the Committee on Banking and Currency, 71st Cong., 3rd sess., 1931, pursuant to S. Res. 71 (Washington, D.C.: Government Printing Office, 1931), p. 76.

[39] A survey made in the Bank Examinations Department of the Federal Reserve Bank of New York in 1959 showed that forty large corporations, each representing $1 billion or more of annual sales, in every instance distribute their borrowing over more than one and, in one case, as many as ten of the

It is likely that the larger banks in the major business centers have more in common with each other than they do with the small community banks in the hinterlands of their own states. A nation-wide branch system, composed just of "reserve city" banks [40] and serving the larger national corporations might well be more logical than the union of the city banks with their country cousins. The trend, however, has not been in that direction. Where branch banking is permitted, the city banks have already spread out into their suburban and rural areas or throughout the entire permissible area where regional or statewide branching is authorized. Even the former purely "wholesale" banks in New York City have, in a number of instances, merged with "retail" banks.

The concept of regional banking has long held considerable ap-peal for those who recognize the economic need for and the poten-tial economies of larger banking organizations but who, at the same time, either harbor lingering fears of too much bigness in banking or simply recognize the unfavorable popular and political climate.[41] Regional banking, in effect, represents a compromise between the the unit or purely local bank and its opposite extreme, statewide or even nationwide branch banking. A regional bank presumably can retain the local flavor but is large enough to benefit from the econo-mies of operations and the broadening of services discussed above.

In *The Banking Situation in New York State,* Nadler says:

> The term "regional bank" may be applied to an institution which serves either a trading area or an entire banking district through its main office and a number of branches scattered over the territory in which it operates. A regional bank may be large enough to have customers throughout the entire state and often it seeks national ac-counts throughout the country. Whether a bank may be classified as a regional institution depends not so much on its size as upon the

---

large New York City banks. (*Banking Concentration and Competition in New York City;* Unpublished study prepared under the author's supervision, May 25, 1959).

[40] Reserve City Banks are larger banks located in cities directly served by a Federal Reserve Bank or branch thereof or in a few other cities so designated by the Board of Governors.

[41] In the 1931 Hearings before the Senate Committee on Banking and Cur-rency (*op. cit.,* p. 118), Senator Glass, the Committee Chairman, said, "You see the difficulty is that we have to deal with this much contemned specimen of humanity, called a politician, and there are some in Congress, as well as a large number of statesmen, and we cannot jump right into nationwide branch bank-ing."

territory it serves. . . . A regional institution may be the result of
natural growth through the opening of branches or, what is more
likely, it may be the outgrowth of a number of mergers and absorptions.

Indeed, if regional banking is a step between small-town unit
banking and something else that is not yet palatable to the public
and its representatives in Congress and state legislatures, it rests
with the management and directors of regional banks to see to it
that their branch offices not only operate profitably and efficiently
but that they serve the community effectively and not lose the
"local touch."

Competition in Banking. Public concern with the adequacy of
competition generally is expressed in the anti-trust legislation of
the late nineteenth and early twentieth centuries. The Sherman
Act of 1890 prohibited restraints of trade and made monopolizing
trade a misdemeanor. The difficulties of administering the Sherman
Act led to the passage, in 1914, of the Clayton Antitrust Act, Section
7 of which prohibits acquisitions of stock if the "effect of such acquisition may be substantially to lessen competition, or to tend to
create a monopoly." Until recently the only case involving banks
to come before the courts under the provision of either act was the
attempt of the Board of Governors to prove that Transamerica Corporation, through the acquisition of the stock of banks in a five-state
area, was tending to create a monopoly.[42]

More recently the Department of Justice has invoked both the
Sherman Act and the Clayton Act in suits to prevent bank mergers
or holding company acquisitions approved by the supervisory authorities.[43] Even before these actions, however, supervisory authorities have been guided by their interpretation of the principles of
the Clayton Act in their administration of other laws pertaining to
bank mergers and the establishment of bank branches. They have
taken into consideration the competitive factors and denied applications which they considered to "tend to monopoly." [44]

The uncertainty of this application and the trend to bank mergers

---

[42] *Transamerica Corporation* v. *Board of Governors*; 206 F. 2nd 163 (1953).
[43] *United States of America* v. *Philadelphia National Bank and Girard Trust
Corn Exchange Bank defendants.* Civil action No. 29287 in the U. S. District
Court for Eastern Pennsylvania.
[44] *Old Kent Bank and Trust Company* v. *William McC. Martin et al.* (U. S.
Court of Appeals for the District of Columbia, No. 15244.)

which developed after World War II led to agitation for more specific Federal controls over bank mergers and the formation and expansion of bank holding companies.

After many years of discussion, bank holding company legislation was passed in 1956 and Federal control over mergers of all insured banks was legislated in 1960. Both laws made competition a factor to be considered by the supervisory authority. The Bank Holding Company Act specifies that the Board of Governors of the Federal Reserve System should consider, among other things:

> (5) . . . whether or not the effect of such acquisition, or merger or consolidation would be to expand the size or extent of the bank holding company system involved beyond limits consistent with adequate and sound banking, the public interest, and the preservation of competition in the field of banking.

The Federal Merger Act provides:

> . . . the appropriate supervisory agency shall also take into consideration the effect of the transaction on competition (including any tendency to monopoly), and shall not approve the transaction unless, after considering all of such factors, it finds the transaction to be in the public interest.

Both statutes stress the public interest as the final criterion; a concept not easy to define. For example, in ruling on the application of the First New York Corporation, et al., to form a bank holding company, the Board of Governors of the Federal Reserve System found: [45]

> . . . Thus the question whether the size or extent of the proposed holding company system would be consistent with . . . the public interest must depend largely upon preservation of competition in the field of banking.

Thus the "public interest" is equated with adequacy of competition although the latter has not been specifically defined either by the Congress or the supervisory authorities.

Much of the confusion that results from attempting to apply Federal antitrust standards to bank mergers, or bank holding company act criteria to bank holding company acquisitions derives from the

---

[45] Statement supporting Order of July 10, 1958, Federal Reserve Bulletin, Vol. 44 (1958), p. 912.

fact that the public concept of competition itself is changing. In the classical sense of "perfect competition," it has long since been virtually eliminated from most of our business enterprise. It is disappearing rapidly from banking as well wherever even limited branching is permitted. A large number of small banks may possibly have provided adequate competition in the past. Each had roughly equal competitive power and provided alternative choices of approximately equal facilities because none was equipped to render much more than the rudimentary banking services required by a relatively simple economy.

The classical economist contrasted competition—in the sense described above—with monopoly, as good is contrasted to evil. What has developed, and is still developing, is neither. The emerging banking structure is constituted of a fewer number of relatively larger banks in much keener competition with each other, and with a number of smaller banks as well. The larger banks tend to broaden the scope of their services more and more; the smaller banks tend to specialize in the kinds of business in which they can compete most effectively.

This development is itself the result of competition. An expanding economy, a growing population, the amazing improvements in transportation and communication, the integration of business into large national corporations and their geographical dispersion, have all called for numerous new and improved banking services which the nonspecialized small bank was not, and is not capable of performing adequately.

Banks compete with each other (and with many other financial organiaztions) to render the banking and financial services demanded by all segments of the public. These are many and varied —far more so than in the past. Dozens of banking services common today, from drive-in tellers to account reconciliation, were unheard of forty years ago. The extension of credit is, of course, the basic banking service, but even here the forms and varieties of loan arrangements, from term loan to "boat loan," have multiplied beyond the wildest imagination of a previous generation of commercial bankers. Nor can it be assumed that these developments have come to an end: to serve a dynamic economy the banking structure must remain flexible and must find the resources, primarily of management and organization, to meet even more challenging demands in the future. Only banks which can develop such services will prosper in a competitive banking world.

One cannot stress too often that banking competition is primarily a matter of rendering banking services more effectively than one's competitors. To succeed in doing so attracts depositors whose funds, wisely invested, yield the profits of the banking business. Rate or price competition is rare in banking except in the sense that rate changes by one bank are generally quickly followed by its competitors. The real nub of competition is the ability to attract and satisfy customers, large and small.

Large banking organizations can specialize in many fields: small banks can specialize effectively only in a few. Thus larger size, in itself, has become both a means of competing more effectively by broadening the scope of a bank's ability to render service and a measure of competitive success (sometimes overrated) which tends to attract large customers.

Few informed persons would disagree with this analysis up to a point; the point at which each person feels that size has become overwhelming or that number has become too few.[46] Perhaps our economic and political heritage has led us to look at competition too much as an end in itself, or (in banking) as the means of preventing the evil envisaged as some sort of financial stranglehold on the economy by a concentrated "money power." It is more useful and realistic to look upon the actual results of the concentration that has already taken place. In doing so, one can find little evidence of evil and considerable evidence of public benefit.[47] In general, the

[46] *Cf.* Federal Deposit Insurance Corporation, *Annual Report* for the year ended December 31, 1960, p. 60. "Banking is perhaps the only industry in which attempts to demonstrate a decline in competition invoke the size of the 100 largest—or 50 or 25 or 10 largest units in the industry in the nation. With the greatly increased facilities of transportation and communication of recent years, there is more competition of this sort now than formerly, regardless of the changes which have occurred in the number of banks or the number and location of banking offices."

[47] *Cf.* Paul D. Butt, *Branch Banking and Economic Growth in Arizona and New Mexico*, New Mexico studies in Business and Economics No. 7. (Albuquerque: Bureau of Business Research, University of New Mexico Press, 1960). Among the findings of this study were that ". . . The evidence strongly supports the contention that during the period (1947–1959) the unlimited branch banking system of Arizona contributed more to Arizona's economic development than the limited branch banking system of New Mexico contributed to New Mexico's economic development."

largest banks have demonstrated their advantage to the public not only by developing and offering a wide variety of improved services, but by paying the maximum rates of interest and charging the lowest rates on loans as well. Their ability and willingness to do so results not only from their somewhat greater operating efficiency but, more importantly, from the fact that they generally face more direct and aggressive competition from other large banks and the smaller specialists than do small banks doing a general banking business in relatively isolated communities.

There are, furthermore, two aspects of banking competition that are frequently overlooked. One of these is that even the largest bank is small in comparison with its largest customers. The big national corporations, with their huge holdings of cash and liquid assets, are in a dominant position when they come to negotiate loan rates and terms with, or to ask for special services from even the largest banks in the country. The other fact is that in nearly every aspect of commercial banking, except the provision of demand deposit facilities, commercial banks face strong competition from other financial institutions. On the deposit side are the savings banks and savings and loan associations, unregulated in most instances as to the maximum rates they can pay. On the asset side are a host of institutional lenders, insurance companies, pension funds, savings institutions in the mortgage market, commercial factors, finance companies, and, in many communities, even individuals. With respect to prime borrowers the acceptance and commercial paper markets provide additional competition.

If the preservation of competition "in the field of banking" is to be a meaningful criterion in judging merger or holding company applications, the supervisory authorities cannot rely on size or number of banks alone. The so-called concentration ratios do not, in themselves, tell the whole story. Rather the authorities should seek to preserve or foster a competitive pattern in which no one bank overshadows all others and where a reasonable number of choices of alternative banking facilities is maintained at various size levels, for the entire range of banking services, at reasonably convenient locations within meaningful market areas. At the same time they should permit sufficient consolidation to make it possible for commercial banks to compete effectively on a wide scale and not be overshadowed by their largest customers.

The Bank Holding Company Act specifically refers to the convenience, needs, and welfare of the community to be served. In a broad sense this criterion encompasses the maintenance of soundly managed, progressive banks motivated by a real desire to serve their communities to the fullest possible extent. This kind of banking service depends heavily on competent and progressive management. It is spurred on by the kind of keen competition that obviously exists between large and aggressive banks. It will be in the public interest therefore to sacrifice in some degree the existence of a larger number of banks if the consolidation results in more effective banking services, lower costs, better management, provision for management or ownership succession—all provided that a reasonably balanced pattern of competition is preserved.

III

THE STRUCTURE OF A BANK

A bank is much more than a building, however imposing. It is an organization of human effort. Its purpose is to perform the banking functions required by the community it serves. Banks and banking offices have character; a unique personality that closely reflects the way in which they function as organizations.[1] A bank's character mirrors the personality and purposes of its management, the objectives it has set for itself and the methods it has chosen to carry out those objectives. A person who is in frequent contact with banks, such as a bank examiner, can sense the personality of a bank almost as soon as he enters its lobby. In some banks he finds alertness, in others indifference; in some a sense of mission, in others an air of smug self-importance.

In some small part these impressions can be derived from the physical appearance of the bank. Low inviting counters, and tasteful decorations bespeak a certain warmth while old-fashioned floor-to-ceiling cages, in the few instances where they still are found, may well represent an ultra-conservative approach to lending as well as to changing times. In large measure, these impressions are a reaction to the attitudes of officials and employees; the helpful guard, the cheerful teller. These outward appearances are not accidents. They are the product of management decisions and management policies and they lie at the heart of a bank's willingness and ability

---

[1] Cf. William H. Newman, "Basic Objectives Which Shape the Character of a Company," *The Journal of Busines of the University of Chicago,* XXVI, No. 4 (October 1953), p. 211. "In addition to a separate legal existence, every company develops its own traditions, habits, and reputation which gives it individuality. This body of habits and attitudes endows a company with character and personality quite beyond the people who work for it at any given time."

to perform its functions well. The character of a bank, its appearance, its personnel, and all the rest, reflect its organization and is a vital determinant of its ultimate success or failure.

The structure of a bank, in the dynamic sense, involves varied characteristics which shape or determine its individuality. Among these are its size, its location, and, above all, its own institutional organization. These characteristics, of course, are interrelated. They are varying aspects of a bank's nature which can be separated only for the purpose of study and discussion. But thus to separate them helps to shed light on what makes up the structure of a bank.

SIZE

In this country, banks range in size from those with deposits of less than $1 million to the very largest banks with deposits in the billions. Size, of course, is relative but, by any reasonable measure, the small bank is still the typical bank in the United States. Out of approximately 13,000 insured commercial banks, about two-thirds have total deposits of less than $5 million. These are small banks by today's standards. About 3700 additional banks have assets between $5 million and $25 million and could be designated as small-to-medium sized institutions.

For the sophisticated city-dwelling student of finance, a really small country bank has to be seen to be believed. To anyone who grew up in a rural community and still remembers the general store, the operations of a small bank are nostalgically familiar. It is a friendly place where every customer is known, usually by his first name. The chief executive officer is as likely as not to be found at a teller's window or proving the incoming exchanges. His desk will be piled high with banking literature and the latest banking regulations which he has no time to read, but his knowledge of the bank's clientele is intimate and extensive.[2]

Major decisions in such very small banks are seldom made by the

---

[2] Cf. Edward H. McMahan, Hearing Examiner, *Report and Recommended Decision*, in Re Application of BANCOHIO CORPORATION Pursuant to Section 3(a)(2) of the Bank Holding Company Act of 1956, for approval of acquisition of up to 100 per cent of the voting shares of The Hilliard Bank, Hilliards, Ohio. (Docket No. BHC-56) heard in Columbus, Ohio, May 31–June 2, 1960. The examiner's findings of fact with respect to The Hilliard Bank constitute a classic description of a small bank (deposits $2,900,000).

active management but by the directors who are the prominent and
usually prosperous businessmen and farmers of a rural community.
The president is frequently a local merchant who spends little time
in the bank but is available for consultation to the operating officer.
As a merchant he is thoroughly familiar with the credit standing of
every citizen in the community. He has their accounts on his own
books as well as on those of the bank. Typically, he has a fairly
large stockholding in the bank and whatever he receives in salary is
secondary in his consideration to the increase in the value of his
investment.

Small banks fill an important need in the small communities they
serve, but they seldom serve those communities to the fullest possible extent. Their loan-deposit ratios are below average, they are
seldom interested in consumer lending, and they have neither the
time nor the technical knowledge to accommodate an unusual or
complicated request for credit.[3]

Small banks tend to be director-managed because they do not
earn enough to be able to afford top-grade operating management
in today's competitive market for banking talent. A study of 42
banks in the Second Federal Reserve District which had total deposits under $2 million showed that the average salary of the highest
paid officer was slightly less than $7,000 per annum and this was
seldom supplemented by any pension or insurance benefits. The
average age of these officers was 57 years. In other words, near
the peak of their earning power, the officers of very small banks are

---

[3] *Cf.* McMahan, *op. cit.* "The bank has never offered any consumer credit
program. . . . It has turned away installment loan applications because the
cashier has so many duties he is physically unable to handle them. . . . The
cashier is reluctant to make any loans when it appears that out of the ordinary
procedures will have to be followed to handle or collect them. In his own
words he says he prefers 'to make a loan and collect it when I make it.'"
(Finding No. 15, p. 12.)

"In February 1951, the most substantial business establishment at Hilliards
presented negotiable warehouse receipts on soybeans to the bank in an effort
to secure funds to finance the soybean crop. They were turned down by the
bank and moved their account to a Columbus bank in order to secure adequate
financing for their business." (Finding No. 17(a), p. 13.)

"A real estate broker in Hilliards refers to the continuing growth of the community over the past few years, and points out that there is only one general
banking facility. He states that the service which the bank . . . can provide
the community is entirely inadequate." (Finding No. 17(c), p. 13.)

being paid less than a junior bank examiner or a senior clerk in a large bank. In most cases these salaries are substantially lower than those paid by large branch banking organizations to the managers of comparable offices.

The second officer in these 42 banks was paid, on average, $4,500 per annum, less than large banks pay college-graduate trainees with no banking experience whatsoever. In 13 of these 42 banks the second "officer" was a woman whose official capacity was largely a convenience for signing purposes.

In most of these banks the examiner rated the management as ranging from fair to poor.[4] In 46 per cent of the cases the examiner considered the problem of management succession to be an immediate one. In most of the remaining instances the problem was present but not acute, only because the managing officer had not yet reached the age of 60.

The inability of small banks to attract and keep highly competent management is inherent in their limited earning power.[5] The problem is particularly acute for the very small bank but is still present in significant degree with respect to the two-thirds of all insured commercial banks in the United States with deposits under $5 million. In 1960, for example, member banks with deposits under $5 million earned an average of 4.2 per cent on total assets, and spent about 30 per cent of gross earnings on salaries and wages.[6] Thus a bank with resources of $5 million earned about $205,000 and had about $61,500 with which to compensate a staff that would average four officers and six to ten clerks. Such a bank might afford to pay from $15,000 to $20,000 for a top man and perhaps $9,000 to $15,000 for a second man, but, after the clerical personnel have been adequately compensated, there is usually too little left over for junior officers of the caliber that would assure competent management succession from within the organization. As one goes down the scale from deposits of $5 million the problem becomes more acute. One result

---

[4] National Bank Examiners frequently characterize such management as being "of mediocre ability but sincere in effort."

[5] Most small banks have charged rates at or close to the usury ceilings for years. They cannot increase their earnings to offset steadily rising costs.

[6] Board of Governors of the Federal Reserve System, *Federal Reserve Bulletin,* May 1961.

is that the better junior officers all too frequently leave small banks to obtain higher remuneration and wider opportunity in larger ones, making the problem even more difficult.

Small banks persist in large number partly because of the senti- mental attachment of important segments of the American public to home-town unit banking, and partly for psychological and economic reasons. The directors of small banks, who are usually also the principal stockholders, take a great deal of pride in the banks they direct as well as a paternalistic view of the communities they serve.[7] They have the time and the knowledge of local affairs to supply management at the relatively low cost of directors' fees, and they manage most small banks safely and soundly, if not progres- sively.

Small banks can still justify themselves in terms of profitability partly because their salary scales *are* low, partly because the interest rates they charge are somewhat higher than average, and partly because their net profits (to the extent that they do not exceed $25,000) are subject to a Federal income tax of only 30 per cent as compared with the 52 per cent tax on corporate profits in excess of $25,000.[8]

Because of these "advantages" the net profits of banks under $5 million in deposits compare favorably with those of larger banks. In the nation, for example, in 1960, they exceeded the profits of the larger banks as a percentage of assets, and were less in terms of return on invested capital only because of the smaller banks' higher capital ratios, as shown in Table 1.

While small banks are numerous and not unprofitable despite their management problems, it is the large banks that control the major portion of the nation's banking resources. Banks with total assets of $50 million or more held over three-fourths of the aggregate

---

[7] *Cf.* McMahan, *op. cit.* "The President is Minar W. Schofield, age 75, who has been engaged in farming all his life on the farm operated by his father and grandfather. His father was one of the founders of the bank and its first presi- dent. . . . Dr. Jesse Jasper, a physician, and Jack Alder, owner of the Chev- rolet agency in Hilliards, whose grandfather was one of the founders of the bank, are the two other shareholders who, together with the officers, compose the Board of Directors." (Finding No. 2, p. 7.)

[8] Based on average operating ratios a bank would have to have deposits in excess of $2,300,000 before any of its operating earnings would be subject to taxes at the higher rate. Inclusion of tax-exempt income would increase this figure.

TABLE 1

PROFITABILITY OF MEMBER BANKS

Deposits in Millions	Net Profits as Per Cent of Assets	Net Profits as Per Cent of Capital Funds	Capital Funds as Per Cent of Total Assets
Under 1	.82	6.7	12.7
1 to 2	.89	8.4	10.9
2 to 5	.84	9.0	9.5
5 to 10	.80	9.7	8.5
10 to 25	.76	10.0	7.9
Over 25	.76	10.2	7.6

Source: Board of Governors of the Federal Reserve System, *Federal Reserve Bulletin,* May 1961.

assets of all member banks in December 1960. Table 2 is illuminating.

TABLE 2

DISTRIBUTION OF MEMBER BANK ASSETS BY SIZE OF BANK

Deposits in Millions	Number of Banks	Per Cent of Assets
Under 2	847	0.6
2 to 5	1,939	3.4
5 to 10	1,421	5.1
10 to 25	1,085	8.4
25 to 50	378	6.7
50 to 100	188	6.7
Over 100	265	69.1

Source: Board of Governors of the Federal Reserve System, "1960 Member Bank Earnings," *Federal Reserve Bulletin,* May 1961.

As banks become larger they acquire a greater degree of flexibility but at the same time their management problems become more complex. Fortunately, they are able to attract the necessary competency with which to deal with such greater complexities. Most of the discussion of bank policy formation in subsequent chapters is pertinent primarily to the bank with resources of at least $10 million. Until a bank reaches approximately that size it cannot afford the management specialization which can study its problems separately. There is little point in designing an organization chart for the very small bank where the cashier plays in turn all of the executive and some of the clerical roles. By contrast, organizational responsibility needs to be clearly defined in larger banks where personnel administration, for example, is a separate function.

Large size entails its own special problems. The cashier of a $2 million bank not only knows most of his customers intimately but works in constant close association with the people under his direction. In large banks, not only do the customers tend to become impersonal individuals known chiefly through the medium of account numbers or financial statements and trade checkings, but even the employees lose their individuality for the senior officers. In very large banks it is not unusual for the officers themselves to complain that they have little personal contact with the "Head Man" who is often also the mysterious fountainhead of policies that may seem arbitrary and unrelated to the reality of the officers' daily and practical problems.

Larger banks, in short, require the decentralization and delegation of management problems. Such decentralization and specialization calls for greater management skills. At the same time their greater earnings and economies which derive from size and specialization should provide the means to attract and train officers of the requisite caliber.

LOCATION

The structure of a bank is shaped in a number of ways by the community it serves. The credit needs of the community largely determine the fields of lending in which a bank will specialize and the nature of the community will determine the other banking services expected. Rural banks tend to engage in farm lending, whereas suburban banks specialize in mortgage loans and consumer credit. A bank's location also affects its costs. Salaries, as shown above, tend to be lower in small rural communities and higher where there is active competition for clerical personnel from industry or government.

Location affects a bank's needs for liquidity. For example, banks in resort and farm areas tend to have wider seasonal swings in loans and deposits than do banks of comparable size in suburban areas. In similar fashion, a bank's exposure to risk may be heightened by the lack of diversification in the business of the community it serves. One of the advantages of regional branch banking systems is their ability to average out the problems that arise from serving particular localities.

It is the specific locality served by a bank that affects its operations rather than any marked differences between broad geographical areas. For example, comparisons between similar groups of banks in New York and Iowa or Kansas show only minor variations in their asset distribution ratios or operating results. The differences between individual banks, even in neighboring localities, are usually far greater.

One of the important tasks of bank management is to keep fully aware of local banking needs and to seek in every appropriate way to contribute to the health and growth of the community which the bank serves.

CHARACTER OF BUSINESS

The character of a bank's business, as stated previously, is largely determined by the community it serves. Nevertheless, within larger communities some banks specialize in serving particular segments of the market for banking services. Thus, among the big banks in New York City can be found the predominantly "wholesale" banks whose business is largely with other banks and national corporations. Their character is clearly different from the equally big (or even bigger) banks which, through extensive branch networks, do a retail as well as wholesale banking business. By the same token the smaller banks which serve only particular neighborhoods or trades within the city have a still different character.

Whenever there are two or more banks serving the same community such specialties are likely to be found. One bank will have stressed trust services, another consumer lending or service tailored to the needs of smaller businesses. One bank will aggressively seek savings deposits, another concentrate on commercial lending. This kind of specialization reflects the predilections and special skills of management and represents still another facet of a bank's individuality.

MANAGEMENT ORGANIZATION

Size, location, and the special nature of a bank's business may
delineate the potentialities of a bank but its own organization determines its individual character. Banks of like size, located in similar
communities, and doing about the same kind of business still differ
markedly in individual character and, what is even more significant,
in results. Some banks grow and thrive in areas with seemingly
low potential while others stagnate in thriving communities. The
difference lies at the heart of the problem of bank management.

The organization of a bank, in the sense that it is used here, is the
unique management arrangements which have been devised and
put into practice by an individual bank to enable it to perform the
banking functions in its community or trade area. This organization represents those too often silent and neglected partners, the
bank's shareholders, who have placed their capital at risk in the hope
of profit to be derived from the lending and investing of deposits.
To perform its functions well, a bank needs a balanced combination
of sound direction and competent executive management. All three
elements in the organization of a bank—directors, officers, and shareholders—have vital roles to play if the individual bank is to develop
its potentialities to the fullest extent.

Board of Directors. Direction, ideally, should spring from the
directors of a bank who have the responsibility for determining its
policies and the opportunity of doing so in ways that will make it
effective in the community and profitable for the stockholders. The
Board of Directors, therefore, appropriately heads the organization
charts that visually depict the management arrangements devised
by most banks.

A great deal has been written about the duties and responsibilities
of bank directors; much of it by the courts. In a leading case,
judge Finkelburg stated: [9]

Briefly summarized, I understand the law on this subject to be as
follows:

---

[9] *Rankin* v. *Cooper,* 149 Fed., 1010. *Cf. Briggs* v. *Spaulding,* 141 U.S. 132,
and *Gibbons* v. *Anderson,* 80 Fed. 345.

(1) Directors are charged with the duty of reasonable supervision over the affairs of the bank. It is their duty to use ordinary diligence in ascertaining the condition of its business, and to exercise reasonable control and supervision over its affairs.

(2) They are not insurers or guarantors of the fidelity and proper conduct of the executive officers of the bank, and they are not responsible for losses resulting from their wrongful acts or omissions, provided they have exercised ordinary care in the discharge of their own duties as directors.

(3) Ordinary care, in this matter as in other departments of the law, means that degree of care which ordinarily prudent and diligent men would exercise under similar circumstances.

(4) The degree of care required further depends upon the subject to which it is to be applied, and each case must be determined in view of all the circumstances.

(5) If nothing has come to the knowledge to awaken suspicion that something is going wrong, ordinary attention to the affairs of the institution is sufficient. If, upon the other hand, directors know, or by the exercise of ordinary care should have known, any facts which would awaken suspicion and put a prudent man on his guard, then a degree of care commensurate with the evil to be avoided is required, and a want of that care makes them responsible. Directors cannot, in justice to those who deal with the bank, shut their eyes to what is going on around them.

(6) Directors are not expected to watch the routine of every day's business, but they ought to have a general knowledge of the manner in which the bank's business is conducted, and upon what securities its larger lines of credit are given, and generally to know of and give direction to the important and general affairs of the bank.

(7) It is incumbent upon bank directors in the exercise of ordinary prudence, and as a part of their duty of general supervision to cause an examination of the condition and resources of the bank to be made with reasonable frequency. . . .

Thus it has been well established that the legal responsibility for the operations of a bank devolves upon its directors and that they "are under a duty to use ordinary care and prudence in the administration of the affairs of the bank and if through their failure to do so a loss to the bank results, they may be held liable for such loss in a civil action for damages." [10] This legalistic concept of respon-

---

[10] *Duties and Liabilities of Directors of National Banks,* Form 1417, Treasury Department, Office of the Comptroller of the Currency (Revised September 1956), p. 25. *Cf. The Bank Directors Responsibility: A High Public Service,* by Averell Harriman, Governor, and George A. Mooney, Superintendent of Banks. Issued by the New York State Banking Department, September 1957.

sibility, important and binding as it is,[11] only scrapes the surface of the directional function.

In his challenging book, the *The Practice of Management,* Peter Drucker raises a question as to whether Boards of Directors are on their way out as functioning organs of enterprise. He concludes that they are not, even where the law does not specifically charge them with financial responsibility, because:

> . . . there are real functions which only a Board of Directors can discharge. Somebody has to approve the decision as to what the company's business is and what it should be. Somebody has to give the final approval to the objectives the company has set for itself and the measurements it has developed to judge its progress toward these objectives. Somebody has to look critically at the profit planning of the company, its capital-investment policy and its managed-expenditures budget. Somebody has to discharge the final judicial function in respect to organization problems, has to be the "Supreme Court." Somebody has to watch the spirit of the organization, has to make sure that it succeeds in utilizing the strengths of people and in neutralizing their weaknesses, that it develops tomorrow's managers and that its rewards to managers, its management tools and management methods strengthen the organization and direct it toward its objectives.[12]

These functions of a Board of Directors have as much significance for banking as for any other enterprise. The degree to which the directors actually perform these functions will, in large measure, determine the character of their bank and be an important factor in its successful operation.

The first responsibility of the directorate is to define the business of the bank and to determine what its objectives are in terms of the stockholder, the depositor, and the community it serves. Herein lies the importance of a clear understanding of the banking functions discussed in Chapter I. If the directors are aware, in general terms, that it is the essential business of a bank to supply the legitimate credit needs of the community, it is a natural second step to determine what kind of loans and how many of each the bank should make. The directors will thus formulate a lending policy in terms of the bank's objectives.

---

[11] Clarence G. McDavitt, Jr., *If You're a Bank Director* (Cambridge, Mass.: Bankers Publishing Company, 1950). Chapter IV discusses "38 Ways to Get Into Trouble."

[12] Peter F. Drucker, *The Practice of Management.* (New York: Harper & Brothers, Publishers, Inc., 1954), p. 179.

If the directors are aware that deposits are the raw material of the bank's lending and investment business, they will be in a better position to establish the bank's objectives with respect to the deposit and other services it should render to its customers. These considerations will have important bearing on banking hours, physical facilities, and the rate of interest paid on savings deposits. If the directors are conscious of their responsibility to shareholders they can more effectively consider and plan the level of profits required to keep its capital attractive to the public while maintaining a competent and adequately paid staff. Objectives can and should be set with respect to public relations, personnel training and development, and community progess. Directors, too, should be aware of the risks in banking, discussed in the following chapter, and establish objectives in terms of minimizing those risks for the bank they are directing.

All too often the objectives of bank directors, like those of individuals, are taken for granted. They are considered to be implicit in the day-to-day decisions that absorb man's time and energies. The explicit written statement of an objective, however, is far more valuable not only *per se,* but also for the discussion and thinking, the process of mental sharpening that must of necessity go into its formulation.[13] It is for this reason that bank examination reports contain questions as to whether a bank has a written investment policy and whether the directors have set specific limitations on

---

[13] The following opening paragraphs from the "Loan Policy and Procedures Statement" of The Simsbury Bank and Trust Company, Simsbury, Connecticut, illustrate a broad and comprehensive approach to the establishment of lending policies:

"These statements, based on present practices, are for the guidance of the Bank's Credit Department, the lending officers and the Executive Committee. They will be reviewed at least annually first by the Executive Committee and then by the Board in order to assure adjustment of the Bank's policy to changing conditions.

General

"The Bank's charter implies deployment and use of depositors' and stockholders' monies so as to benefit the economy as a whole and the users of it in the Bank's trade area. Its loan transactions must be conducted on such terms and bases as will provide income sufficient to pay the attendant costs, with sufficient margin remaining to cover losses and contribute a major portion of earnings necessary to pay a reasonable dividend to stockholders and accumulate some reserves."

The Statement proceeds to discuss in detail the Bank's territory, ethics, insistence on financial statements, interest rates, prompt service, et cetera. It is quoted by permission of George H. Stebbins, President.

the various types of loans. What the policy may be is less important than that a policy exists. The specific policy may rightly vary
widely in different communities. The important thing is that the
directors have taken the time to consider the matter thoroughly and
have arrived at well-considered decisions.

Policies and objectives once arrived at are, of course, not im-
mutable. They must be periodically reviewed in the light of changing conditions, new facts, and new factors.

Having determined the objectives, the next duty of the directors
is to measure the bank's accomplishments. One way of doing this
is by self-comparison. Most directors are furnished with monthly
and other periodical statements of the bank which form a basis for
judging the bank's progress. It is especially helpful to chart or
graph the principal asset and liability accounts and the chief components of the bank's earnings so that self-appraisal may be visual
as well as statistical.[14]

A second method of measuring a bank's accomplishments is to
compare it with similar banks. All supervisory authorities and
many banking associations publish, at least annually, average ratio
figures of earnings, expenses, and asset distribution for banks in
similar size groupings. In making such comparisons, however, the
director should not let himself be lulled into a false sense of com-
placency merely because his bank is "as good as the average."
Average is but a synonym for mediocre, particularly when applied
to bank statistics.

The most important but least frequently used method of measuring a bank's success is to compare its results with its clearly defined
objectives. Every bank is required to publish its assets and liabilities periodically. As a part of establishing its objectives each bank
should also have unpublished figures for six, twelve and, perhaps,
twenty-four months ahead. In order thus to budget or forecast the
bank's asset and liability accounts, the directors should take a close
look at what is going on in their community. The record of building permits and mortgage recordings will provide valuable clues.
Management of local industry and the important retailers of the

---

14 *Cf.* Denton Fuller, "Reports to Directors," *Bankers Monthly*, Vol. LXX,
No. 4 (April 1953). Some banks have found that the display of charts by
means of slide projectors helps to focus and heighten the directors' interest.

community, who should be represented on the Board of Directors, are able to provide much useful information concerning the trend of future business activity. A simple discussion with each of the bank's important borrowing customers regarding his probable needs for credit in the months ahead will help management and the directors to set the bank's goals intelligently and realistically.

In establishing objectives and measuring accomplishments the directors must "look critically at the profit planning of the company, its capital-investment policy and its managed-expenditures budget." In banking terms this means that the directors should see to it that the bank has some form of cost analysis and a carefully planned budget. It means that the directors should be thinking about the adequacy of the bank's capital and should be aware of its liquidity needs. It means that the directors should be formulating the bank's lending and investing policies and planning its new business development program.

Directors also have to serve as the court of last resort to which all unresolved problems and policy questions are referred. This is a responsibility that directors seldom escape, but they have the opportunity to avoid many emergency problems by careful forward planning. A periodic review of the organization and a clear delineation of responsibility, preferably in writing, will prevent many problems from arising. The establishment and supervision of effective personnel policies is a clear directorial duty.

Another responsibility and opportunity of great importance is what Drucker calls fostering the "spirit of the organization." This may seem to some directors to be rather an intangible assignment but teamwork, cooperation, and loyalty can contribute far more to community welfare and net profits in the long run than any amount of astute bond trading. In small and medium-sized banks the directors can be close enough to the personnel to provide a personal touch by attending staff meetings and bank social affairs. Even in large banks there is more opportunity for evidencing personal interest in people and policies than directors usually take advantage of. In any event, spirit is always set at the top and, if it exists there, will sift down readily through the official staff to the newest employee.

Lastly, the directors have the responsibility for developing managers, and for assuring that the rewards to management, the tools furnished management and management methods are adequate.

These duties involve seeing to it that the staff has adequate space in which to work, and that it is not handicapped by antiquated methods and equipment. It means that adequate salary incentives be provided and a well functioning training program be kept in operation. The widespread failure of directors to meet this particular group of responsibilities, has been an important contributing cause to bank mergers.[15]

It should be emphasized that it is the function of directors to direct and not to manage.[16] In small banks directors may be required to make executive decisions because the bank cannot afford (or at least does not have) adequately trained executive management. Sometimes, however, the habit of managing tends to persist with the directors as the bank grows larger and, in too many moderate-sized banks, the officers are not granted adequate executive authority to make on-the-spot decisions. Nevertheless, while directors should not, ideally, exercise executive authority, they should keep closely informed concerning the actions of the executive officers and remain vitally interested counselors to those officers.

A Board of Directors functions most effectively through committees or, if the number of directors is small, through the assignment of areas of special knowledge to individual directors. In the case of large boards it is customary to establish a smaller Executive Committee which meets more frequently to review the bank's operations. While certain outstanding directors may constitute the core of this committee, other directors should be required to serve on it in rotation. An examining committee and, if the bank exercises trust powers, a trust committee are required by law. Banks frequently have loan committees and sometimes investment committees. Too

---

15 *Cf.* McMahan, *Report and Recommended Decision, Bancohio Corporation op. cit.* The examiner's findings with respect to the management situation perfectly illustrates this point. "Since there is no assistant with authority to act for the cashier, and no employee trained to take his place, in the event of absence on the part of the cashier for a period of time, the bank, as presently operated, is without a credit or lending officer on active duty at such time. . . . The situation, as it is, has existed for some time, and although it is critical, and the directors recognize such, they continue to take no action. . . . They hesitate to take the steps they know they should take, because of the dread of responsibility with regard to enlarging the space so as to provide room for any addition to the Bank's staff, and because of the extra expense involved." (Finding No. 12, p. 11.)

16 *Cf.* McDavitt, *op. cit.*, p. 31. "Matters of policy can be, should be, and rarely are the principal function of the board of directors."

few banks, however, have directors' personnel or operations committees, or even business development committees.[17]   For a board to function at its best each of the important areas of the directors' responsibility should be assigned to a special committee (or even an individual director) and its actions in planning for and making progress should be frequently reported back to the full board.

Probably no bank ever has quite the ideal Board of Directors but many banks have more talent on their boards than they recognize or use.   Most communities, furthermore, have more people of talent and usefulness than are ever selected to be bank directors. Above all, directors should be sincerely interested in the welfare of their communities and look upon their bank directorship as a form of public service.[18]   Directors should be mature, but vigorous. They should be open to new ideas but essentially cautious in adopting innovations.   Directors should be representative of the community served by their bank.[19]   These are obvious truisms not always found in actuality.

It is difficult to generalize about the composition of bank directorates.   The size and location of the bank affect this aspect of a bank's nature as they do others.   Larger banks tend to have a greater number of directors.   Federal law sets a minimum of five and a maximum of twenty-five.   According to a study made by the Federal Reserve Bank of Richmond for the Virginia Bankers Asso-

---

[17] A country bank in New York State recently developed a "director-officer program."   Each of its directors is assigned to work with the officers in one or more of twelve different areas: investments, loans and mortgages, records and building, personnel and salaries, business development, branch advisory, audit, methods and systems, cash and tellers, insurance, public relations, and installment loan policy.

[18] Self-serving directors, unfortunately, are not uncommon.   Only recently a bank president complained about a director "whose only interest in the bank is the business his law firm gets from it."

[19] The Sullivan County Trust Company of Monticello, New York, a moderate-sized bank, has for many years operated on the basis of a policy declaration which, among other things prescribes the following standards in the selection of members of the Board of Directors; (1) Local business interest must be predominant, (2) A Director must hold a position of responsibility in his business (must represent himself, not outside interests), (3) Directors must have demonstrated community interest, (4) They must be in agreement with the bank's written policy, (5) They must have substantial investment in the bank (a minimum is stated in excess of the minimum required by law, and a maximum to prevent domination by any one shareholder), and (6) They must be under 45 years of age when elected.   *American Banker,* August 30, 1961, p. 7.

ciation a few years ago, the typical $5 million country bank had an average of eight directors. In such banks 45 per cent of the directors were businessmen, 17 per cent professional people, 13 per cent farmers, 14 per cent bank officers, and 11 per cent "retired and other." Twenty-five per cent of the directors were over 65 years of age, 52 per cent over 55. This distribution is probably typical of banks throughout the country.

Most successful and responsible businessmen and professional people enjoy being bank directors. To be a director of the local bank seems to carry an extra measure of prestige, and bank directorships tend to be among the last that men give up as they retire gradually from full and active participation in business life. As a consequence the aging of directors is a problem that faces many banks. There is no certain age at which all men cease to think imaginatively and constructively, but the tendency to resist change increases observably with age.[20] Since the ability to adapt to an ever-changing environment is a requisite of survival to which banks are no exception, the problem of an aging board can be a serious bar to progress. Increasingly, banks are facing up to this problem by setting a retirement age for directors (usually around 70).[21] Directors reaching this age are designated as "honorary" or "emeritus." They continue to attend meetings and to give the bank the benefit of their experience but they have no vote in the final decisions of policy. What is more important, their places on the board are thus made available for younger and perhaps more progressive directors, the new blood that is needed to keep an organization alert to the changing conditions in the community it serves.

Executive Management. Up to this point discussion has emphasized the role of the directors in establishing policy. Important as that role is, it is seldom performed (except in very small banks) without the active leadership and participation of the senior executive officers. It is the function of executive management not only to carry out policy but even more important to propose it.

---

[20] In the late 1930's, when Federally-insured mortgages were still an innovation, an informal survey of member banks in the Second Federal Reserve District showed that the proportion of such mortgages to total loans was in roughly inverse proportion to the age of the bank president.

[21] *Cf.* "Directors' Retirement: Some Pros and Cons," *American Banker,* July 27, 1961.

The chief executive officer of the bank, and often two or more of the senior officers, serve a dual role as both officers and directors.[22] As officer-directors it is their function to provide leadership and direction to the board. As professional bankers, the officer-directors can be presumed to have the technical training and experience to analyze the banking problems that face the institution and to present them to the full board in sufficient detail and with enough background for the board to perform its policy-determining function wisely and effectively. If the Board of Directors is not informed and interested, the fault generally lies with senior management.

Competent management actively seeks the advice and counsel of the directors. It assumes the responsibility for keeping the directors interested as well as informed. It provokes discussion and works diligently to keep board meetings from becoming merely routine, seeking ways to present the bank's problems that will stimulate director participation. Management of this caliber is constantly seeking for new directors who will add varied viewpoints to the counsels of the board; who will bring new ideas as well as new business to the bank.

By contrast, some bank officers seem to mistrust their directors. They like to keep the number small and to avoid different viewpoints on the board in order to escape what they would term "controversy" or "interference." They try to insulate the board from bank examiners [23] and other outside influences apparently for fear

---

[22] The president of a national bank is required by law to be a director (U.S.C. Title 12, Sec. 76). Similar provisions are contained in most state banking laws. When the president is inactive (as in many small banks), the cashier may or may not be a director. If he is not, one can be certain that the bank is director-managed.

[23] The Federal Reserve Bank of New York, for a number of years, has included in its letters transmitting reports of examination to member banks an invitation to the directors, individually or collectively, to discuss any phases of the report with the officers in charge of the Bank Supervision Function. In ten years this offer has not been accepted more than a dozen times. Similarly, the Bank Relations Department of the Federal Reserve Bank of New York has made cost analyses of small banks; analyses which are especially revealing of the strengths and weaknesses of a bank's operations. Specific offers on the part of Reserve Bank officers to discuss these reports with directors in their own communities, at their own convenience, have been largely ignored. The only apparent conclusion is that such meetings are discouraged by management which may fear that its policies or its competence may be questioned. When held, such meetings are exceptionally constructive.

that management policies or practices may be questioned. Life may be easier for the senior executive if he knows that the board meetings will hold no surprises and no searching or perhaps embarrassing questions, but this is a shortsighted approach which eventually will slow down the bank's progress.

When policies and objectives have been established by the board under the leadership of senior management, it becomes the duty and responsibility of management to carry them out. In general terms, the fundamental principles of good bank management call for a clear definition and explicit delegation of management responsibilities. These are often depicted on an organization chart, but such a chart bears only the same relationship to actuality as a two-dimensional photograph bears to the flesh-and-blood reality of the human personality. It is the way in which the officers and directors work together to build a structure based on a combination of teamwork and individual responsibility that will give each bank its unique personality.

Stockholders. Part of a bank's special character results from whether a majority of its stock is closely held by a single individual or a relatively small group, such as the Board of Directors, or whether its shares are widely distributed in the community. The directors and management of some banks deliberately seek to maintain close control. This is true of many small banks and even of some fairly sizable ones. In other banks management seeks to distribute the stock as widely as possible. Such wide distribution in small lots tends to make a bank more community-minded. Ownership succession is facilitated and a bank's ability to remain independent is enhanced.

A large group of informed and loyal shareholders can be a valuable asset in a bank's public relations and business development programs. And with respect to a bank's individual character, the width of stock distribution is itself a significant factor. Bank directors who represent numerous small shareholders are more likely to put the bank's interest and that of the community before their own and to look upon their directorships in the nature of a public service. While these comments are broad generalizations to which many exceptions can be found, nevertheless in recent years, aside from defalcations, most of the banks which the supervisory authorities would consider "problem" banks have been institutions owned or controlled by a single individual or a small group.[24]

---

[24] The problem of "dominated banks" is not a new one. Comptroller of the Currency Pole, testifying before a Subcommittee of the Senate Committee on Banking and Currency, indicated that supervisory persuasion was effective in some cases but ". . . in others, Mr. Chairman, where the board may be obdurate or the bank may be under the domination of a single person, which is very often the case, you can exact any sort of promise but performance is another thing." "Operations of the National and Federal Reserve Banking Systems," *Hearings* Pursuant to Senate Resolution 71, January 19, 1931, p. 5.

IV

BANKING RISKS

The previous discussion of the functions and structure of commercial banking did not emphasize sufficiently one essential element of the *nature* of banking—its risk. Subsequent explorations of specific bank policies will be meaningful, of course, in terms of increased effectiveness and profitability of banking operations; but such policies must always be adopted with an eye to minimizing risks as well. A brief review of the principal risks of banking and an appraisal of their magnitude in the past, therefore, will serve as a useful backdrop for further discussion of specific policies.

Taking risks can almost be said to be the business of bank management. A bank that is run on the principle of avoiding all risks, or as many of them as possible, will be a stagnant institution and will not adequately serve the legitimate credit needs of its community. On the other hand, a bank which takes excessive risks or, what is more likely, takes them without knowing the extent of them, or even that they exist at all, will inevitably run into difficulty. Particularly in times of expanding business activities some of the risks of banking may be obscured beneath the general economic prosperity and banks may seem to take large risks without apparent penalty; however, the seeds of unwise banking will sprout inevitably into losses in the first serious business recession. They always have in the past.

This chapter will analyze the nature of the principal banking risks and evaluate the impact they have had on banking in the past. Subsequent chapters will be concerned with some of the management techniques which enable banks to guard against, or minimize these risks.

THE CREDIT RISK

The most obvious risk in banking is the credit risk; the possibility that loans will not be repaid or that investments will deteriorate in quality or go into default with consequent loss to the bank. Few bankers ever knowingly make poor loans or investments. It is what occurs after a loan or investment is made that causes it to deteriorate in quality. Such adverse circumstances may sometimes be foreseen, as when obvious credit weaknesses are overlooked or ignored. However, many are unforeseeable. One cannot extend credit successfully on the premise of a major economic downturn in the foreseeable future. One cannot predict the impact of war or threats of war on the economy; one cannot even predict, very far ahead, changes in consumer demand which may affect the business of a borrower or even the business of an entire community. These risks to the quality of bank credit are ever present.

The protection against the risks of lending and investing consists in maintaining high credit standards, appropriate diversification, intimate knowledge of the borrower's affairs, and, of prime importance, alert collection procedures. These principles, as they apply to various kinds of loans and investments, will be discussed in detail in Chapters X–XII.

THE RISK OF FORCED LIQUIDATION

Another ever-present risk in banking is the possibility that customer demands for funds will require the sale or forced collection of credit-worthy assets at a loss. A depositor's demand for his money is one that a bank must meet promptly or go out of business. In times of rapid economic decline, such as the depression of the 1930s, such demands come primarily from depositors seeking to convert their bank deposits into currency because of lack of confidence in banks generally. The danger of such "money" panics and their attendant runs on banks has been greatly reduced, if not eliminated, by the reform banking legislation of 1933 and 1935. Federal deposit insurance has become a stout bulwark of confidence; and greatly improved bank supervision and stricter banking laws have materially strengthened the banking structure.

Of more immediate importance to banking policy are the demands for funds that are made on banks in times of high economic activity and active demand for credit. In such times depositors tend to use their funds more actively, to invest surplus funds in short-term money-market instruments, thus rapidly drawing down deposit balances. This increase in demand deposit velocity does not decrease the aggregate of demand deposits but the rapid shift of deposits from one bank to another can prove embarrassing to the bank which loses them.

Of even greater significance is the fact that at such times banks are also subject to heavy demands for loans from their customers. The banking system cannot increase loans or investments without creating new deposits. For the latter, additional reserves must be found and the Federal Reserve System, in the interest of preventing unsound speculative credit expansion, would be reluctant to supply them. As a result banks would be able to meet large loan demands with funds derived solely from the sale of securities. Under the pressures of extensive demand for credit, interest rates rise and the prices of fixed-interest obligations fall. Thus the liquidation of investments to increase loans could be, and in recent times has been a costly process, particularly if a bank were forced to sell bonds of intermediate or longer-term maturity, the price of which could be substantially affected by even modest changes in interest rate levels.

One might imagine that a bank could always refuse to make additional loans, and in some cases it could, but when the request for credit comes from a depositor of long standing who normally maintains sizeable deposit balances, the refusal to lend could easily lead to the withdrawal of deposits and the loss of a valuable customer. A community bank, for example, could hardly afford not to accommodate its local municipality which has maintained sizeable balances for years, when it wants to negotiate bond-anticipation notes for a new school project.

To protect itself against the risks of forced liquidation a bank must maintain adequate liquidity in the form of assets readily convertible into cash at minimum risk of loss. A discussion of how banks can estimate their liquidity needs, both short- and long-term and of the provisions that can be made to meet these needs is contained in Chapters VII and VIII.

THE RISK OF DEFALCATION

The credit risk and the risk of forced liquidation are normal banking risks. Unfortunately there is, in banking, another risk from which not even the cash-in-vault is safe; *i.e.*, the risk of defalcation. This risk is present in good times as well as bad and will remain a banking risk as long as banks employ people and as long as people are subject to the financial, social, and moral pressures of a free society. Internal controls and audits, along with adequate fidelity insurance, are essential to a bank's protection from the risks of loss and embarrassment resulting from the dishonest acts of its officers or employees. These will be discussed in Chapter VI.

EMERGENCY RISKS

In recent years there have been added to all of these other potential banking difficulties the risks inherent in atomic warfare; the possibility of massive destruction of banking facilities and bank records. It has been painfully difficult to persuade banks adequately to recognize this risk or to take even the simplest forms of protection against it.[1] It may be that the horror of atomic destruction paralyzes thought and action, or that human beings can only be persuaded to guard against dangers which they have actually experienced. Nevertheless, as the authorities responsible for emergency planning have repeatedly pointed out, the survival of a nation so heavily dependent upon its financial mechanisms may depend upon the *degree* to which its banking system can be quickly restored to functioning form.[2]

Banks hold in custody for safekeeping, in the broadest sense, not only the evidence of the existence of their depositors' money (their deposit ledger records) but much of the evidence of their tangible wealth in the form of abstracts of title to real property and securi-

---

[1] As of December 31, 1960 less than 6 per cent of insured commercial banks had so much as delegated the responsibility for coordinating the program to an officer or a committee. Source: James Louis Robertson, Member of the Board of Governors, Letter of May 19, 1961 addressed "To Whom It May Concern."

[2] Recent letter to all banks from the three Federal supervisory agencies.

ties pledged as collateral or held in trust. The duplication and remote storage of these records reduces by at least 50 per cent the chances of their destruction. The acceptance of this responsibility is a duty of bank management. Other measures of protection, some of them costing virtually nothing (such as provision for successor management in an emergency) are outlined in a series of five booklets prepared by the Advisory Committee on Commercial Bank Preparedness and the Banking Committee on Emergency Operations. These booklets have been distributed to all commercial banks in the nation.

PAST EXPERIENCE WITH BANKING RISKS

It can be claimed with considerable justification that the American financial system has been strengthened to the extent that banking panics and serious prolonged depressions will never again occur. It may be that the record of the 1930s is merely historical and has little practical significance. Nevertheless, the bankers who experienced the bank holiday of 1933, now steadily decreasing in number, were profoundly influenced by it and familiarity with the record may serve as a salutory and sobering warning to those younger bankers who have never lived through a similar period. The bank officers of the late 1920s were not fools; they were intelligent men carried away by the spirit of the times. The same thing can happen to intelligent men again.

To point up this record a study was made of fifty state member banks chosen at random in the Second Federal Reserve District. Each of these banks survived the depression although more than half of them were reorganized and required outside assistance in the form of additional capital funds or the removal of unacceptable assets. In 1929 these fifty banks had risk assets (assets other than cash and U. S. Government securities) aggregating $373,325,000.[3] By 1933 the total of risk assets had shrunk to $258,809,000, a decline of approximately 30 per cent. In this forced liquidation of assets the banks took the following losses:

---

[3] All figures from Reports of Examinations made during the year specified (Federal Reserve Bank of New York, confidential files).

	Amounts (000 omitted)
Losses on loans	$ 9,590
Losses on securities	27,040
Other losses	2,287
Total losses	$38,917
Recoveries	3,659
Net losses	$35,258

Net losses in the five years from 1929 to 1933 amounted to approximately 9.5 per cent of 1929 risk assets, and about 30 per cent of the risk assets liquidated during that period. This, however, was not the full extent of the banks' problem because in the examinations made during 1933 the remaining assets were classified [4] by the examiners as follows:

	Amounts (000 omitted)
Security depreciation	$21,009
Estimated losses	12,080
Doubtful assets	5,899
Slow (substandard) assets	30,378
Total classified	$69,366

The total of assets classified in the 1933 examination reports represented 27 per cent of the remaining risk assets. The total of losses net of recoveries for the five years from 1929 to 1933 plus the classified assets in 1933 was about 28 per cent of total 1929 risk assets.

The aggregate portrait of the effects of depression on bank assets does not quite tell the whole story because it is an average picture. The following summary schedules from a 1934 examination report of

---

[4] Examiners classify bank assets "loss," "doubtful" or "substandard" (formerly "slow"). Estimated losses are required to be charged off immediately. Doubtful assets are usually considered to require reserves of 50 per cent. Substandard assets are defined as "containing more than normal banking risk," but not necessarily a loss potential. In 1934 security depreciation was considered as "loss." Since 1938 depreciation on investment grade securities has not been classified adversely, depreciation on lower-grade bonds, not in default is classified as "doubtful" and depreciation on stocks and defaulted bonds would be classified as "loss."

an "example" bank show in dramatic form some of the banking risks with which bank management and bank supervisory authorities have had to cope in the past.

"EXAMPLE" BANK
STATEMENT OF CONDITION
March 23, 1934
(000 omitted)

Assets		*Liabilities*	
Loans	$30,830	Capital	$ 5,400
Mortgages owned	18,030	Surplus	3,000
Investments	14,370	Undivided profits	
Banking house and		and reserves	837
fixtures (net)	3,830	Deposits	46,765
Other real estate	910	Bills payable	9,616
Cash and due from banks	3,754	Mortgages payable	193
Other assets	735	Mortgage participations	
		outstanding	5,971
		Other liabilities	677
Total	$72,459	Total	$72,459

ASSETS CLASSIFIED
(000 omitted)

	Slow	*Doubtful*	*Loss*
Loans	$13,658	$1,137	$4,022
Investments	804	31	5,226
Other real estate	826	30	55
Bonds and mortgages	4,346	–0–	101
Total	$19,634	$1,198	$9,404

RECAPITULATION OF CAPITAL
(000 omitted)

Total capital funds	
Capital	$5,400
Surplus	3,000
Undivided profits	232
Reserves	605
Total book capital funds	9,237
Less classified losses	9,404
Capital deficit	$ 167

CLASSIFICATION OF SECURITIES
(000 omitted)

	Book	Allowed	Depreciation
Group I bonds	$ 5,530	$5,435	$ 96
Group II bonds	2,822	1,449	1,373
Defaulted bonds	1,830	523	1,307
Stocks	3,936	1,485	2,450
Federal Reserve Bank	252	252	–0–
Total	$14,370	$9,144	$5,226

REAL ESTATE ACTUAL AND POTENTIAL [5]

(000 omitted)

	Book
Other real estate owned	$ 910
Other real estate owned by affiliate (carried in loans)	3,265
Potential O.R.E. in loans	1,089
Potential O.R.E. in mortgages	1,403
Other real estate in name of affiliate or nominee	393
Other real estate in investments	350
Total	$7,410

The problems of this "example" bank in 1934 were not untypical. They were centered in stocks and bonds which had depreciated drastically in quality and market value and in loans based on real estate values that had seemed most conservative ten years before but which, by 1934, had largely faded into thin air. These values were to shrink still further in the next few years and this bank took substantially more losses than the examiner "estimated" in 1934. It is true that most of the mortgage loans it made had never been amortized and that banks are no longer permitted to buy stocks and bonds of the quality which studded this investment portfolio. Nevertheless banking still involves risk, and it is the task of bank management to be alert to unknown and perhaps unknowable eventualities.

---

[5] Potential other real estate included properties in the process of foreclosure or loans and mortgages so badly in arrears of interest or taxes as to make foreclosure appear inevitable.

V

BANK EARNINGS

Bank earnings are the foundation upon which rest the two main pillars of banking strength—adequacy of capital and competency of management. The experience of the 1930s showed that even in the most serious and prolonged depression of our recent history, nearly 95 per cent of the losses taken by banks were absorbed through earnings over a ten-year period.[1] Thus, earning power proved to be the first line of defense against the risks inherent in banking. In other words, bank earnings, current and accumulated, serve to protect the stockholder's investment in times of economic adversity, just as his stockholdings, the bank's capital, is the ultimate protection for the depositor.

In more normal times bank earnings provide the income on capital investment in banks. It is for the sake of this income that the stockholder is willing to supply the capital that enables a bank to engage in the risky business of creating credit, and it is out of retained earnings that the major portion of bank capital has been accumulated.[2] Even when bank earnings are paid out as dividends, by enhancing the marketability and increasing the value of the

---

[1] Comptroller Pole testified in 1932 that the same had held true for all national banks since the inception of the National Banking System.

[2] R. B. Wiltse, "Bank Capital," Report to the Executive Committee of the Federal Reserve Bank of New York, June 8, 1950 (unpublished). ". . . of the approximately $1 billion of capital additions . . . made by Second District banks during the past ten years, 92 per cent came from retained earnings. . . ." In the ten years since 1950 sales of new stock have played a more important role but retained earnings still accounted for 73 per cent of the aggregate additions.

stock, they make it possible for the bank to raise additional capital when needed.

Perhaps even more important to the strength and soundness of the privately-owned banking system is the fact that out of earnings banks must find the wherewithal to recruit and keep competent management. All too frequently the complaint is heard that banks "cannot afford" to meet competitive wage and salary rates. But unless banks do attract their fair share of the ablest young men and women, the strength and caliber of the banking system will inevitably diminish. Only out of ample earnings can banks afford to bid in today's highly competitive market for the best of prospective talent.

TREND OF BANK EARNINGS AND EXPENSES

Bank earnings have been rising in recent years but increasing expenses have nearly kept pace with earnings. Chart I shows the growth of both income and expense, as a percentage of assets, during the past ten years. As a percentage of income, expense has remained fairly constant. It has been the steadily rising levels of bank assets, the larger proportion of assets held in loans, and the resulting higher level of total earnings that have enabled banks to show a rising level of dollar net income.

SOURCES OF BANK INCOME

Banks derive their income primarily from lending and investing and, to a lesser extent, from fees and charges received for services rendered. Income from loans constitutes more than 60 per cent of the total. Interest on investment securities accounts for another 22 per cent. All other income, including fees from trust department activities, makes up only about 14 per cent of the total.

Chart II illustrates the significance of rising loan income to bank earnings.

Bank income is also affected by the kinds of loans banks make. For example, the increase in the proportion of consumer credit loans, made on a discount basis which effectively doubles the gross yield, has increased the average rate of return for many banks.

CHART I

EARNINGS AND EXPENSES AS A PERCENTAGE OF ASSETS
ALL INSURED COMMERCIAL BANKS IN THE UNITED STATES
1950–1960

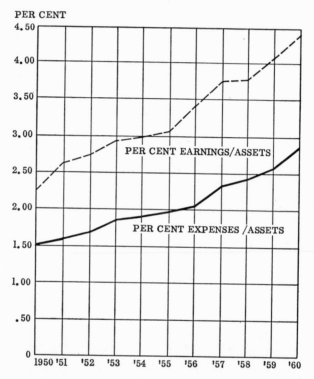

Source: Board of Governors of the Federal Reserve System, *Federal Reserve Bulletin,* 1950–1960.

DISTRIBUTION OF EXPENSE

Insured commercial banks spend about 26 per cent of their gross income for salaries and wages; about 22 per cent for other operating expenses; and about 17 per cent of gross income for interest on time and savings deposits.[3] The latter cost, together with relatively

[3] Board of Governors of the Federal Reserve System, *Federal Reserve Bulletin,* May 1961.

CHART II

EARNINGS OF ALL INSURED COMMERCIAL BANKS
IN THE UNITED STATES
1950–1960

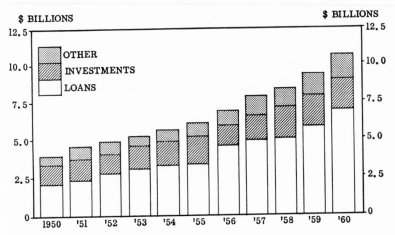

Source: Board of Governors of the Federal Reserve System, *Federal Reserve Bulletin,* 1950–1960.

minor charges for interest on borrowed money, represents the cost of acquiring funds rather than a true operating cost. Interest cost is a measure of management policy rather than management efficiency and is strongly influenced by the competitive situation in which a bank finds itself.

Chart III shows the relative growth of these items of bank expense from 1950 to 1960.

FACTORS AFFECTING BANK EARNINGS

Some of the causes of rising bank earnings are beyond the control of bank management. Interest rates on loans rise where a strong demand for credit exists, and frequently run into the ceilings imposed by the usury laws if such demands persist. Many small banks have never charged much less than the legal maximum. Banks could, conceivably, increase service charges further but, as a practical matter, are being forced by competition to render even

CHART III

EXPENSES OF ALL INSURED COMMERCIAL BANKS
IN THE UNITED STATES
1950–1960

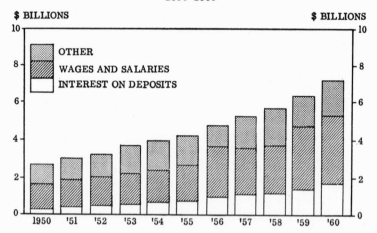

Source: Board of Governors of the Federal Reserve System, *Federal Reserve Bulletin,* 1950–1960.

more costly services. In some banks there still may be an opportunity to expand loan portfolios, but for many, minimum liquidity
needs already restrict further loan expansion.

In short, the credit demands which have enabled banks to expand
their loan portfolios and to increase their interest rates have been
the result of a high level of business activity coupled with the restraints which the monetary authorities have placed on the rapid
expansion of the money supply. This combination has placed commercial banks in the enviable position (from the standpoint of earnings) of having a well regulated monopoly on the creation of a
commodity (credit) that has been in relatively short supply. The
recessions which have interrupted the upward sweep of the economy
on three or four occasions since 1945 have been short lived. Loan
demand in these periods slackened only slightly,[4] and banks were

---

[4] What slackening took place was in commercial loans and was offset by the
almost continuous rise in mortgage loans and consumer credit.

not forced to liquidate assets drastically as they were in the 1930s. In fact, during these periods of recession, the Federal Reserve System expanded credit by increasing liberally the supply of bank reserves. Banks used these reserves to acquire additional securities so that total earning assets as well as total deposits expanded, and current earnings no more than leveled off despite falling interest rates.

Even more importantly, the policy of "active" credit ease in times of recession has usually resulted in rising bond prices. As a result reductions in current earnings, where they have occurred, have been more than offset by security profits.[5]

The record of bank earnings in recent periods of both expansion and recession might cause the casual observer to view prospects for bank earnings as favorable indeed, but it is well to remember that bank costs have risen steadily and that costs are far less flexible than the more volatile earnings rates or the volume of credit demand. A severe recession, characterized by a falling-off of loan demand and a prolonged reversal of the Federal Reserve's restrictive monetary policy, could seriously affect bank earnings. Salary scales, once increased, are not easily or quickly reduced. New buildings and modernization programs commit banks to higher occupancy costs for years ahead. Branch offices established in anticipation of a rising level of business activity and suburban expansion can become a drain on income if that activity fails to materialize. If loan demand and interest rates were to decline to the levels of only a few years ago while expenses remained at present levels, the recently satisfactory earnings of commercial banks would virtually disappear.

Although banks might improve their gross earnings through aggressive lending, realistic interest rate policies and the imposition of higher service charges, they are still to a considerable extent at the mercy of the market and subject to the vicissitudes that may beset the economy. The fact makes all the more vital the control and reduction of bank expense through an increase in the productivity

---

[5] In the recession year of 1958 net earnings of all insured banks declined by $43 million but net profits on securities aggregated $775 million as compared with net losses in the previous boom year. Source: *Federal Reserve Bulletin,* May 1960.

of the banking operation. This is the prime challenge to bank management and a few banks have already pioneered in this direction. They are the banks whose earnings are well above average. The comparisons in Tables 3 and 4 of two very profitable banks, one a unit bank with resources of a little over $10 million, and the other a large branch banking system with aggregate assets well in excess of $500 million should serve as a challenge to the management of banks of any size.

TABLE 3

EARNINGS OF PROFITABLE BANKS

% Assets	Deposits $5–20 million		Deposits Over $50 million	
	Bank A	Average	Bank B	Average
Total Earnings	5.67	4.40	4.96	4.76
Total Expenses	2.83	3.38	2.90	3.48
Net Earnings	2.84	1.02	2.06	1.28

Source: Reports of Earnings and Dividends (1961) and Operating Ratios of Second District Member Banks (1961).

At first glance it would appear that the high net earnings of both these banks resulted primarily from their relatively high gross earnings. Of course, earnings are an important factor but they do not tell the whole story. Ordinarily as bank earnings rise in relation to assets, expenses increase commensurately. High income is often derived from consumer credit, which is a high cost form of lending, or earnings are swelled by banking activities unrelated to total assets, such as a profitable trust department or a substantial income from mortgage servicing. Such extraneous activities require staff and cost money. The profitability of Banks A and B in the comparison in Table 3 derives from the fact that they have been able to increase gross income while keeping expenses well below average in relation to total assets. The degree of this efficiency is evident in Table 4 which shows the main categories of expense as related to gross income.

The below-average salary costs shown by these banks are not the result of lower unit salaries; they reflect the ability of management to get the banking job done with fewer people. While others wait

TABLE 4

EXPENSES OF PROFITABLE BANKS

% Total Earnings	Deposits $5–20 million		Deposits Over $50 million	
	Bank A	*Average*	*Bank B*	*Average*
Salaries and Wages	12.2	25.3	14.8	26.6
Other Operating	10.0	21.6	17.8	23.0
Subtotal	22.2	46.9	32.6	49.6
Interest on Deposits	27.8	29.9	26.0	23.5

for the electronic age to solve bank operating problems, these banks, both big and relatively small, have demonstrated that the greatest savings are to be found not in better machinery alone, but in more efficient procedures and more effective management organization.

High productivity reflects not only simplicity of method but the effectiveness of personnel training and the elimination of waste time and effort which, in the aggregate, still cost banks millions of dollars every month. To attain these results and control rising costs, a precise knowledge of the factors that go into bank income and expense is essential. It is the long-range hope for the maintenance of an adequate level of bank earnings.

ANALYSIS OF INCOME AND EXPENSE

For analytical purposes the published figures of bank income and expense leave much to be desired. On the expense side in particular they do not provide an adequate basis for comparison between banks. Salary figures, for example, include trust department salaries for those banks which have such departments so that comparison with a bank which does not operate a trust department is essentially meaningless. Of even greater significance, since it affects many more banks, is the fundamental difference between the operating cost of handling demand and time deposits. The latter, because of their low rate of turnover, are substantially cheaper to process than active checking accounts. A bank with a high volume of savings deposits, therefore, can easily show below-average salary costs while it is actually operating inefficiently. The published figures consequently need to be subjected to closer analysis.

Detailed analysis of income and expense, often loosely referred to as "cost analysis," serves a number of useful purposes. In the first place bank management cannot successfully plan a broad lending and investing program unless it knows the net yield as well as the gross return on various types of loans and investments. There is no point, for example, in attempting to expand a consumer lending operation or enter some new phase of it, such as check credit, until management is reasonably sure that the *net* return will be commensurate with the risk. The fact that such lending is considered profitable by other banks is no guarantee that it is, or will be equally profitable in a particular bank.[6]

Secondly, bank management should have a reasonably concise idea of the relative profitability of its various classes of deposits if it is to intelligently establish interest rate policies or decide what services it can afford to render to depositors. All too frequently such policies are established with little reference to their cost or profitability.

Income and expense analysis is also vital to cost control and cost reduction. For this purpose it is usually desirable to obtain departmental and branch office breakdowns of income and expense so that particular segments of the bank's earnings can be made the direct responsibility of individual supervisors, department heads, or branch managers.

By relating expense to volume, expense analysis can be used to determine per item costs. Such figures are widely used as a basis for determining or justifying service charges and are also a measure of efficiency on the basis of which operating standards can be established.

Finally it is essential to establish "functional costs" which can be defined as the direct costs of performing specific operations such as bookkeeping or consumer lending. Such knowledge is necessary for comparing systems and procedures, and functional costs are the most nearly comparable between different banks.

----

[6] An income and expense analysis of one consumer credit department, made under the author's supervision, revealed the fact that the net income of that active but inefficient department was less than the return on the bank's government securities; a fact that shocked management into remedial action.

METHODS OF
INCOME AND EXPENSE ANALYSIS

To a considerable extent the purposes for which a bank analyzes its income and expense will determine the form of the analysis. Many of these purposes are interrelated, and there is no reason why more than one approach should not be followed. At best, any analysis will involve a number of arbitrary decisions and no one method can be said to be completely or scientifically accurate. The allocation of senior officers' salaries to departments or functions, for example, and especially to item costs, can only be based on subjective judgments.

One cannot accurately determine what the president of a bank spends his time thinking about. He himself would find the keeping of a record of his varied activities, even for a few days, to be intolerably burdensome. Moreover, even if such a record could be kept, it would be largely meaningless because the work of senior management seldom follows established patterns. The president may spend a week working on a merger, half the next week attending a bankers' convention, two days working out a complicated loan agreement, and the next day catching up on a pile of neglected and quite miscellaneous correspondence. Some of his most productive effort is likely to be spent entirely outside of regular banking hours in the form of new business garnered on the golf course or the sudden insight that flashes across his mind as he is about to fall asleep.

In small and medium-sized banks even the work of the junior platform officer is equally varied. In the course of any business day he may take loan applications, open new accounts, sell savings bonds or travellers' checks, interview an equipment salesman, a representative of the bank's correspondent, and a wealthy woman customer who wants to know what stock to buy. Such efforts cannot be accurately allocated to the cost of processing a check.

Even so, from the viewpoint of the individual bank, and for many of the purposes for which banks analyze their income and expense, the inaccuracies of expense allocation are not seriously detrimental. For the purpose of comparing the bank's own performance year by year, for budgeting and cost control, consistency is more important

than absolute accuracy.[7] And whether 5 per cent or 10 per cent
of the president's salary is distributed to the check department will
not alter the per item cost of processing a transit check by as much
as a tenth of a mill.

TRADITIONAL METHODS OF
INCOME AND EXPENSE ANALYSIS

There is not room in this work for an exhaustive analysis or cri-
tique of cost accounting theory.   Many articles on varying aspects
of the problem have appeared in banking magazines, and there are
nearly as many approaches and refinements as there are analysts.
A very comprehensive study is contained in *Bank Costs*, a project
of the Bank Cost Committee of the National Association of Bank
Auditors and Comptrollers.[8]

The traditional methods of bank cost accountants have involved
the distribution of the income and expense accounts shown on the
bank's general ledger, first to departments and then to fund-using
(lending or investing) or fund-supplying (deposits and capital
funds) functions.   The emphasis may be either on the ultimate
profitability of lending and investing, or it may be on the profitability of deposits and capital, taking into account their investment
return, net of their cost.   The essence of this approach is that all
expense is distributed to departments and then to functions where
per item costs can be computed by comparing cost, thus determined,
with the number of items processed.   Chart IV, reproduced from
Bank Costs Manual by permission of The Association for Bank
Audit Control and Operation, illustrates these principles.

---

[7] A typical bank controller's view is expressed by William J. Boyle: "Without
cost accounting management can only *guess* what departments are unprofitable.
When a department is shown to be unprofitable, a program of cost control gives
management a tool to take corrective measures through either a revision in rate
charges or an examination of existing work procedures that may prove to be
too costly.   I dare say that we would find in this gathering a variance of opinion with respect to the *technique* of the system of cost accounting.   These
differences, in my opinion, are relatively unimportant. . . . What *is* important, however, is for us to discuss the need for such a program."   William J.
Boyle, Assistant Vice President, Providence Tradesmens Bank and Trust Company, Philadelphia, Pa., in "Cost Control," address delivered during Group III
Regional Meeting of Pennsylvania Bankers Association, *Bank Management Sym-
posium 1958* (New York: The Consolidated Reporting Company, 1958).

[8] A loose-leaf cost accounting manual published by the Association in 1951.

GENERAL FLOW CHART OF EXPENSE

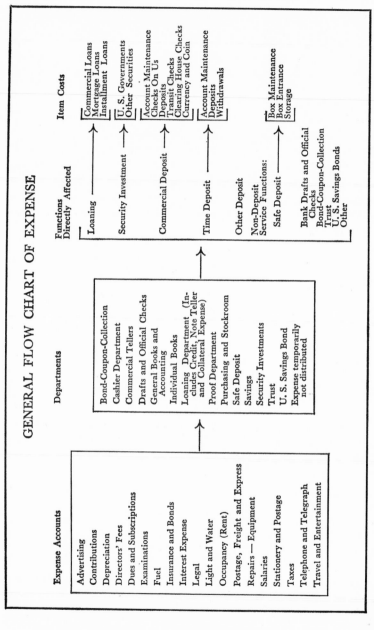

Expense Accounts

Advertising
Contributions
Depreciation
Directors' Fees
Dues and Subscriptions
Examinations
Fuel
Insurance and Bonds
Interest Expense
Legal
Light and Water
Occupancy (Rent)
Postage, Freight and Express
Repairs — Equipment
Salaries
Stationery and Postage
Taxes
Telephone and Telegraph
Travel and Entertainment

Departments

Bond-Coupon-Collection
Cashier Department
Commercial Tellers
Drafts and Official Checks
General Books and
  Accounting
Individual Books
Loaning Department (Includes Credit, Note Teller and Collateral Expense)
Proof Department
Purchasing and Stockroom
Safe Deposit
Savings
Security Investments
Trust
U. S. Savings Bond
Expense temporarily
  not distributed

Functions Directly Affected

Loaning ⟶

Security Investment ⟶

Commercial Deposit ⟶

Time Deposit ⟶

Other Deposit

Non-Deposit
Service Functions:

Safe Deposit ⟶

Bank Drafts and Official
  Checks
Bond-Coupon-Collection
Trust
U. S. Savings Bonds
Other

Item Costs

Commercial Loans
Mortgage Loans
Installment Loans

U. S. Governments
Other Securities

Account Maintenance
Checks On Us
Deposits
Transit Checks
Clearing House Checks
Currency and Coin

Account Maintenance
Deposits
Withdrawals

Box Maintenance
Box Entrance
Storage

CHART IV

77

"FUNCTIONAL ANALYSIS"
OF INCOME AND EXPENSE

Traditional cost accounting approaches suffer from two important defects. First, the allocation of overhead and supervisory or administrative salaries is a complex task, as suggested above, from which most small and medium-sized banks have shied away. Secondly, the resultant figures are seldom comparable as between banks because purely operating costs are combined with administrative costs on the basis of estimates made individually and subjectively by each bank. Does it really cost Bank A more to process a check or handle a loan because the President of Bank A receives a higher salary than the President of Bank B? Even the fact that Bank A has a more modern and expensive bank building does not necessarily add or detract from the efficiency of the systems and procedures carried on therein. It is these costs, the pure or direct costs of performing each operation, which need to be isolated and controlled if efficiency and productivity are to be increased. And it is these processing costs which are most nearly comparable between banks and between alternative systems.

The more highly a bank is departmentalized the more readily can a major portion of its income and expenses be objectively distributed to clear-cut departments and functions. For the very small bank, where three or four employees participate actively in nearly all of the bank's operations, cost distribution is virtually impossible. For the majority of banks, those with resources of say $4 to $20 million, something less complex than the NABAC manual is called for, but some form of cost control is nevertheless essential.[9]

In an attempt to simplify the methods of traditional cost accounting and to provide, particularly for smaller banks, a sound basis for interbank comparison, the author devised [10] a simplified "Functional

---

[9] At the annual "audit clinic" of the Association for Bank Credit Control and Operation held in Boston in 1958 a "cost panel" was presented for the first time. The "small bank" there represented was the $40 million South Shore National with seven offices in Quincy and Weymouth, Mass., and with $25 million in trust assets. "Cost Accounting," *Auditgram*, XXXIV, No. 11, (November 1958) p. 5.

[10] Presented to the Investment Seminar of the New York State Bankers Association (Co-sponsored by the Graduate School of Business of New York Uni-

Analysis of Income and Expense" which has been widely applied to banks with resources between $5 million and $20 million in the Second Federal Reserve District.[11]

This approach to the problem of bank costs is basically an attempt to provide the majority of banks under $20 million in total resources with the means of comparing the efficiency of their various operations (as measured by cost) from year to year and with other banks of comparable size. Such comparisons should indicate the areas in which management needs to concentrate its efforts to reduce costs or increase income. The analysis form also shows the relative profitability of demand and time deposits as one guide to interest rate policy.

The method starts with the assumption that the principal function of a bank is the making of loans and investments. Banks have other functions, as Chapter I pointed out, but the essential economic role of a commercial bank is the creation of credit, and its primary source of income is the interest on its loans and investments.

By rough analogy, therefore, a commercial bank is conceived as a credit factory (with some incidental sidelines) of which the raw materials are the funds placed at its disposal principally by depositors and in part by stockholders. Using these funds, a bank creates credit and sells it at a price which is termed "interest." The cost of its principal raw material (deposits) consists of the interest which the bank in turn pays to its time and savings depositors and the cost of the services which it renders primarily to its demand depositors over and above its service charges. The costs of making and servicing loans and investments are considered as "manufacturing costs" and deducted from the income received thereon. Other costs which cannot be directly related to processing assets or deposits—the hard core of overhead and administrative costs— are distributed to both the asset and deposit operations in proportion to processing or direct operational costs.[12]

versity) in September 1955, as "Profit Analysis: A Guide to Bank Policy." *New York State Banker* (September 1955), Vol. 16, Issue 52.

[11] A project of the Technical Assistance Division of the Bank Relations Department of the Federal Reserve Bank of New York. Beginning in 1958, the Federal Reserve Bank of Boston has compiled a similar form of analysis from figures submitted to it by its member banks of comparable size.

[12] This method of overhead distribution is recommended by the New York Clearing House Association in its booklet, *Bank Cost Accounting Principles and Procedures,* New York, 1961.

A second assumption on which this method of analysis is based
is that, having provided for adequate liquidity in the form of primary and secondary reserves,[13] a commercial bank for all practical
purposes invests its remaining funds without particular regard to
whether they are demand or time deposits; *e.g.,* when a customer
comes in to borrow $10,000, the average banker looks at his cash
position to see if he has any available funds to lend without asking
whether they came in through the savings deposit window or the
commercial tellers.   The bank's portfolio of loans and investments
represents a pooling of funds, the composition of which is more
likely to be determined by the credit needs of the community than
by any preconceived ideas of some ideal conversion of funds.

Carrying out the analogy with a manufacturing enterprise, the
various kinds of loans and investments a bank makes might be
considered as different product lines.   Each has a different sales
price and a varying direct cost of manufacture.   Installment loans,
for example, which have the highest gross yield are also the most
expensive loans to make and service.   It is the net return on the
various kinds of loans and investments which, other things being
equal, will indicate to bank management their relative merits as
portfolio ingredients.   An adequate cost accounting method, therefore, must distinguish the direct costs of making and servicing specific kinds of loans from the administrative and overhead costs that
apply to the whole banking operation.

The final assumption upon which this simplified functional analysis is based is that profits must be related to capital to determine
profitability.   Capital is required in a bank in some relationship to
the risk factor in its assets.[14]   In determining the relative profitability of demand and time deposits, therefore, capital is allocated
to such deposits respectively in proportion to their investment in
the portfolio, or risk assets of the bank.

The eight steps of this simplified form of analysis are shown be-

---

[13] See Chapter VIII for a method of determining minimum liquidity requirements for demand and time deposits.

[14] Bank supervisors and others use a number of so-called "risk-asset" ratios
to determine the adequacy of bank capital.   The ratio used in the funtional
analysis described here is the "measure of minimum capital adequacy" devised
by the author and used by the Federal Reserve Bank of New York.   It is described in detail in Chapter IX.

low in condensed form.[15] Many of the captions, obviously, can be refined in detail and the analysis expanded for use by larger banks.

STEP I

ANALYSIS OF INCOME
(000 omitted)

Account	*Amount*
Income from short-term (secondary reserve) assets	$ 63
Remainder of income from loans and investments (portfolio)	595
Service charges on demand deposits	68
Miscellaneous department income (Safe deposit rental, trust fees, etc.)	23
Total Income	$749

The first step is a simple analysis of income. Interest on loans and investments is split between income on portfolio assets and income from secondary reserve assets (see Chapter VII). Service charge income is shown separately so that it may be deducted later from the cost of servicing deposits. Income from noncredit-creating functions is separately controlled. The income from various types of loans and investments can be shown separately if desired.

STEP II

ANALYSIS OF EXPENSE
(000 omitted)

	Direct Cost	*Overhead Allocation*	*Total*
Demand Deposits			
Tellers	41	28	69
Transit	14	9	23
Bookkeeping	54	35	89
	109		181
Time Deposits			
Processing	17	10	27
Interest paid	199	–	199
	216		226

15 The figures shown in the tables which follow are the averages for the 27 banks with total assets ranging from $12 million to $20 million which participated in the 1960 Functional Analysis Program of the Bank Relations Department of the Federal Reserve Bank of New York.

STEP II—Continued

Loans and Investments			
Commercial loans	21	14	35
Mortgage loans	14	10	24
Consumer loans	34	23	57
Subtotal	69		116
Security Investments	5	3	8
	74		124
Miscellaneous Departments			
Trust	12	8	20
Safe deposit	4	3	7
Other	1	–	1
	17		28
Administration and Overhead	143	143 *	x
Total Expense	559		559

* Distributed in proportion to direct processing cost.

Step II separates bank expenses into four major groupings. The direct costs of servicing deposits include the salaries of those staff members who actually process deposits and checks—the teller-transit-bookkeeper operations—and the salaries, or related portions thereof, of the senior clerks or officers who directly supervise these operations. Also included are the cost of materials, supplies, machine rental or depreciation, and other costs directly related to processing deposits.

Loan and investment processing costs likewise are the direct costs of putting loans and investments on the books, collecting and accounting for interest payments, and the ultimate collection of the assets themselves. These are the more or less mechanical costs of lending and investing, rather than the costs involved in decision-making. These processing costs are important to isolate because they are a measure of the efficiency of the bank's credit-creating operation. On a functional basis they are quite comparable between banks. For more detailed analysis these direct costs of lending can be broken down as between mortgage loans, consumer credit and all other.

The direct costs of rendering miscellaneous services are also separately controlled so that the profitability of these activities, which are essentially sidelines of the banking business, may be accurately determined.

Finally, the costs which cannot be directly allocated to specific operations, *i.e.*, overhead and administrative costs, are determined. This category can be readily refined into a number of sub-groups for more detailed analysis, such as occupancy costs, credit department, advertising, etc., and these areas separately controlled or compared with other banks. In the smaller bank, however, the separation of the different components of overhead and administrative costs is often difficult.

The allocation of overhead costs to the operations of a bank is probably the most controversial aspect of any cost-accounting procedure. In the approach shown in Step II, overhead costs are distributed pro rata to each processing operation. The result of this method of overhead distribution is to charge demand deposits with a relatively larger proportion of overhead, a result with which most practical bankers would agree because a large portion of administrative effort is devoted to customer relations with business accounts which are almost exclusively demand depositors and commercial borrowers.[16]

STEP III

ASSET ALLOCATION
(000 omitted)

| | | Allocation | | |
| | | Primary | Secondary | |
Source of Funds	Amount	Reserve	Reserve	Portfolio
Demand deposits	$ 7,522	$1,593	$1,413	$ 4,516
Time deposits	7,598	676	697	6,225
Capital funds *	1,446	—	—	1,446
	$16,566	$2,269	$2,110	$12,187

* Available for investment: Book capital funds and reserves less fixed assets, plus or minus the net of accruals and deferred items.

---

16 Most bank presidents in banks of the size considered here would estimate the administrative and overhead expenses of their banks at three or four times as much per dollar of demand deposits as per dollar of savings deposits. The method of overhead allocation used in this analysis allocates approximately three times as much overhead to demand deposits as to time deposits in an "average" bank in which time deposits slightly exceed the aggregate of demand deposits.

Step III is a simplified conversion of funds table showing the extent to which three categories of funds are invested in a like number of asset classifications. Few banks allocate primary and secondary reserves specifically to demand or time deposits, although they should. The legal reserve against time deposits for member banks is 5 per cent including cash on hand. For demand deposits the legal reserve in banks outside of reserve cities is 12 per cent. Most banks, however, hold more cash and bank balances than they need for reserve purposes. They maintain excess balances with correspondents to compensate them for a variety of services, some of which, like check collection, are directly related to the demand deposit function. Others, such as investment advisory services or loan participations, are related to portfolio assets. If a bank consistently holds more primary (cash) reserves than it needs its earnings will suffer. Rather than assess this penalty (if it exists) against demand deposits alone, it has been prorated in this method of analysis to demand and time deposits in proportion to required reserves.[17]

Secondary reserve requirements vary from bank to bank. They are related to the demands for funds made on each bank by its depositors and borrowing customers. A method of estimating such requirements is described in Chapter VIII and average requirements over the course of a year, as estimated by that method, are used in the asset allocation shown in Step III. To fulfill this secondary reserve requirement any excess of primary reserves is first assigned and the balance is made up of readily marketable short-term assets which qualify as liquidity instruments (see Chapter VII).

Most banks hold more liquid assets than their estimated needs would require. These "excess" liquid assets are transferred to, and treated as part of, the "portfolio" in the above analysis. Thus the aggregate of primary and secondary reserves should be the total of the bank's legal reserve and minimum liquidity needs averaged over the period under study.

---

[17] Required reserves are computed for demand and time deposits and the proportion of each to the total requirement established. These proportions are then applied to acutal primary reserves to establish allocation. The amounts in excess of legal requirements are considered "excess" primary reserves and are used to fulfill secondary reserve requirements.

STEP IV

COMPUTATION OF YIELDS
(000 omitted)

Asset Breakdown	Amount	Earnings	Expenses	Net	Yield
Cash and due from banks (primary)	$ 2,269	0			0
Secondary reserve	2,110	63	4	59	2.79
Portfolio	12,187	595	120	475	3.90
	$16,566	658	124	534	

Step IV is designed to compute the yield on the three major asset categories. The earnings figures are taken directly from Step I. Expenses are the cost of lending and investing (including related overhead) brought forward from Step II, with a pro rata share of investment expenses allocated to the secondary reserve category. Net earnings on each category of funds is then expressed in terms of yield.

STEP V

COMPUTATION OF EARNINGS
(000 omitted)

	Allocation	Amount	Yield	Income	Net Earnings
Demand Deposits					
	Primary	1,593	0	0	
	Secondary	1,413	2.79	39	
	Portfolio	4,516	3.90	176	
				215	
	Cost of processing		181		
	Less: Service charge		68	113	102
Time Deposits					
	Primary	676	0	0	
	Secondary	697	2.79	20	
	Portfolio	6,225	3.90	243	
				263	
	Cost of processing		27		
	Interest Paid		199	226	37
Capital Funds					
	Portfolio	1,446	3.90	56	56
Miscellaneous Operations					
	Gross income			24	
	Less: Expense			28	(—) 4
Total Net Current Earnings (before taxes)					191

In Step III various sources of investable funds were allocated to three asset categories. In Step IV the average earnings on those three categories were computed. Step V combines Steps III and IV to determine the net income (before taxes) from the investment of each of the three categories of funds and from the other noncredit-creating operations of the bank. This is a total functional accounting for the net income from the bank's operations.

STEP VI

ALLOCATION OF INCOME TAXES
(000 omitted)

	Net Current Operating Earnings	%	Applicable Federal Taxes *	Net Earnings After Taxes
Time Deposits	$ 37	19.1	13	$ 24
Demand Deposits	102	53.7	36	66
Capital Funds	56	29.6	20	36
Miscellaneous Departments	—4	—2.4	—2	—2
	$191	100.0	67	$124

* This "average" bank had $52,000 of tax-exempt income. Tax liability, therefore, was 30 per cent of $25,000, or $7,500, plus 52 per cent of $114,000, or $59,200.

Step VI allocates applicable Federal income taxes to the earnings on the various classes of funds and miscellaneous operations pro rata. These taxes are computed (for comparative purposes) as being 30 per cent on the first $25,000 and 52 per cent on additional taxable income. This of course may not represent the individual bank's actual tax bill which will be affected by "below-the-line" adjustments resulting from profits or losses and transfers to tax free reserves. State income taxes in some states will have to be added. These tax adjustments, however, are not operating results (in a strict sense) which this method of analysis attempts to measure.

At this point the net profits of the bank can be recapitulated in terms of the net financial return, after taxes, on each of the classes of investable funds and on other operations. At the same time the profitability of the bank as a whole can be computed by relating total profits to available capital funds. This, however, does not reveal the relative profitability of each category of deposits. To determine this figure it is necessary to allocate capital funds to demand and time deposits separately. This is done in Step VII.

STEP VII

CAPITAL ALLOCATION
(000 omitted)

	Participation in Portfolio	Per Cent of Participation	Book Capital Allocation	Uniform Capital Allocation
Demand	4,516	42.0	607	463
Time	6,225	58.0	839	639
	10,741	100.0	1,446	1,102

All of a bank's risk assets are included in the portfolio. Primary and secondary reserve assets consist only of those assets against which the various capital adequacy tests used by bank supervisors (Chapter IX) require no specific capital allocation. Available capital (book capital net of fixed assets) is allocated to demand and time deposits, therefore, in the same proportion as such deposits are invested in portfolio or risk assets. Thus, since demand deposits account for 42 per cent of the deposits at risk they are considered to be supported by 42 per cent of the available capital funds.

The smaller the amount of a bank's capital funds in relation to its earning assets the more profitable it will appear. In order to be able to compare one bank with another on an equitable basis, it is necessary to compute a theoretical capital requirement that is directly related to risk assets. This can be done uniformly on the basis of any "risk-asset" formula. In the step above the uniform capital allocation is based on the capital adequacy computation, devised at the Federal Reserve Bank of New York, which will be described in detail in Chapter IX. The theoretical capital requirement is allocated to two classes of deposits in the same proportion as actual capital. This allocation of capital makes it possible to compute the profitability of demand and time deposits separately as is done in Step VIII.

STEP VIII

PROFITABILITY OF DEMAND AND TIME DEPOSITS
(000 omitted)

	Capital Allocation	%	Earnings on Deposits	Earnings on Related Capital	Total	Per Cent Earned on Capital
Actual Capital						
Demand	607	42.0	66	15	81	13.34
Time	839	58.0	24	21	45	5.36
	1,446	100.0	90	36	126	
Theoretical Capital						
Demand	463	42.0	66	11	77	16.63
Time	639	58.0	24	16	40	6.26
	1,102	100.0	90	27 *	117	

* Earnings on reduced amount of theoretical capital computed at net yield on portfolio assets of 3.90%, adjusted for income taxes.

In Step VIII the proportionate earnings on the amount of capital funds allocated to demand and time deposits, respectively, are added to the net earnings from the direct investment of these funds as determined in Step VI. The total is then related to the amount of capital funds allocated to each class of deposits in Step VII to determine their relative profitability. In effect, each class of deposits, together with its related capital funds, is treated as a separate "bank."

To make the profitability ratios comparable with other banks, they are also computed in relation to the theoretical minimum capital required by the risk factors in the asset structure of the particular bank.

It appears from this analysis that demand deposits are more profitable than time deposits and, for banks of this size, with average asset distribution this is probably true. According to this analysis the interest cost of time deposits is roughly equal to the cost of servicing demand deposits but about one-third of the latter cost is recouped through service charges. In addition, the profitability of demand deposits is enhanced by the fact that, being invested in a higher proportion of riskless assets for liquidity reasons, they require relatively less capital protection.

For the well-managed bank, however, with above-average earnings and below-average costs, time and savings deposits can be profitable even at higher-than-average (maximum permitted) interest rates. If there is a strong demand for loans from a bank's service area the portfolio can contain a relatively greater portion of higher-yielding assets which will justify the bank's bidding aggressively for deposits.[18] Furthermore, no cost analysis can reflect the collateral advantages of a bank's remaining competitive—the potentially profitable volume of related business obtained from savings deposit customers.

Some cost analysts attempt to prove the profitability of savings deposits by "converting" such funds exclusively into the highest yielding loans in the bank's portfolio. If assets are thus "allocated," related capital should also be allocated and, when this is done, profitability is not greatly increased since high-yield assets generally contain a larger degree of risk and consequently require proportionately more capital.

SIGNIFICANCE OF FUNCTIONAL ANALYSIS

The significance of an analysis of bank income and expense does not necessarily lie in the demonstration that demand or time deposits are more or less profitable *per se*. The principal benefit will be found in the individual cost ratios that can be derived from such an analysis; their year-to-year comparison within the bank as a measure of progress in controlling and reducing costs, and their comparison with similar figures for other banks as an indication of the cost areas which may require intensive examination and corrective action.

The intriguing thing about comparing the ratios of different banks is the wide variation invariably found between the highs and the lows in every earning and expense ratio. The individual bank which finds itself very far removed from the best performance should ask itself the reason. It may not be due to differences of efficiency of operation in every case. Widely varying results may be occasioned by differences in the character of the business handled, its volume, and its complexity. Thus, a large number of small deposit accounts are more expensive to handle per dollar of deposit than are a few

---

18 *Cf.* Howard D. Crosse, "Profitability of Savings Deposits," address to Mid-Winter Meeting, New York State Bankers Association, January 22, 1962, published in *The New York State Banker,* Vol. 23, Issue 18, February 5, 1962.

large accounts adding up to the same totals. By the same token, service charge income is proportionately reduced if the major part of the deposits consists of large accounts that carry themselves or are otherwise profitable. Nevertheless, wide deviations from the income and expense records posted by the few banks which show the best results should challenge management to re-examine its portfolio management, its systems and procedures, and its staff organization.

FACTORS OF PROFITABILITY

A detailed study of the banks which show up best in any analysis indicates that there are three main factors contributing to above-average profitability. The first of these is likely to be a higher than average gross income, resulting from an aggressive lending policy and relatively high loan totals. The second most important profit factor is relatively low expense, particularly in the administrative and overhead categories. This usually betokens an effective delegation of decision-making responsibility, a well-trained and experienced staff which lends flexibility to the bank's operation, and a sound salary administration. Finally, intelligent management of the bank's tax liability is a major contributor to high profits. The maintenance of an adequate level of tax-exempt income, taken together with the willingness to absorb security losses for the purpose of increasing income or ultimate capital gains, helps materially to maximize profits. This subject will be further discussed in Chapter XII.

BUDGETING OR "PROFIT PLANNING"

One of the principal by-products of an effective analysis of income and expense is a budget or planned projection of the bank's operations into the future. A budget is much more than a simple forecast of income and expense. It is a pattern to follow, a measure against which performance may be judged, a set of goals that an organization may strive to exceed.

Bank budgets do not start with income and expense. They are derived from forecasts of the volume and character of the bank's assets and liabilities: how many loans of what kind and how many deposits with what degree of activity. When volume and activity have been projected they can be combined with estimates of cost to forecast earnings and profits.

One vital function of the budget is to divide the bank's operations into manageable and visible components so that management and the directors can see the problems of the bank as distinct and separate entities. Last year's experience must be combined with next year's expectations to establish the pattern. The attainment of budgeted results is not as important in itself as the explanation of the failure to do so. A budget should be a guide, not a strait jacket; an intelligently established set of goals and not a flat prediction. The goals which management is willing to set for itself provide powerful incentives for improved performance.

Budgeting should start with the people primarily responsible for performance, the department heads and branch managers. Their estimates should be checked by top management in the light of economic conditions, community growth, competitive factors, and comparisons with other banks in similar circumstances. It is the task of top management and the directors to see to it that budgetary goals are set high enough to provide a realistic challenge to the entire organization. Deviations of performance in either direction should require formal explanation, because the principal function of the budget is to act as a control of the management's ability to plan intelligently and to execute a plan successfully.

No bank is too small to have a budget, even if its form is relatively simple. On this all bank directors should insist, for it is the directors' most effective tool in the execution of their important function of giving guidance to the bank in its service to the community and its rewards to the stockholder.

DIVIDENDS

Dividends are the objective and end-product of earnings in a privately-owned banking system. The amount of dividends which can be paid is, of course, limited by the bank's rate of earnings but, with a given amount of earnings, various dividend policies can be followed. Among the important considerations in deciding dividend policy are the bank's rate of growth, the adequacy of its capital funds, the distribution of its ownership, and its plans for expansion.

The basic question is, "What portion of earnings *should* the bank retain?" An adequately capitalized bank in a stable or economically declining community needs, in fact, to retain none. Many a small bank finds itself in this condition and yet the directors continue to hoard capital as a squirrel hoards nuts. The reason is usually found in a small list of stockholders more interested in capital gains than in income.

In growing communities where the bank itself is expanding and can see the need for additional capital in the future the choice lies between retention of earnings and a dividend policy that will maintain the market price of the bank's stock and its desirability as an investment at attractive levels so that additional capital, when needed, can be readily obtained in the market place. The choice taken in individual circumstances is likely to depend upon whether the directors want the widest possible distribution of the bank's shares, or whether they want to perpetuate close control. For the latter, minimum dividends and maximum earnings retention are the most effective program. It is a program, however, of self-interest, rather than community interest, and its unfortunate prevalence has been a contributing factor to the merger trend.

Stock dividends have become increasingly popular in recent years as a compromise between earnings retention and distribution. The declaration of small stock dividends, sometimes in addition to regular cash dividends, gives the stockholder the choice between keeping his additional shares for capital gains or disposing of them for maximum income. Although there is no logical basis in arithmetic for it, the receipt of a marketable stock dividend has had the effect of increasing the apparent dividend and thereby increasing the market value of the bank's stock. As the market value increases the sale value of the stock dividends increases further, making the stock still more attractive on the market. This can be a potentially dangerous pyramiding of values. If the stock dividend is not maintained, or if market values decline for other reasons, the fall in price of the stock of an individual bank can have an adverse effect on public relations. It is for this reason that bank supervisors have generally insisted that stock dividends should not be continuous, year after year, and that in any event the market value of the stock dividend should bear a reasonable relationship to the actual current earnings of the bank. As a rule-of-thumb, 75 per cent of earnings is considered the maximum limit to the market value of a "regular" stock dividend.

On the average, commercial banks pay out only about half of their net profits as dividends.[19] More attention is paid to this average performance than it deserves. It has become a kind of traditional rule-of-thumb which many banks follow despite the fact that, in particular circumstances, the payment of a greater or lesser percentage might be more advantageous. As long as there is a ready market for bank stock and, if a bank seeks wide local distribution of its shares to improve its community relations and facilitate successor ownership, a more liberal dividend policy is warranted. New capital can then be readily sold as it is needed.

---

[19] Dividends paid by all insured commercial banks in 1959 were equal to 52 per cent of net profits. *Federal Reserve Bulletin,* May 1960.

VI

AUDIT AND CONTROL

It is unfortunate that bank directors and supervisors have to concern themselves with the possibility of losses resulting from the dishonest acts of bank officers and employees. Yet such losses are a real and ever-present danger because, in banking, people handle money. Bank officers and employees are human beings subject to all the pressures and temptations of a society that perhaps puts too much emphasis on the things money can buy. Unlike other people subject to similar pressures, bank employees are daily faced with the physical availability of money in large quantities. In the United States the problem is made even more serious by the multitude of small banks, any one of which may be seriously embarrassed, if not ruined, by a major defalcation.[1]

A less publicized, but no less effective pilferer is the inefficiency which inevitably creeps into banking operations when left without adequate supervision or review. Even minor inefficiencies such as the paper that is needlessly handled twice, or the figure that is copied when it could be reproduced by carbon paper, can result in slow but steady drains on a bank's resources. Over a period of time, these losses probably exceed the more dramatic losses from dishonest acts. Errors, too, can be an important source of loss of money, time, and prestige. All these kinds of losses, the risk of which is inherent in banking, can be reduced by the formulation and implementation of a soundly conceived program of control and audit

---

[1] Most of the banks closed since 1945 have been victims of employee dishonesty. Source: Federal Deposit Insurance Corporation.

94

which covers not only financial transactions and book entries but operating procedures as well.

ASSESSMENT OF THE RISK

The record of bank defalcations in the United States is a sorry one and shows no indication of diminishing. The American Bankers Association reported 256 cases for the three years 1957 through 1959, each in an amount of more than $10,000, and totalling $20 million.[2] Although this is not a large amount in relation to the total resources of all banks, a single defalcation can loom shockingly large in a particular institution.

Most dishonest acts are unpremeditated. They take place when money, which is readily available, appears to be the only solution to a problem brought on by the pressures to which some individual bank officer or employee may become subject. Such pressures may be social or psychological (the desire to be a good fellow or to live up to the style of the Joneses), or they may be simply accidental, *e.g.*, illness in the family or the need to correct some personal mistake or involvement. In most cases the individual convinces himself, in the first instance, that he is "borrowing" the money and only gradually becomes more deeply enmeshed as he finds he cannot pay it back. The longer such a crime goes undetected the more brazen and cynical the individual is likely to become.

In the course of an ordinary lifetime there are few individuals who are not subjected to financial pressures of one kind or another. A bank examiner, on entering the cage of a girl teller, once facetiously enquired, "And how much are *you* short?" The young lady burst into tears and confessed that she had "borrowed" ten cents for bus fare the night before. This rather pathetic incident is but one end of a scale that leads to the respected bank president who, ostensibly to finance a new industry in his community, permitted and engineered illegal overdrafts in excess of $1 million which bankrupted his institution.[3]

Although the larger number of fidelity losses are attributable to

---

[2] Insurance and Protective Department, American Bankers Association, "Directors Responsibility for Defalcation Losses," *Protective Bulletin*, LII, No. 10 (June 1960), p. 1.

[3] *American Banker*, January 16, 1957.

bank employees, the larger amounts, and the most serious cases, are the peculations of bank officers. In nearly every case, the person involved had been respected in his community and considered entirely trustworthy by all his friends and associates. In many cases he completely dominated the operations of his bank, a situation which is always fraught with danger. The bank director who deprecates the need for an audit program because he "knows his people" has been repeatedly proved to be living in a fool's paradise.

Each fidelity loss, whatever its size, is a study in human nature. It is difficult to prove from the record that there exists a person who, if subjected to sufficient pressure, would not resort to unauthorized borrowing *if he were convinced he could escape detection.* Individual resistance to pressure, of course, varies widely, and people without a strong sense of the difference between other people's money and their own should not be working in banks. It is virtually impossible, however, to predict who will succumb to a specific amount of pressure.

Losses through inefficiency are more difficult to measure but they are unquestionably large. The differences in operating costs between clearly well-managed banks and the average bank, noted previously, are one measure. In 1955 the Bank Relations Department of the Federal Reserve Bank of New York, aware of these marked differences in operating results, undertook a series of programs devised to call to the attention of its member banks the opportunities for cost saving through review and simplification of procedures. Representatives of the department, skilled in bank operations, undertook to review individually the operating procedures of those banks having assets ranging from $5 million to $20 million, a size group which generally lacked the internal resources to review its own operations effectively.

During the period 1954 through 1959, the operating costs of all member banks in the United States (excluding interest on time deposits) increased by an average of about .45 per cent of total assets. The increase in the Second District, the only district where so much emphasis had been placed on procedural reviews, averaged only .31 per cent, the lowest increase shown by any of the twelve districts. Of even greater significance, moreover, was the fact that Second District banks in the $5–20 million size group showed an increase of only .19 per cent (the procedures of most of these had been reviewed by the Reserve Bank's technical representatives). The difference between this increase and the average increase in the entire Second District was .12 per cent. This may seem small but when applied to the total assets of this group of banks it represented a saving of over $2.7 million a year. By contrast, total losses from dishonest acts in the Second District have averaged under $1 million a year. Inefficiency is clearly the greater thief. The problem for bank management is to prevent crime and waste to the greatest possible extent and to see that it is promptly detected when it occurs. The audit and control function is the principal tool of management in this regard but not the only one. The first line of defense consists of following basic personnel policies which are too frequently lost sight of.

PERSONNEL POLICIES
IN RESTRAINT OF CRIME

A discussion of the means of minimizing fidelity risk would not be complete without mention of certain aspects of personnel policy that have special significance in this respect. Rotation of employees, for example, serves not only as a method of training but as an effective control principle. This will be discussed further below.

It is almost self-evident that banks should be especially selective in their hiring policies. Too frequently, however, under the pressure of needing hands to get a job done, banks have not thoroughly investigated prospective employees and have known too little of their background. An employee, dismissed by one bank under suspicious circumstances, turns up working for another.[4] References should be meticulously checked and all shadows of doubt eliminated.

It should be equally clear that an adequate salary scale is an important factor in minimizing the pressures which may lead employees astray. Yet, all too often, the courts have excoriated the bank rather than a confessed defaulter when a teller's salary became a matter of public record. The excuse that banks cannot afford to

---

[4] Examples of such laxity are the person who was dismissed for check kiting by one bank and hired as an auditor by another, or the note teller who was fired for holding his own worthless checks as cash items and subsequently turned up as a bank examiner.

pay salaries comparable with those for similar jobs in the community or commensurate with the responsibility of the position is little more than an admission of the inefficiency with which too many banks are operated.   One of the principal aims of the kind of control and audit program advocated herein, with its strong emphasis on increasing operating efficiency, is a bank staff of fewer but better paid people.

Salary scales alone are not the sole answer to the problems of temptation.   Most poorly paid bank clerks never steal.   The character and integrity of the individual are the essential deterrents to crime.   This fact points up the vital need for bank management really to know something about the people who work in banks. Bank directors and senior management often think they "know their people" without having made any systematic effort to do so.   After a defalcation has come to light they frequently wonder how they could have failed to recognize situations which, after the fact, suddenly appear to have been so obvious.

Particularly in small banks in small towns there is little excuse for the directors and senior management not to be familiar with the scale of living of their employees or of the problems with which they may be faced at home.   In larger institutions it is perhaps more difficult, but no less necessary, for management to keep reasonably close personal contact with the junior officers and employees.   Periodic interviews with each individual at which time his progress, aspirations and problems are frankly discussed will generally bring to light an indication of the kind of problem or pressure which might lead to wrongdoing.

Finally, banks should make abundantly clear, in practice as well as in theory, their willingness to assist their employees with financial problems.   The provision of health insurance, and especially "major medical" coverage would have removed the source of temptation in many known cases of fraud.   In addition, loans to employees should be freely available at favorable interest rates together with sympathetic financial counseling.   Legitimate borrowing should be made easy enough to avoid the temptation to indulge in the illegitimate variety of raising funds.   Employees who abuse such privileges are not likely to be good fidelity risks in any event and severance pay, in the long run, will represent cheap insurance.

JUSTIFICATION OF AUDIT COST

Despite the most careful and progressive personnel policies some fidelity losses are likely to occur. A bank may insure itself, of course, against the results of defalcation as well as against losses from burglary, forgery, misplacement and risks of a similar nature. The Insurance and Protective Department of the American Bankers Association recommends specific minimum amounts of coverage for banks of different deposit size. Bank examiners usually check to make sure that banks do hold at least this minimum coverage. In recent years there has also become available a form of excess fidelity coverage in the amount of $1 million which supervisory authorities and others are strongly urging all banks (and especially the smaller ones) to acquire.[5]

The importance of fidelity insurance cannot be overemphasized, but it is not a substitute for adequate controls and effective audits. Too often bank directors, particularly those in smaller banks, take this point of view. Relying on surety bonds and so-called "knowledge of their people," they resist spending the bank's money for auditing because it is not "productive." All authorities are agreed that this attitude is short-sighted and represents a failure of bank directors to live up to their responsibilities.

Defalcations can be a source of extreme embarrassment to bank management even though protected by insurance. Screaming headlines always ask, in effect, how management could have been so incompetent to permit such a thing to happen. The bank's good name is besmirched even though its assets may be recovered.[6]

The prevention of crime is even more important than its detection, and the avoidance of loss is better than its recovery. No one

---

[5] *Cf., American Banker* (New York), April 7, 1961, Editorial, "Money Well Spent—$1 million Excess Fidelity Bonds That Save Banks."

[6] Syracuse *Herald-Journal*, April 29, 1951, "$2,100,000 Overdraft Revealed." The former Syracuse Trust Company ultimately recovered all of the loss occasioned by the collusion between its head bookkeeper and several customers. The adverse publicity, nevertheless, resulted in the resignation of a senior officer (not implicated but who *might* have known what was taking place), the subsequent sale of the bank, and possibly the untimely death of its president from a heart attack.

would deliberately leave oily rags and litter in the attic of his home merely because the house was insured against fire. The temptation to which all bank employees are subject increases as the chance of immediate discovery diminishes. Bank directors have a moral obligation to protect their employees as well as their depositors and stockholders by removing, as far as possible, the opportunities for wrongdoing and providing for the probability of swift detection of misbehavior.

A well-conceived and carefully executed control and audit program will "protect weak people from temptation, strong people from opportunity, and innocent people from suspicion." [7] If the audit program includes a regular and formal review of operating procedures as well as a check on the bank's assets, liabilities, and income, a competent auditor can more than earn his salary by suggesting or instituting cost-saving methods.

The cost of an adequate audit program should be considered as much a fixed cost of banking as the cost of depreciating the building and fixtures, and if the money is spent for a thoroughly competent person and the audit function enlarged as suggested below, the cost of audit can be a far more productive expenditure than many bank directors realize.

AUDIT AND CONTROL—DEFINITIONS

The words audit and control are usually referred to in that order but controls, as a matter of necessity, come first. There can be no meaningful audit without established controls.

A control is a mechanical or procedural device introduced into a process or chain of events which will automatically require that something be done in a specified and predetermined manner. Thus a lock on a door is a control requiring that the door may be opened by inserting and turning a specific key. Physical controls of this kind play an important role in banking operations. They range from the time-lock on the vault door to the locked control in the savings posting machine. But of even greater importance are the procedural rules which are devised and enforced to the end that banking transactions will follow certain specified channels which

---

[7] Marshall C. Corns, *Bank Auditing* (Cambridge, Mass.: Bankers Publishing Company, 1955).

provide predetermined safeguards. The requirement, for example, that a bank's drafts, over a certain amount, must bear two official signatures, and the instructions to that effect given to the correspondent bank, constitute a control designed to make certain that at least two of the bank's officers will have knowledge of any transaction by which the bank's funds are expended.

Another common form of control is the proof. One can hardly think of banking transactions in any other terms than those of double-entry bookkeeping. Every debit must have its opposite credit and at the end of the day, or at intermediate intervals, the sum of debits must be equal to the sum of credits. Proofs which demonstrate this fact are controls to assure accuracy and absence of error, vital conditions of a successful banking operation. It is for the purpose of making certain that he has committed no errors that the teller "proves" his work at the end of the day or that the bookkeeping department adds up all the checks paid and the deposits credited to ascertain that the net figure agrees with the changes in the controlling deposit ledgers. No operation in the bank should be without its control or proof.

The audit function, on the other hand, is concerned with making certain that controls are maintained and that proofs are accurate. It is for this reason that the auditor makes an unexpected count of the teller's cash and reviews the proof, or makes an additional audit run of the day's checks and deposits. It is for this purpose, also, that he reviews actual operating practices to make certain that the controls, established as a matter of policy, have not broken down in day-to-day operations. Too often the control of a locked door to the vault, established to limit access to authorized persons, is vitiated by having the key hang on a peg readily accessible to anyone.

The initial responsibility for devising and establishing adequate controls rests with senior operating management. Every system and procedure in the bank should be set up with control in mind. Each suggested short-cut in operations needs to be viewed in the light of control as well as efficiency. Every piece of new equipment should be examined in the light of the controls which it will afford, as well as the speed of its operation.

In making decisions about controls senior management can and should rely heavily on the auditor since the latter will have the responsibility for maintaining and checking them. Bank directors, too, although not expected to be expert in operating procedures, should be aware of the need for control so that they may intelligently appraise audit reports and understand, in general terms at least, some of the operational complexities they are called upon to consider.

Many banks use an operating manual or manual of procedures as a kind of master control; a control of controls, as it were. Such a manual will contain a description of the approved procedure to be followed in every operation of the bank The preparation of such a manual entails a very valuable discipline; in the process every one of the bank's controls and procedures must be reviewed and evaluated. Rarely will such a process fail to result in material improvements. A manual of operations provides an invaluable training guide as well as a compact reference work with respect to transactions which take place infrequently.[8] Along with its advantages, however, a manual of procedure, once adopted, may increase the danger of inflexibility and resistance to change. It should always be in loose-leaf form.

PRINCIPLES OF CONTROL

There is not space here for a discussion of all of the controls which have a part in banking operations. Nor does a person responsible for bank policy need to know all the details with which his operating people should be completely familiar. A few basic principles, however, should be well known to anyone, including bank directors, who is generally responsible for bank policy and supervision of operations.

The first principle, and one which underlies most bank controls is that, wherever possible, the handling of funds should be separated from the posting of related records. A division of responsibility and a dual accountability are thus immediately established. Where this kind of inherent double-check cannot be conveniently built into

---

[8] During World War II a small bank was successfully operated by a junior officer and nine female high school graduates on the basis of an operating manual which the bank's chief operating officer had prepared as his thesis for the Graduate School of Banking.

the system, the responsibility for checking devolves immediately upon the audit function.

A second basic principle of control is to require that money and securities, again where possible, be held under dual control. In this case the two responsible parties act jointly, keeping watch over each other. Double locks on vault doors are examples of this form of control. Conversely, however, if dual control of valuables is *not* possible, as in a teller's cage, then the sole responsibility must be clearly isolated and enforced. Thus each teller should have complete control over, and sole access to his own cash while he is using it, accounting for it, *in toto*, through his proof at the end of the day. Similarly, each bookkeeper is responsible for his own ledgers, lest, among other things, he be blamed for the errors of others.

A third general principle of bank control is the ideal requirement that no person shall work at the same job without interruption. Rotation of assignment between bookkeepers (exchanging ledgers) or between bookkeepers and mortgage clerks (exchanging jobs) is a device to assure that control over any series of transactions or any set of records will not permanently rest with one individual.

Unfortunately complete rotation of assignments is extremely rare in banks. It requires a good deal of extra training and runs into the resistance of bank employees (and officers) who are comfortable in well-accustomed routines. Rotation, however, will pay dividends in staff flexibility and efficiency as well as in improved control.

Enforced vacations of at least two weeks continuous duration, including the bank's senior officers, is another form of the same control principle. It is one on which bank directors should adamantly insist, no matter what the pressure of business or how selfless may appear the chief executive officer's devotion to duty. Few of the major defalcations in small banks would have gone undetected for so many years had the officer-perpetrators been required to be away from the bank for at least two consecutive weeks each year.

Finally, an important set of controls over bank income and expense, too infrequently availed of by smaller banks, is the accrual system of accounting. Accruals are independent calculations of the amount of income or expense the bank should incur with respect to the total of its various assets and liabilities, or in connection with other services rendered on a fee basis. If demand loan interest, for example, actually collected and credited to undivided profits, does not at least roughly equal the amount of interest forecast by the accrual process, the auditor has some important questions to ask. Accruals fundamentally serve the function of accurately prorating income and expense over time and of showing the bank's true earnings. They are well worth the small effort to maintain for control purposes alone.

As has been indicated above, many controls can be effectively introduced into systems and procedures; others are physically built into bank equipment. An effective and inexpensive method of control which is often overlooked is the simple carbonized form. With no additional time or effort, it produces an extra copy of bank entries for the auditor. Costing little more than the paper it is written on, the "auditor's copy" provides the auditor with a means of checking most bank entries when he has the time to do so. The knowledge of its existence can be a powerful damper on temptation.

AUDIT PRACTICES

It is not the intention here to describe how banks should be audited. A number of excellent manuals are available for the professional auditor or the member of a directors' examining committee who wishes to familiarize himself with specific audit techniques.[9] Rather, this discussion will concern itself with those fundamental audit concepts with which every bank director should be familiar.

Good auditing can be said to consist of substantial verification of the accuracy and completeness of a bank's records and of the safety and efficiency of its operations. The auditor of a large New York City bank [10] has stated the audit responsibility as:

1. To see that the assets of a bank are safeguarded.
2. To see that all liabilities are properly recorded.

---

[9] *Cf.*, The National Association of Bank Auditors and Comptrollers, *Bank Accounting, Auditing, and Operations*, 1951, and *Audit Program for the Smaller Bank*, 1946.

Roy F. Buchanan, *Audit Aid for Small and Moderate-Sized Banks* (New York: The Surety Association of America, 1950).

[10] Morris A. Engelman, Auditor, Bankers Trust Company, "Auditing Under Automation," *Auditgram*, March 1961.

3. To see that all income to which the bank is entitled is received and
    recorded in the proper income account.

    Additionally, continuous appraisals of operating systems assure
    that internal controls are providing adequate protection and that
    waste and unnecessary expense are eliminated.

The most direct form of auditing is simple rechecking: having a
second person re-do what someone else has already done. Obviously such procedures would be intolerably time-consuming and
wasteful. The first problem of good auditing, therefore, is to devise satisfactory methods of ascertaining that a series of transactions
has been correctly performed without having to recheck each one.
This, of course, is where control fits into auditing. Generally,
where controls are effective the auditor's task tends toward seeing
that they are maintained and to checking totals. Where controls
cannot be (or are not) built into the procedural system, auditing
tends to require more direct rechecking.

Some direct checking, on a spot-audit basis, has an important place
in the audit program even where controls are well developed. Although he may be generally satisfied that he has checked all the
entries and withdrawals of securities in and out of the vault, the
auditor, nevertheless, will occasionally wish to count them to make
sure he has not missed anything. For similar reasons he periodically
counts the tellers' cash or makes a proof of the notes.

The principal problem in auditing is to determine how much
checking needs to be done to accomplish the purposes listed above.
No auditor would have time to check the proceeds of every note
to the deposit ledgers; nor does he need to. Accuracy is generally
assured by the system of proofs, and, to serve as a deterrent to
wrongdoing, auditing needs merely to create a knowledge in the
minds of bank employees that some number of every variety of transaction will be checked, that there is no way of knowing which
transaction will be checked, and that *any one* transaction might be
checked.

The two basic elements of sound auditing practice are surprise
and variation. There should be no discernible routine to the auditor's work aside from his daily matching of controls to assure accounting accuracy. Both the timing and the scope of audit work
should vary, and vary unpredictably. If these elements are carefully maintained, spot auditing and sampling will provide effective
audit control.

One specific audit procedure perhaps requires special comment. It is the procedure of verifying loans and deposits directly with the bank's customers. Many banks, particularly the smaller ones, have resisted this practice,[11] although it is urged by every authority as the *sine qua non* of a well-rounded audit program.[12] The fact is the only matching records or controls for many of a bank's accounts are the records of its customers. No auditor or examiner can be absolutely certain of the accuracy of a bank's record of a savings account unless he sees the customer's passbook, or be sure of the validity of a note unless the customer acknowledges his debt. Direct verification is most effective when conducted on a "positive" basis, *i.e.*, requesting the customers to reply positively to the request for confirmation of balances. Verification on a "negative" basis involves a request to a customer to check the information supplied by the bank with his own records and to notify the auditor only if there appears to be a difference. Thus negative verification assumes the account is correct if the customer does not reply. Both kinds of verification are usually conducted with respect to a random sampling equal to at least 20 per cent of the accounts each year, including some accounts audited during the immediately preceding years.

No one, of course, can verify ledger records which have been abstracted or destroyed. Such has occasionally been the case in large defalcations. This has been particularly true with respect to small banks operated or dominated by one man.[13] It has been suggested that this loophole could at least be partially closed in communities where customers are used to the verification process, by advertising in the local press the fact that certain accounts of

---

[11] Stanley E. Shirk, "Special Problems of Bank Audits," *Journal of Accountancy*, April 1960, p. 39. "In bank auditing, confirmation procedures present a special problem as many bankers are reluctant to permit the use of the procedure. They are concerned both with the cost and the possible impact on depositors and borrowers. They feel that the cutomers will think that there is something wrong with the bank."

[12] The NABAC manual devotes an entire chapter to the techniques of this procedure.

See also "Direct Verification for Smaller Banks," American Bankers Association, Country Bank Operations Committee and Insurance and Protective Committee, New York, 1961.

[13] When a large defalcation which has been going on for a number of years is discovered, people always ask how the examiners failed to discover it. The examiners prove the books as they find them but cannot be aware of liabilities which are not shown in the records.

the bank are in process of being verified by the bank's auditor. A request might be made through this medium that the auditor be notified immediately if any customer should fail to receive a request for confirmation if he has an account of the kind being verified.

THE AUDIT PROGRAM

The audit program is a formal summary or schedule of audits to be performed. It stems from policy decisions with respect to the scope and frequency of individual audits. How often and how completely shall the various operations and accounts be checked? What percentage of transactions and accounts shall be verified both internally and directly with customers? These policy decisions should be made by the bank's directors taking into consideration the recommendations of operating management and the auditor, their own common sense, and the suggestions contained in a recognized audit manual.

Many auditors set up their programs on a set of file cards. Each card covers a specific audit procedure, describes briefly the audit to be performed, indicates the scope and frequency approved by the directors, and provides space to record the work done. The cards can be filed to provide a "tickler" or time schedule for the program. Each month the auditor should report directly to the Board of Directors or its Examining Committee the progress made with the program and the full details of any unusual findings.

OPERATIONAL REVIEWS

The most effective way for the auditor to review operating procedures is to prepare and periodically review a manual of procedures. Methods and procedures, of course, are not established by the auditor, but rather by the operating officers of the bank or the heads of departments who are responsible for the work done. The auditor's interest in them is from the dual viewpoint of control and efficiency. He has the primary responsibility for the former but only an advisory role with respect to the latter. His effectiveness, in this respect, will depend heavily on his competence and his ability to sell ideas.

If the bank is large enough to have an officers' operating committee, and even very small banks would benefit from some such formal attention to operating problems, it is well to include the auditor as a member of it. In this capacity he can take part in the development of new systems and procedures and make suggestions with respect to the old ones. Whether the system change be the introduction of a new carbonized form or a new electronic computer, the auditor's role is essentially the same. He must understand the new system and what it is intended to accomplish, and he must satisfy himself on behalf of the directors that the new procedure provides adequate controls and will contribute to the overall efficiency of the bank's operations.

As every bank clerk knows, proofs do not always prove, and looking for differences is one of the most time-consuming and wasteful efforts in daily bank operations. One of the auditor's principal responsibilities should be to review all the proof errors that occur and to try to analyze the reasons for them. It is easy to attribute most of the errors to employee carelessness or failure to follow directions, but perhaps the opportunities for carelessness might be reduced if the directions were made more explicit.

A New England banker,[14] who made something of a hobby of reducing errors and simplifying his bank's operations, found that the use of numbers keyed to the bank's records, the use of different colored tickets and plus and minus signs for debits and credits, together with explicit instructions printed on every entry ticket virtually eliminated proof errors in his bank. He also found that these same innovations greatly reduced the time needed to train new employees and substantially reduced the time previously spent by officers in answering the same questions over and over again. Work simplification is a veritable gold mine which few banks have adequately tapped. It poses a real challenge to an imaginative auditor.

EXAMINATIONS

A distinction is sometimes made between "internal" and "external" audits as well as between audits of all kinds and examinations. The examinations made by the supervisory authorities are clearly stated not to be audits, although in most cases they include a verifi-

---

[14] Charles N. Bachelder, former president, Hanover National Bank, Hanover, N. H.

cation of some of the assets and liabilities and a proof of the general ledger controls. Examinations made by directors, or by accountants engaged by the directors, may include a considerable amount of auditing, including proof of income and expense and direct verification of assets and liabilities.

Functionally, an examination is primarily concerned with an *evaluation* of assets, procedures, policies, and the effectiveness of management. Supervisory authorities are also directly concerned with a bank's compliance with the law.[15] In the same functional sense, auditing is the process of verifying the existence of assets and the accuracy of accounts whether it be done as a continuing process internally, or periodically by outside accountants or directors.[16] Unquestionably there is a good deal of overlap. When the auditor counts the teller's cash he is doing the same thing an examiner does and he is doing it for the same reason; namely to make sure it is all there. To the extent that internal auditing is effective, however—and it is the examiner's duty to determine if it is—the examiner may withdraw from the audit field; and he has done so. For a number of years some supervisory authorities have conducted "balance sheet" examinations of very large banks. Such an examination assumes the correctness of the bank's statement in reliance upon elaborate and complete internal audit procedures which are carefully reviewed in the course of the examination.

National banking regulations and the laws of most states require that, in addition to the supervisory examination, the directors themselves make examinations of the bank. The fact of the matter is that few bank directors have the necessary competence to make an adequate examination.[17] Those who take their obligations se-

---

15 Russell G. Rankin, *Safeguarding the Bank's Assets* (New York: New York State Bankers Association, 1953), p. 5. "The prime objective of examination by federal and state examiners is to evaluate the financial condition of the bank on a given date and to ascertain whether or not the management of the bank is conforming to the requirements of the applicable banking statutes and regulations. It is not to detect fraud."

16 Corns, *Bank Auditing*, p. 65. He makes the distinction between an "examination . . . for the purpose of reviewing and determining the make-up of individual figures which represent assets and liabilities; while an audit . . . for the purpose of verifying that the individual items represented by the figures . . . are correct and reflect the results of normal business transactions."

17 *Cf.* Stanley E. Shirk, "Are Your Directors' Examinations A Sham?", *Auditgram*, September 1960, pp. 20 ff.

riously in this regard engage the services of public accountants to assist them. This group includes nearly all of the major banks in the country and an increasing number of the smaller ones. The State of New Jersey requires that the directors' examination be conducted by public accountants and that it include a direct verification of at least 20 per cent of the loans and deposits. The Financial Institutions Act which passed the Senate but failed of passage in the House would have given the three Federal supervisory authorities the right to require an audit be made by a certified public accountant if they found internal conditions warranted such action.

There are three principal reasons for the failure of more banks to use outside accountants to conduct comprehensive audits or directors' examinations; (a) banks which do not have well-developed internal audit programs are generally those which have less than $10 million in assets and whose management mistakenly believes the cost of an outside audit to be too large, (b) directors tend to place too much reliance on the examinations of the supervisory authorities despite the protests of the supervisors that they do not audit, and (c) only relatively few of the thousands of smaller accounting firms working regularly in communities where small banks are located have sufficiently familiarized themselves with bank audit problems and procedures. A well-known bank accountant has said that "In a sense, banking is one of the last frontiers for the public accounting profession." [18] It is to be hoped this frontier will gradually become settled and populous, for the outside accountant can effectively complement and support the internal audit program and, in small banks, substitute for it. The certified public accountant, in effect, provides the answer to the not entirely facetious question, "Who audits the auditor?"

THE CONTROLLER-AUDITOR

Up to this point the term "auditor" has been used in a generic sense as anyone who performs the audit function. This function has been described to include the duties often performed by a person designated as controller or, more accurately as auditor *and* controller. For it should be emphasized again that the institution of

---

[18] Shirk, "Special Problems of Bank Audits," *op. cit.*, p. 42.

controls and the review of systems and procedures is part of the function of preventing both crime and waste, and inefficiency is probably a more important thief of bank profits, day in and day out, than the unfortunate bank officer or employee who makes the headlines as the result of a defalcation.

The control and audit functions go hand in hand. It should not detract from the importance of auditing to say that, in all probability, the control portion of the dual function is, in the long run, the more important. It requires more skill and talent, it calls for more initiative and imagination to establish effective controls and efficient systems and procedures than it does simply to check to see that they are properly executed.

In large banks, as a matter of organization, the two related functions are often separated and placed under the direction of different persons called "controller" on the one hand and "auditor" on the other. The controller is nearly always the more important and incidentally the higher-paid individual. He is usually a member of the senior management group with primary responsibility for financial planning, cost-accounting, budgeting, systems control and methods analysis. The auditor frequently works under the direction of the controller even though he should report his audit findings directly to the Board of Directors.

In medium-sized banks the auditor and controller are likely to be the same person. He directs the work of the audit staff, reports their findings to the Board, and at the same time participates actively in the planning and accounting functions of the bank. In still smaller banks, the control function tends to be assigned to, or assumed by, the chief operating officer who is probably designated as cashier or treasurer, leaving the auditor, if there is one, as a more or less dignified clerk with little more than audit duties to perform. In very small banks (assets under $5 million) auditing, if performed at all, is a part-time job. It can most effectively be assigned to one of the officers or senior employees who should be formally designated as "control officer" by the Board of Directors and made responsible for the administration of the audit program. Ideally in small banks such purely audit duties can be most effectively assigned to an outside accountant who assists the directors with their annual examination and spends one or two days a month performing audit duties in the interim. The officers and employees of such smaller banks cannot readily be separated from their operational duties.

Over the years there has been a good deal of debate on how large a bank should be to justify the appointment of a full-time auditor-controller. As a kind of informal rule-of-thumb, supervisory people have taken the position that the dividing line lies somewhere in the $12 to $15 million size range. In banks of approximately this size there is no question but that a capable person can profitably spend full time supervising the audit work and reviewing and strengthening procedures. To the extent, however, that the duties and responsibilities of the auditor-controller can be enlarged, the position can be justified in even smaller banks.

Cost accounting and budgeting, too infrequently found in smaller banks, fit naturally into the area of the control officer's responsibility. In fact, almost any job which does not involve the making of original book entries or the receiving and disbursing of funds can be assigned to the individual who is responsible for audit and control. The maintenance of credit files, so often neglected in small banks, the review of outstanding loans, or the supervision of a program of rotational training are ideal tasks for such a person. The latter, particularly, can be worked in with the audit program which in itself can be an effective training medium. Other possible duties for the control officer in a small bank could include watching the reserve position, the preparation of reports to directors and to supervisory authorities, and the preparation of at least rudimentary market research studies of the community served by the bank.

Many of the duties suggested for the controller-auditor are far closer to the real problems of bank management than the ordinary platform work or operational responsibilities to which junior officers are usually assigned. This fact suggests that the position of auditor-controller is an ideal training ground for management succession, particularly in moderate-sized banks. The more duties that can be assigned to this position, the more a bank is justified in going into the market for a person with more than average potential. Auditing duties, in themselves, require a higher caliber person[19] than is fre-

---

[19] *Cf.* Walter Kennedy, *Bank Management* (Boston, Mass.: Bankers Publishing Company, 1958), p. 154. "An efficient bank auditor must be a versatile person. While he must be necessarily thoroughly versed in banking operations he must remain objective and refrain from engaging in activities which he

quently assigned to them. Too often, in medium-sized banks, management has reluctantly established the auditor's position under pressure from the supervisory authorities and has assigned to the task the least capable and effective person in the organization, *i.e.*, a long-service employee who does not meet the public well and who has little prospect for future promotion. This is a short-sighted policy. The position of controller-auditor is *not* a necessary evil; it is one of the most challenging opportunities in banking today.

will be called upon to check or evaluate. His close contact and association with all departments necessitates that he be a person of tact and skill in his human relations. The fact that the auditor's duties frequently require him to correct or criticize makes it important for him to maintain a constructive attitude and not become a chronic fault-finder. The auditor must be articulate and able to express himself both orally and in writing in a clear and concise manner."

VII

LIQUIDITY–CONCEPTS & INSTRUMENTS

The problem of liquidity for commercial banks is essentially that of having available at all times sufficient funds to meet the demands for money that may be made upon them. As stated in Chapter IV, liquidity is the protection against the risk that losses may develop if banks are forced to sell or liquidate credit-worthy assets in an adverse market. In this sense liquidity is protective. In a more positive sense, liquidity can be defined as a bank's (or the banking system's) ability to meet not only possible withdrawals of deposits but to provide for the legitimate credit needs of the community (or the economy) as well. It is in the latter sense that bank liquidity has been most sharply questioned in recent years.[1]

The liquidity of the banking system as a whole, the ability of all banks, or groups of banks, to meet the credit demands that may be made upon them, is the aspect of bank liquidity that has been most measured and discussed.[2] For the individual bank, however, the problem of liquidity can become even more acute because transfers of deposits between banks, which do not affect the aggregate

---

[1] Alfred Hayes, President of the Federal Reserve Bank of New York, in an address to the New Jersey Bankers Association in Atlantic City, May, 1960, said ". . . at some point, banks and their customers quite naturally feel a bit uneasy with their high loan deposit ratios, raising questions as to whether their banks can contribute their share toward further needed growth in the economy."

[2] Cf. inter alia; The Institute of International Finance, "The Problem of Bank Liquidity," Bulletin, New York University, February, 1957.

Economic Policy Commission, "The Problem of Commercial Bank Liquidity," Booklet, American Bankers Association, 1957.

Federal Reserve Bank of St. Louis, "Commercial Bank Liquidity," The Monthly Review, September, 1960.

liquidity of the banking system, may be of major concern to the individual bank from which the deposits are withdrawn. It is the purpose of this chapter to examine the concept of bank liquidity both from the viewpoint of the commercial banking system in its entirety, and from that of the individual commercial bank, and to review the instruments of liquidity available to the banking system. The following chapter will explore some ways of measuring and forecasting liquidity needs.

GENERAL MEASURES OF LIQUIDITY

Liquidity is most frequently measured in terms of certain balance-sheet ratios. The ratio of loans to deposits, for example, is often used to demonstrate the degree to which banks have already used up their available resources to accommodate the credit needs of their customers. The presumption is that the higher the ratio of loans to deposits, the less able a bank (or all banks) will be to make additional loans.

The loan-deposit ratio undoubtedly has a psychological effect on bank management. As the ratio rises management may tend to become more cautious and selective in its lending policies and, quite obviously, the total of funds available, roughly measured by deposits, sets an upper limit to a bank's ability to make additional loans without recourse to more or less continuous borrowing. Loan-deposit ratios for member banks in the three reserve categories for selected years are shown in Table 6.

TABLE 6

LOAN-DEPOSIT RATIOS—SELECTED YEARS
Member Banks by Reserve Classes
(Year-end figures)

Year	Central Reserve City Banks	Reserve City Banks	Country Banks
1920	81.0	83.4	77.8
1928	60.0	67.0	65.4
1934	31.6	35.0	40.7
1945	23.3	17.3	12.9
1954	42.2	39.3	36.3
1958	52.8	48.4	43.7
1959	56.0	51.8	46.0
1960	58.9	55.2	49.6

Source: Federal Reserve Bulletins.

The ratio of loans to deposits has been rising steeply in recent years in all categories of banks.[3] Historically, however, if one goes back forty years or more, present-day ratios do not appear unduly high and history may well repeat itself in this respect.

The mere ratio of loans to deposits, however, reveals little about the banks' other assets available for conversion into funds with which to meet deposit withdrawals or to make additional loans. A more significant ratio for the latter purpose is the ratio of short-term assets [4] to deposits. This ratio, for four recent years, is shown in Table 7.

TABLE 7

SHORT-TERM LIQUID ASSETS RATIO
All Weekly Reporting Member Banks in the
United States
(Dollar Figures in Millions)

Liquid Assets	1961	1960	1959	1958
Vault cash	$ 1,417	$ 1,240	$ 1,103	$ 996
Balances with other				
commercial banks	2,956	2,830	2,634	2,570
Loans to banks	2,008	2,067	1,789	1,540
Loans to brokers and				
dealers	2,432	1,916	2,109	2,179
Treasury bills and				
certificates	6,279	3,294	4,324	4,446
Treasury notes and bonds				
maturing within 1 year....	5,028	1,433	1,252	3,125
Less borrowings	1,749	2,316	1,966	1,170
Net liquid assets	18,371	10,464	11,245	13,686
Short-Term Liabilities				
Total deposits	$105,342	$95,233	$91,725	$86,135
(Less cash items in				
process of collection				
and required reserves)				
Ratio of net liquid				
assets to net short-				
term liabilities	17.4%	11.0%	12.3%	15.9%

Source: Federal Reserve Bank of New York.

---

[3] The higher ratios in reserve and central reserve cities reflect a slower deposit growth rather than a substantially higher loan demand.

[4] Defined as assets of the highest quality maturing within one year.

The ratio of liquid assets to deposits is a more accurate indicator of the amount of funds still readily available to a bank than is the ratio of loans to deposits. However, both measures leave out of consideration the flow of funds from loan repayments as well as the *demand* side of the equation; *i.e.,* the amount of funds that a bank or banks may be called upon to supply. The liquidity position of a bank is like a reservoir. It may be adequate, although nearly depleted, just before the season of heavy rains. Or it may be inadequate, although three-quarters full, just before the summer drought. To appraise the liquidity requirements of the individual bank one needs to know more than either of these ratios shows. A method of making such an estimate will be discussed in the next chapter. First, however, it will be useful to examine the liquidity problem in a broader perspective.

DECLINE IN LIQUIDITY AND ITS CAUSES

Table 6 shows that bank liquidity, measured by loan-deposit ratios, has been declining steadily since the end of World War II. During the depression of the 1930s and continuing through the war years, the Federal Reserve System supplied sufficient reserves to the market so that banks seldom had to worry about the availability of funds. Excess reserves, in fact, piled up in the banking system beyond the ability of banks to invest them. With the prices and yields of Government securities effectively stabilized by Federal Reserve action, government bonds of any maturity were, for all practical purposes, "liquid" in the sense that they could be readily sold without loss. Bankers literally forgot that a liquidity problem could exist.

EFFECT OF LOAN EXPANSION

With the return to more or less free markets after the Treasury-Federal Reserve "accord" in 1951,[5] and as the result of the rapid expansion in the private sector of the economy, the demand for

---

[5] An agreement which freed the Federal Reserve from its obligation to support fixed prices for government securities. Board of Governors, *Annual Report for 1951,* p. 4.

bank loans began to rise very sharply. In view of the inflationary potential of rapid credit expansion, the Federal Reserve System supplied reserves to the banks sparingly. Bank loans were expanding at a more rapid rate than the economy as a whole, as measured by GNP, because of the shift from government to private economic activity. Meanwhile deposits, particularly demand deposits, lagged behind the rise in GNP.[6]

To make the loans that were sought, therefore, banks had to reduce their holdings of U. S. Government securities. These sales resulted in falling prices (rising yields) for such securities. By 1953 the liquidity problem in the form of substantial depreciation in U. S. security holdings was clearly in evidence. It subsided temporarily in the recession of 1954 but, with the upsurge in loan demand in 1956 and in 1957, the need for more effective liquidity provisions came directly into the limelight.

EFFECT OF INCREASED DEPOSIT VELOCITY

In addition to the fact that bank deposits had not grown as rapidly as the demand for bank credit, bank liquidity was adversely affected by the increase in demand deposit velocity or turnover. As interest rates rose in the face of expanding demands for funds, the use of money acquired a rising value and, since banks could not pay interest on demand deposits and were limited in what they could pay on time and savings deposits,[7] there came into being, outside the commercial banking system, a vast market for liquid credit instruments, which assumed the character of near money.

Traditionally, commercial bank deposits have been the form in which the liquid assets of the economy were held. In recent years, however, a large portion of the liquid assets of individuals and corporations came to be held outside the commercial banking system. Deposits of individuals in mutual savings banks (in areas where they are well represented) and in savings and loan associations, which are not as closely regulated as banks as to the rates of interest

---

[6] Between 1945 and 1960 loans at all commercial banks increased from 10.5% of GNP to 22.9%, while total deposits declined from 68.6% of GNP to 42.5%. Most of this relative decline took place before 1951. Since then, time deposits have just about kept pace with economic growth.

[7] Until the spring of 1961 large banks in the principal money centers did not accept time deposits from domestic corporations as a matter of policy, largely because they feared a massive shift to such deposits from demand accounts.

they may pay, have grown far more rapidly than time deposits in commercial banks.[8]   Corporations, at the same time, have invested the major portion of their temporarily excess funds in various money-market instruments.

When the holder of a bank deposit elects to use his money to acquire some other form of liquid asset or money substitute, the effect is to transfer deposits and not to extinguish them (if he acquires such assets from someone other than a bank).   When a corporate treasurer, for example, draws a check on his bank to purchase Treasury bills from another non-bank holder, the existing deposit is merely credited to the account of a new owner, in all likelihood on the books of another bank.   When an individual decides to save some of his money (whether currency or demand deposits) by placing it in a mutual savings bank, he is transferring to the savings institution, temporarily, the *use* of existing money. The first result will be an increase in "due from banks" on the books of the savings institution.

On the other hand if a holder of money uses it to purchase liquid or other assets from a commercial bank, or to repay existing loans, the immediate effect is to reduce bank deposits.   When deposits decline, however, a portion of the bank's reserves become "excess," and, in the absence of offsetting action by the Federal Reserve System, these excess reserves can be ('and in times of high credit demand quickly will be) used by the commercial banking system to recreate substantially the "lost" deposits by the making of new loans and investments.   When credit demand is strong the banking system tends to use all available reserves promptly and fully.   That this is true is evidenced by the fact that the sizable growth in near money, noted in Chapter I, took place with no net decrease in the aggregate demand deposits in commercial banks.

However, when holders of demand deposits use them actively and invest them fully, the velocity or turnover of deposits rises.   With increased velocity the level of deposits in each individual bank tends to fluctuate both more rapidly and more widely.   Surplus

---

8 "Although savings deposits at member banks have doubled since 1945, their growth has nevertheless been slower than that of their closest competitors; deposits at mutual savings banks have risen by 125 per cent, while savings and loan associations have grown sevenfold."   Federal Reserve Bank of New York, "Time and Savings Deposits at Member Banks," *Monthly Review*, Vol. 42, No. 7 (July 1960), p. 119.

deposits, not needed for working balance purposes, are quickly withdrawn for investment in other liquidity instruments and the bank is unable to use these funds to make even short-term loans or investments. At best a bank may sell the funds for a day or two in the Federal funds market. Increased deposit velocity, therefore, has had an adverse effect on bank liquidity that is not fully reflected by loan-deposit ratios or the ratio of short-term assets to deposits.

If this point seems belabored it is because its understanding is so essential to comprehending not only the role of money transfers within the banking system but also the nature of the competition for liquidity instruments (near money) and real savings funds between commercial banks, the money market, and other financial institutions.

EFFECT OF CHANGES
IN LOAN CHARACTERISTICS

Loan repayments are often considered to be a factor in a bank's liquidity position.[9] Over time they constitute an important source of funds with which to make new loans (to the extent that total loans do not increase) and loan repayments can be used to repay deposits (to the extent that the total of outstanding loans decreases). If the rate of loan repayments is reduced, that is if the loan turnover diminishes, then this source of liquidity is also reduced. Loan turnover tends to decline when the terms of repayment are extended.[10]

It has been many years since short-term, self-liquidating paper made up the bulk of commercial bank loan portfolios. The integration of industry and commerce into larger and more extensive business organizations has long since eliminated much of the need for the kind of short-term credit that historically financed, in separate stages, the transfer of goods from raw material producer, to fabricator, to wholesaler, to retailer, and to consumer. Moreover,

---

[9] *Cf.* Milton J. Drake, Presentation before National Credit Conference, American Bankers Association, Chicago, January 1961, "Some Concepts of Bank Liquidity." Reprinted in *Bulletin* of the Robert Morris Associates, Vol. 43, No. 6, February 1961.

[10] *Cf.* Federal Reserve Bank of Chicago, "Liquidity of Business Loans," *Business Conditions,* March 1961, pp. 9–10. Also, Federal Reserve Bank of New York, "Turnover of Business Loans at New York City Banks," *Monthly Review,* Vol. 44, No. 1 (January 1962), 10.

the increasing importance of time and savings deposits has resulted in the availability of at least theoretically longer-term funds. In any event, capital loans and other longer-term loans have assumed a position of considerable prominence in the vast growth of commercial bank lending since World War II. More than half of the business loans in the New York City banks, for example, have original maturities of more than one year.[11] In smaller banks the growth of mortgage loans and consumer credit, and particularly the tendency to lengthen the terms of such loans, has raised questions concerning the banks' ability to meet short-term credit needs in their communities in the event of a further upsurge in loan demand.[12]

The fact of the matter is that commercial bank loans today are probably more "liquid" than they appear. The regular amortization of term loans, mortgage loans, and consumer credit provides a steady flow of funds for re-lending. While half of the New York City banks' business loans had original maturities of more than one year, it has been estimated that at least a third of the loans outstanding at any time fall due within a year. Mortgage officers know "how hard they have to run in order to stand still" in the matter of just maintaining an amortizing mortgage portfolio, and experience shows that the average actual life of a twenty-five year mortgage is something under twelve years. Few banks have tried to determine what percentage of their loans will in all probability be repaid in given periods of time.[13]

It is also probable that many of the so-called short-term loans which historically graced commercial bank loan portfolios were short term in name only. Ninety-day notes were all too frequently renewed over and over again with little or no payment. The "de-

---

[11] Federal Reserve Bank of New York, "Term Lending by New York City Banks," *Monthly Review,* Vol. 43, No. 2 (February 1961), pp. 27–31.

[12] A. L. Mills, Jr., member of the Board of Governors of the Federal Reserve System, in an address before the Bank Management Program of Columbia University, at Arden House in November 1960, said, "The high proportion of long maturity paper carried by the commercial banking system in the form of real estate mortgage loans, consumer installment loans, and term loans has been cited from time to time as a factor that has contributed to high commercial bank loan-to-deposit ratios and a reduced rate of loan expansion."

[13] One fairly typical bank with loans of about $25 million and deposits of about $45 million made such an analysis and found that 47% of total loans would be converted into cash within one year. This represented 20% of mortgages, 58% of consumer loans, and 61% of other loans. Citizens Bank of Sheboygan, Michigan, *Letter* to the author, dated February 10, 1961.

mand" mortgages of the 1920s all too often were not reduced until they were foreclosed in the depths of the subsequent depression. Experienced lending officers will freely admit that demand loans, generally, are among the slowest loans on their books.

One may conclude therefore that loan liquidity has not diminished perceptibly in recent years.[14] It should be emphasized, however, that loan repayments do not supply funds for increasing the total of a bank's loan account or to meet the short-term deposit swings at times when loan demands are pressing on the bank's liquidity position. Loan repayments constitute an important source of "protective liquidity" over time, but affect the current liquidity position only to the extent that *net* loan increases or decreases are predictable.

LIQUIDITY NEEDS

The discussion above has been concerned with liquidity needs in general. More specifically, the liquidity needs of individual banks must be related to the demands made upon them for funds over periods of time. Some funds may be called for tomorrow; some may not be needed for a year or more; and additional liquidity may be needed for unforeseen or unpredictable demands as a margin of safety.

A bank obviously would not be operating efficiently if it held in cash today the funds needed to make loans two years later. Therefore, just as the amount of liquidity is related to the potential size of the demand for funds, the form and maturity in which liquid assets are held should be related to the times at which demands for funds are likely to occur.

LIQUIDITY AND THE MONEY POSITION

Every bank is required by law to maintain a portion of its deposits in the form of cash on hand or demand balances due from specified banks. For banks which are not members of the Federal Reserve System, reserve requirements are established by the laws of the various states and differ widely. A member bank must maintain a minimum percentage of its demand and time deposits in the form of

---

[14] Federal Reserve Bank of Chicago, Business Review, *loc. cit.* draws this conclusion with respect to business loans.

cash in vault or on deposit with the Federal Reserve Bank of its district.[15]   Required reserves may be averaged over reserve computation periods; weekly for reserve and central reserve city banks,[16] and bi-weekly for others, designated as "country banks."

A bank's legal reserve is often considered its most liquid asset. Actually it is not liquid at all in the sense that liquidity has been defined here since it cannot be used (except for very brief periods) to pay deposits or make additional loans.   When it is so used it must almost immediately be replaced, except to the extent that reductions in deposits free a small portion of the reserves.

A bank's legal reserve, however, does serve as a temporary buffer between the demand for funds being made upon it and its true liquidity position.   When depositors' checks are presented for payment the immediate effect is to reduce the bank's reserve account or correspondent balances.   When loans are made the proceeds are usually credited to a deposit account against which checks will be drawn.   Thus, as loan proceeds are drawn down, the bank's reserve account or correspondent balance is reduced in exactly the same way as when other deposits are withdrawn.   In the absence of offsetting credits, a bank must look to its liquid assets for funds with which to restore its reserve to the required amount within the reserve computation period.[17]   Thus a bank's money position immediately reflects the major portion of the demands for funds that may be made upon it.   The management of the money position (the techniques of which will be discussed in some detail in the following chapter) is closely related to, but not a part of the management of the liquidity position.

SHORT-TERM LIQUIDITY NEEDS

The short-term liquidity needs of a bank are largely determined by the prospective actions of its larger customers.   The holders of sizeable deposit balances and the customers who borrow in substantial amounts influence the liquidity position of an individual

---

[15] Board of Governors of the Federal Reserve System, *Regulation D*, "Reserves of Member Banks" (Fed. Res. Act, Section 19).

[16] The designation of New York and Chicago as "central reserve city" banks will expire July 28, 1962.

[17] Some states require that reserves be maintained on a daily basis and Federal Reserve banks expect that their members will make an effort to avoid large deficiencies on any one day, despite the averaging privilege.

bank to a degree that is directly related to their size. The needs of important customers for funds, intermittent, constant, or seasonal will impinge directly and substantially on their banks' liquidity requirements.

Much of the management of a bank's liquidity position, therefore, will revolve around a knowledge of the needs and intentions of large customers and a preparation to cope with them. Alert bank management will endeavor to keep in close touch with those customers whose deposit swings or borrowing needs can substantially affect the bank's own liquidity position in order to learn of their plans as early as possible. This is one important reason for bank officers to visit their customers and to understand the nature of their businesses.

Short-term liquidity needs are also influenced by seasonal factors which may affect the entire level of deposit supply or loan demand. Farm communities, for example, exhibit clear recurrent seasonal patterns of demand and supply of funds that are distinctly different from those, let us say, of suburban communities. Some seasonality of loan demand and deposit flow is found in nearly every community. Certain industries borrow seasonally and corporate needs for funds build up at tax dates.

Most seasonal fluctuations can be quite accurately timed and appropriate liquidity provided on the basis of past experience. In planning for seasonal liquidity needs, the maturity of the liquidity. assets can often be closely tailored to the probable time of the demand for funds.

OTHER LIQUIDITY NEEDS

In addition to providing funds for the known and generally foreseeable short-term demands, banks require a margin of liquidity for demands that can be predicted over the longer range or which may be unforeseen altogether. These may be designated as longer-term liquidity needs. They are generally related to the secular trends of the community or markets which a bank serves. In rapidly expanding areas loan demand grows at a more rapid pace than deposits are accumulated. Funds must be provided for loan expansion or other ways found for coping with these demands. This is one function of longer-term liquidity.

In stable communities, on the other hand, deposits may show a steady rise while loan demand remains virtually unchanged. In such cases the longer view of liquidity requirements may enable the bank to keep currently more closely invested than it would otherwise. In either case, to gauge its needs for longer-term liquidity bank management must attempt some long-range economic forecasting on the basis of which it can reasonably estimate loan and deposit levels for perhaps five years ahead. A later discussion will suggest specific ways in which management may attempt to cope with these fundamental uncertainties of the banking business.

Economic forecasting, however, is at best an inexact science and conservative bank management will maintain some amount of readily available funds to provide for a margin of error. These funds, too, will be included in the bank's longer-term liquidity requirements.

To summarize the foregoing, it should be evident that the management of a bank's liquidity position transcends the simple yardsticks provided by balance sheet ratios. The latter are useful as measures of over-all change, but the position and the need are not always measurable in the same terms. Liquidity needs must be considered both in terms of amount and of the time at which the demands for funds may be made upon the bank (or the banking system). In consequence a bank's portfolio of liquid assets will not be uniform either in its makeup at any given moment, or in its amount over time.

PRIMARY, SECONDARY, AND OTHER LIQUIDITY RESERVES

Writers on the subject of bank liquidity have long recognized the diverse nature of banks' liquidity needs and usually divide a bank's liquidity position into "primary reserves," "secondary reserves," and something variously designated as "tertiary reserve," "Secondary Reserve II" [18] or "Investment Reserve." [19] The latter, whatever it

---

[18] Roland I. Robinson, *The Management of Bank Funds* (New York: McGraw-Hill Book Company, Inc., 1951).

[19] Robert G. Rodkey, *Sound Policies for Bank Management* (New York: The Ronald Press Company, 1944). This term is also adopted by Roger A. Lyon in his recent book *Investment Portfolio Management in the Commercial Bank* (New Brunswick, N.J.: Rutgers University Press, 1960).

is called, represents the "longer-term" liquidity needs discussed above. These categorical separations are perhaps too confining and the term "investment" reserve may tend to confuse the essential difference in purpose between liquidity assets and the "investment portfolio" to be discussed later. The separation between shorter and longer-term liquidity needs and instruments is a fluid and flexible one; what all sections of the liquidity position have in common is the fact that these assets are held to meet estimated needs of funds for other purposes.

Primary reserves are usually defined as cash on hand and demand balances due from banks, or legal reserves plus any excess holdings of non-interest-earning forms of money. They are more readily identifiable than secondary or tertiary reserves, but to a large measure are not part of the liquidity position. To maximize income, excess holdings of money should be held to a minimum. While it is not always possible to attain this ideal fully, especially in small banks where some of the large deposit accounts are of such a temporary nature that they cannot be effectively invested even through the sale of Federal Funds, such banks (if members of the Federal Reserve System) can at least see to it that their excess legal reserves are transferred to their correspondents in the money centers. There the funds will be employed and at least will earn for the small bank, "credit" in terms of expanded correspondent banking services.

True liquidity reserves of both short-term and longer-term nature consist of interest-earning liquid assets which under all foreseeable circumstances can be converted into cash with little or no loss when the needs for which they were provided arise.

INSTRUMENTS OF LIQUIDITY

Before attempting to explore the ways in which banks can estimate and provide for their liquidity needs, it will be useful to examine briefly some of the instruments of liquidity which are available. These consist in the first place of assets in which excess funds can be temporarily invested with the assurance that either the liquidity instruments will mature and be paid when the funds are needed, or which can be readily sold, without material loss, in advance of maturity. In the second place, liquidity instruments include the ways in which banks can borrow funds or obtain them in other ways, such as through the sale or participation of assets.

Most of the instruments of bank liquidity are available through the money market which has been defined as ". . . the active market for money and close money substitutes which financial institutions and others rely on to provide the liquidity needed in the usual course of their operations." [20] Money itself, in the form of excess currency and demand deposits due from banks in excess of minimum working balance needs, is a primary form of short-term liquidity. But money is not an earning asset and is therefore not, in any real sense, a money-market instrument.

FEDERAL FUNDS

Money, in the form of excess balances, may be converted into an earning asset by lending it, usually for one day at a time, as "Federal funds." [21] Federal funds transactions represent a loan of reserve balances by one bank to another.[22] Such loans are often unsecured and, within the same city, may be arranged by an exchange of checks; the borrowing bank's check payable through the clearings on the next business day in exchange for the lending bank's check on its reserve account available on the day of the loan. Between cities (and even within some cities) Federal funds transactions are arranged by telephone and effectuated by transfers of reserve balances through the Federal Reserve wire transfer system under an agreement to reverse the transaction on the following day.

When the transaction is entered into for more than one day, or when the amount exceeds the lending bank's unsecured loan limit,

---

[20] Robert V. Roosa, *Federal Reserve Operations in the Money and Government Securities Markets,* Federal Reserve Bank of New York, July 1956.

[21] Board of Governors of the Federal Reserve System, *The Federal Funds Market* (Washington, D.C., May 1959).

[22] Any transfer of bank balances which is effected by entries on the books of a Federal Reserve Bank in the reserve accounts of a member bank and is available on the same day is a Federal funds transaction. Thus a corporation large and important enough to command this service may instruct its bank to pay Federal funds to a Government securities dealer against delivery of Government securities to be held in custody. By this device the corporation is, in effect, selling Federal funds to the dealer on a secured basis.

a Federal funds transaction may be secured through the device of a repurchase agreement or "buy-back." [23] Under such an arrangement the bank acquiring funds sells securities (usually short-term Government securities) to the bank supplying funds under an agreement to repurchase them at a specified time and at a price representing cost plus an agreed upon rate of interest.

Federal funds transactions between banks represent a liquidity instrument technically classified as a loan by the selling bank (even when it purchases securities under a resale agreement). At the same time it is a form of borrowing for the bank acquiring funds. Because of their very short duration Federal funds transactions are characteristically used for the shortest-term liquidity needs and especially for the temporary adjustment of a bank's money position or reserve requirements.

Most purchasers of Federal funds like to acquire them in amounts of $1 million or more and will seldom bother with amounts under $500 thousand.[24] This effectively precludes the use of the Federal funds market to the vast majority of banks with aggregate deposits under approximately $20 million,[25] except as occasional sellers of excess reserves derived from unusually large short-term deposits.

SHORT-TERM GOVERNMENT SECURITIES

Short-term Government securities, which have a range of maturities suitable for any liquidity needs, are the most widely used money-market instrument. For short-term and seasonal liquidity, Treasury bills have many advantages. Their availability in weekly auctions and their active secondary market at narrow spreads make them, in some ways, the ideal liquidity instrument. Treasury bills are now issued in 91-day, 182-day and one-year original maturities

---

[23] "The Repurchase Agreement in the Government Securities Market," *Treasury-Federal Reserve Study of the Government Securities Market,* Part III (Preliminary) 1959, p. C–20.

[24] Smaller amounts are occasionally purchased by the larger banks as an accommodation for valued correspondents, but such transactions are hardly worth while unless entered into for several days.

[25] If $20 million of deposits were evenly divided between time and demand, the reserve requirement for a member bank would be only $850,000, part of which would be held as vault cash. There would be few occasions when such a bank could sell as much as $500,000 without seriously depleting its reserve account.

and, along with other short-dated Treasury obligations, can generally be acquired in the market with maturities that can be specifically tailored to a bank's expected need for funds.[26]

OTHER SECURITIES

Longer-term Government securities with maturities from two to five years are ideal liquidity instruments for longer-term liquidity requirements such as projected future increases in net loan demand or longer-range protective liquidity. Government agency securities, high-grade short-term municipal securities and railroad equipment trust notes are also sometimes used for these purposes because of their higher yields or, in the case of municipals, their tax-exemption.

COMMERCIAL PAPER AND BANKERS ACCEPTANCES

Commercial paper and bankers acceptances [27] are liquidity instruments which are frequently available at yields somewhat above Government securities of comparable maturity. Both are obligations of private borrowers which are sold through dealers in the money market. Bankers acceptances are obligations of recognized banks as well. Both instruments in recent years have enjoyed virtually unblemished records for safety of principal. Although they lack some of the flexibility of Treasury issues and do not enjoy as extensive a secondary market, these instruments serve many liquidity purposes admirably and are deserving of careful consideration for at least a part of a bank's liquidity portfolio.

BROKERS' LOAN PARTICIPATIONS

In recent years, primarily to relieve their own credit stringency, the large New York City banks have made available to their correspondents participations in their own loans to brokers. These

---

[26] *Cf.* Roosa, *op. cit.*, pp. 37–41 for a description of the various kinds of Treasury issues and the manner in which they are traded.

[27] *Cf.* Goldman Sachs & Co., "Commercial Paper—An Attractive Short-Term Investment," *Brochure* (undated). Also Federal Reserve Bank of Cleveland, *Monthly Business Review*, "Use of Commercial Paper to the Fore," October 1960, and "Rebound in Use of Bankers Acceptances," January 1961.

participations are sold "without recourse" and are not legal obligations of the selling bank. It is understood, however, that the selling bank will ordinarily repurchase the participation, virtually on demand, since it would adversely affect the New York bank's relationship with its broker-customer to have the participating bank call the loan.

When available, these participations are very attractive liquidity instruments as the rate is usually at or close to the prime rate, less a ¼% or ½% retained by the selling bank for servicing the loan. At times of relative credit ease, however, such participations are parcelled out sparingly by the New York City banks to those correspondents which maintain substantial balances.

Brokers' loans made directly by banks to the brokers for their own account and for the account of others were once an important and highly liquid money-market instrument.[28] Today, for New York City banks, brokers' loans are no more liquid than any other well-secured loan which a bank makes to a valued customer and hesitates to call for fear of disturbing a customer relationship. An exception, of course, are the day-loans to dealers in Government securities and acceptances made by the money-market banks at a posted rate.[29] These loans are renewable daily and are a highly specialized form of liquid asset used, like Federal funds, to adjust the money position of the banks in the money centers.

OTHER LIQUID ASSETS

Any credit-worthy loan or investment may be included in a bank's portfolio of liquid assets if its maturity conforms with liquidity needs and if the bank will have no compunction about collecting it at maturity. Among such assets will occasionally be found well-secured notes of nondepositors acquired through so-called money brokers. Such loans are usually secured by cash value of life insurance or marketable securities.

Short-term tax or bond-anticipation notes of municipalities may also be included in the category of liquid assets, as may other cus-

---

[28] Brokers' loans for the account of others were made illegal by amendment of the Federal Reserve Act in 1933 (48 Stat. 181). This provision is contained in Section 19, Paragraph 8.

[29] Roosa, *op. cit.*, p. 21, 31.

tomers' notes of a short-term, self-liquidating nature. Banks which grant lines to national finance companies can sometimes arrange for those lines to be used during periods of seasonal excess of funds and paid off when the local credit needs are at a peak. In such event, these loans, too, may be considered part of the bank's liquidity position.

BORROWING ARRANGEMENTS

A bank's ability to borrow or to dispose of assets either temporarily or permanently is a part of its liquidity arrangements. In this sense a bank's own note discounted with its Reserve bank or correspondent is a prime instrument of liquidity. For the longer term, commitments held from other banks to purchase blocks of mortgages or consumer loans constitute a means of providing additional funds to meet the credit demands of a community.

DIRECT BORROWING

Short-term borrowing from a Federal Reserve bank or correspondent, together with the purchase of Federal funds or the sale of securities under a repurchase agreement, are methods of acquiring funds for relatively short periods of time to restore to required levels reserve balances temporarily depleted by deposit withdrawals. It is not considered sound commercial bank policy to borrow for long periods, or even very frequently, for the purpose of carrying loans or investments or to meet known and predictable recurring seasonal demands for funds. Federal Reserve policy, in this regard, is set forth in the Foreword of Regulation A of the Board of Governors which states:

> Federal Reserve credit is generally extended on a short-term basis to a member bank to enable it to adjust its asset position when necessary because of developments such as a sudden withdrawal of deposits or seasonal requirements for credit beyond those which can reasonably be met by the use of the bank's own resources.[30]

---

[30] Board of Governors of the Federal Reserve System, "Advances and Discounts by Federal Reserve Banks," *Regulation A*, Revised February 15, 1955.

Cf. Federal Reserve Bank of Philadelphia, "Borrowing From the Federal Reserve Bank—Some Basic Principles," *Business Review*, June 1958, pp. 3–9.

The discount officers of a Federal Reserve bank will question a bank's need for borrowing if it remains in debt for more than about 60 days or if it borrows repeatedly in six or seven reserve computation periods. Correspondent banks may be more lenient but bank examiners will question the need for substantial or prolonged borrowing for purposes other than short-term reserve adjustment. It is not considered appropriate for banks to borrow merely to take advantage of a spread in rates such as usually exists between the discount rate and the rate on brokers' loan participations acquired from a correspondent bank.

These comments, of course, do not pertain to situations in which a bank finds itself with the need to help carry its community through a period of unexpectedly adverse economic circumstances such as crop failures, sharp drops in economic activity caused by natural disasters, strikes in major industries, or other comparable and unpredictable circumstances. Under such conditions the Federal Reserve System is designed to function as the "lender of last resort" and to supply liquidity to the banks serving a community in need.

SALE OF ASSETS

For banks operating in areas where the demand for credit chronically exceeds the supply of funds, the sale or participation of assets to other banks offers a convenient method of meeting local loan demands. The practice of originating and selling mortgage loans, for example, has become a business in itself for some banks. The servicing of such loans is usually retained, preserving local customer relationships and providing a source of additional income as well. Banks specializing in mortgage origination often finance home construction while holding commitments from savings banks or others to acquire the permanent mortgages. Additional interim financing or liquidity may be obtained by entering into a "warehousing" [31] arrangement with another commercial bank which will finance the mortgages pending their acquisition by the ultimate investor. Such warehousing agreements represent a source of additional funds to

---

[31] A financial arrangement whereby one bank holds mortgages originated by another pending their delivery to the permanent holder (usually a savings bank) which is committed to acquire them.

the originating bank and a liquidity instrument, or short-term investment, to the warehousing institution.

The sale of blocks of consumer paper, particularly home-improvement loans, has also been widely practiced. Such sales are sometimes made "without recourse"; more often a portion of the proceeds is held as a margin or guarantee fund so that the major portion of the risk remains with the originating bank. Agreements to repurchase delinquent items constitute an effective guarantee so that, in essence, what purports to be a sale of assets may be, in effect, a borrowing arrangement.

The participation of loans to correspondent banks is a method of making loans in excess of the originating bank's legal lending limit and also a method of bringing additional funds into the community.

Frequently small and moderate-sized banks have failed to take advantage of these devices for obtaining additional funds for their communities. They have simply closed their loan or mortgage windows rather than take the trouble to make arrangements for placing a portion of the local loans elsewhere. To maintain such sources of additional funds may, at times, require selling assets which a bank might otherwise hold, but long-range considerations and predictable excess loan demand in the future may well dictate keeping open such channels even at the cost of temporarily excess liquidity.

VIII

LIQUIDITY–PROCEDURES

Having examined the liquidity problem in general, and having reviewed the instruments of liquidity available to banks, the problem of how much liquidity is needed by the individual bank remains.   At any given time the liquidity needs of no two banks will be alike, either in relation to the volume of their deposits or with respect to any other balance sheet ratio.   Similarly, the liquidity requirements for a bank will vary over time as funds flow in and out and the demand for funds, actual and potential, changes from day to day.   It is the task of bank management to measure immediate and prospective demands, and to anticipate them, to the extent possible, by providing an adequate reservoir of liquid assets.

ESTIMATING LIQUIDITY REQUIREMENTS

The best guides available to a bank in estimating its liquidity requirements are its past experience and its knowledge of community events which may affect demands.   As has been previously noted, liquidity needs must be related both to those demands for funds that may be made by depositors and those which may arise from the community's needs for additional credit.   A distinction can be made, therefore, between "deposit liquidity" and what may be termed "portfolio liquidity," or the funds held to make additional local loans and investments.

134

LIQUIDITY FOR DEPOSITS

The more essential, and probably the larger portion of a bank's liquidity needs at any time will be related directly to the volume and character of its deposit liabilities. Not all deposits require the same degree of liquidity. The kind or classification of deposits, *i.e.,* whether they are labeled demand or time, or whether they are deposits of individuals or public bodies, is *not* as important as the likelihood that any specific deposit, or group of deposits, may be withdrawn within a relatively short period of time.

Potential deposit withdrawals may be grouped into those which (a) will surely occur, (b) those which might but are not certain to occur, and (c) those which are unlikely to occur, but under certain circumstances, could possibly occur. In general, the greater the likelihood of deposit withdrawals the larger should be the percentage of liquidity provided and the shorter should be the maturity of the liquid assets held.

As an example of withdrawals which will surely occur, one may cite the payroll account which is deposited weekly and immediately checked against, or the municipal deposit of tax monies which will inevitably be drawn down over a period of months. Seasonal increases in deposits—an important factor in some banks—are another example of temporary deposits. Deposits which in all probability will be withdrawn in a relatively short time (over the course of a year) may be termed "volatile." They are often colloquially referred to as "hot money" and should ordinarily be held in cash or invested in very short-term liquidity instruments.

The volatility of a bank's deposits can be readily shown by charting deposits as of month ends or, more accurately, as of the end of successive reserve-computation periods. A trend line drawn through or near the low points will determine the base or level of nonvolatile deposits and indicate the secular trend of growth (or decline). Fluctuations above this base will represent volatility; at any point in time, the amount of deposits above the base line will be, in effect, the bank's volatile deposits. This is illustrated in Figure A.

Demand and time deposits are charted separately because it is

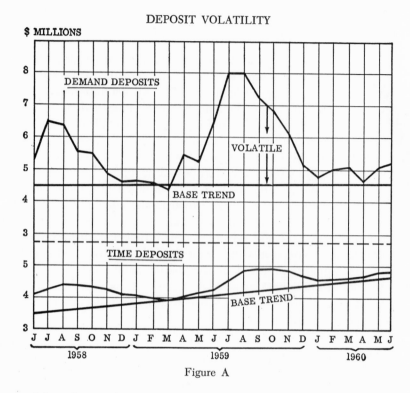

Figure A

useful to know the liquidity requirements for each. The reader
will recall that this information was used in determining the allocation of assets in Step 4 of the Functional Analysis of Income and
Expense, described in Chapter V. If time deposits other than savings deposits are an important factor they, too, may be charted
separately. Such deposits, including "club" accounts, are likely to
account for most of the volatility in the time deposit category.

Fluctuations in time and demand deposits will sometimes tend to
offset each other as when the payment of Christmas club accounts
is quickly followed by an increase in the demand deposits of local
merchants. Therefore, the separate computation of demand and
time deposit volatility may slightly exaggerate liquidity needs. A
check against the fluctuations in total deposits will quickly indicate
any material distortion, but in most banks it is not significant.

Liquidity provision for the volatile portion of deposits should be equal to the total of such deposits less the percentage of required reserves held against them, for as deposits decline, the release of reserves provides a small part of the requisite liquidity. With respect to country member banks, the liquidity requirements for volatile deposits will be 88 per cent of demand and 95 per cent of time deposits.[1]

The second line of liquidity defense is related to those larger deposit accounts, the sudden or unexpected withdrawal of which would make relatively heavy demands upon a bank's liquidity position. Management itself should determine what size is relatively large in any particular bank, but, as a rule-of-thumb, deposit accounts equal to one-half of 1 per cent of total deposits generally may be considered "large" in this connotation.

It will usually be found that the major portion of the bank's demand deposit volatility will be accounted for by the fluctuations in these larger accounts because the holders of sizable demand deposits do not customarily leave them idle for extended periods of time. In computing liquidity requirements against the aggregate of large demand deposit accounts, therefore, the total of volatile deposits may be deducted from the aggregate of large balances to determine what may be termed "vulnerable" deposits. These are deposits that *may* be withdrawn unexpectedly and which are of sufficient size to require special liquidity consideration. On the assumption that a bank might lose one in five of such accounts over the next few years for any one of a variety of reasons, it is suggested that 20 per cent of the vulnerable portion of large deposits be held in liquidity instruments of intermediate term, *i.e.*, with maturities out to perhaps two or three years.

Large time and savings deposits can be vulnerable without having evidenced any previous fluctuations. Therefore, a similar 20 per cent liquidity reserve is suggested for such deposits without deduction for any volatile portion. Careful analysis of large time deposits on an individual basis may indicate that a 20 per cent requirement is, in some cases, too low. With respect to many large time deposits bank management will have a fairly clear picture of their prospective use. The proceeds of a municipal bond issue, for

---

[1] Requirements as of March 1962. For reserve city banks the comparable percentages would be 83½ per cent and 95 per cent. Supplement to Board of Governors, *Regulation D,* effective November 24 and December 10, 1960.

example, may be held in time deposits pending payments on a school construction contract which can be quite accurately timed. Such deposits, like volatile deposits, may require full liquidity protection.

Finally, to meet demands from depositors that might be made in unusual or unforeseen circumstances,[2] and to provide that margin of safety without which no conservative banker feels quite secure, a residual liquidity reserve is suggested equal to 10 per cent of remaining demand and 5 per cent of residual time deposits. These liquidity provisions may be satisfied with liquidity instruments of somewhat longer maturity, perhaps two to five years depending on the state of the market. It is in this area of the liquidity portfolio that maturities can be lengthened when interest rates are relatively high and shortened, or kept short, when interest rates are low in order to maximize income over time.

It should be noted that the liquidity provisions suggested here are related to the normal daily, seasonal, and cyclical swings in deposits, plus a margin of safety. The bank's own liquidity provisions, of course, can be supplemented for short periods by borrowing from its Reserve bank or correspondent. And the liquidity to provide for any long-range secular decline in deposits would normally come from the reduction of outstanding loans or the sale of longer-term securities.

LIQUIDITY FOR LOANS

It has been shown that a major portion of the "liquidity problem" has resulted from rising loan demand rather than from declining deposits and that, to avoid a liquidity squeeze, a bank must maintain a sufficient supply of liquid assets to make the loans that its good customers will require. Such funds, held available to make local loans or investments, may be termed "portfolio liquidity." Part of this demand may be seasonal in character and, like deposit volatility, can be depicted by charting month-end loan totals (exclusive of money market or other loans held for liquidity reasons) as in Figure B.

---

[2] An example of such an unpredictable circumstance was the public response to the issuance of the so-called "magic fives" (5 per cent Treasury notes of Series B 1964) in October 1959. Withdrawals from some savings banks in New York City approximated 5 per cent of total deposits.

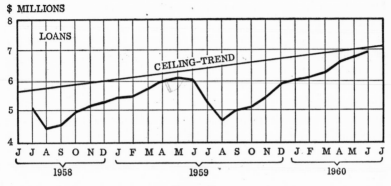

Figure B

The trend line in Figure B is drawn through or near the high points rather than the low points in reeognition of the fact that *increases* in loans make demands on liquidity in the same way as do *decreases* in deposits. The trend line represents a "ceiling," or an amount to which loans may be expected to rise periodically or seasonally. Over a period of time such a chart will reveal cyclical as well as seasonal variations in loan demand. The amount by which loans are below the ceiling, at any given time, represents the amount of short-term liquid assets which a bank should hold to meet these seasonal or cyclical demands for loans.

If loans have been rising more rapidly than deposits and if management expects that they may continue to do so, an additional provision of liquidity may be called for. Future loan expansion, of course, is limited to the funds available to the bank either directly through increased deposits or indirectly through loan participation or the sale of assets. If the bank's loan-deposit ratio is already high it may have to seek other solutions to the problem of high community loan demand, such as active campaigns for new deposits or even a merger with another institution.

Unlike deposit fluctuations, however, the rise in loans is subject to some control by the bank itself. Management can tighten up its lending policies or even refuse entirely to make some loans. Thus the degree to which loans will be increased in excess of additional deposits is a management decision based on an appraisal of the bank's entire situation in the community. If, on the other hand the loan-deposit ratio is not too high, and if the bank holds a portfolio of investments which could be converted over time into local loans, then the planning for such a conversion will play a part in the bank's liquidity calculations. By the same token, if the bank is in a community where loan demand is relatively static and deposits are continuing to rise, its longer-range need for liquidity will be reduced. In the liquidity calculation shown in Table 8 a space is therefore provided for entering management's best estimate of the net effect of secular changes in loans and deposits. A subsequent discussion of loan and deposit forecasting will review in more detail the considerations that should go into making such an estimate.

Finally, to provide once more for the unforeseen and unpredictable, a short-term liquidity provision is suggested to meet the unexpected loan demands of good customers who perhaps have not borrowed in recent years. The amount arbitrarily suggested is 20 per cent of capital and surplus—enough to make two legal-limit unsecured loans. A larger sum might be provided by a bank which is very active in commercial lending since business loan demand is likely to fluctuate more widely over the business cycle than the demand for mortgages or consumer credit.

The figures shown in the following sample computation are those of a bank in a resort community at a time when deposits are just rising from the seasonal low point and when loans are still at the seasonal peak.

TABLE 8

LIQUIDITY POSITION
JULY 1

Deposit Liquidity	Amount (thousands)		%	Liquidity Requirements Under 1 year	1–2 years	2–5 years
Demand deposits						
Volatile		426	88	375		
Vulnerable						
Large	1,170					
(−) Volatile	426	744	20		149	
Residual						
Total	5,193					
(−) Large	1,170	4,023	10			402
Time deposits						
Volatile		–0–	95	—		
Large		60	20		12	
Special		100		50	50	

TABLE 8 (Continued)

LIQUIDITY POSITION
JULY 1

Residual					
Total	4,831				
(—) Above	160	4,671	5		234

Portfolio Liquidity					
Seasonal loan demand		–0–	100	—	
Unexpected demand		116	100	116	
Net secular loan increase				50	50	100
Aggregate estimated requirement				591	261	736

	Under 1 year	1–2 years	2–5 years
Liquidity Instruments Held			
Excess reserves and correspondent balances	304		
Acceptances, commercial paper, and loan participation	—		
High-grade securities			
Under 1 year	100		
1–2 years		500	
2–5 years			600
Firm commitments from others to purchase assets	—		
Totals	404	500	600
Less borrowing	—		
	404	500	600
Excess (+) or deficit (—)	(—)187	(+)239	(—)136

Table 8 shows a modest deficiency in short-term liquidity, but at a time when deposits can be expected to rise and loans to fall. The bank's medium-term liquidity requirements have been well provided for and the excess in this category can be applied against the apparent deficit in the longer-term requirements. It should be emphasized as strongly as possible, moreover, that a calculation such as this is at best a close approximation and a *guide* to policy, not a determinant of it. Bank management, in the light of *all* it knows about the local situation, may well be satisfied with the liquidity position revealed by the table.

In charting deposit and loan figures there sometimes may be evident unusually sharp increases or decreases. These may not represent a change in *trend*, but rather, a change in *level*. For example, if a new large deposit account is obtained (or if one is lost) the level of deposits may be raised or lowered without affecting the direction or trend of deposit growth as a whole. Similarly, if a bank were to purchase a block of mortgages, perhaps on out-of-town properties, the loan total as charted would show a sharp increase although nothing had occurred to change the trend of local loan demand. The base line for deposits and the ceiling line for loans may, therefore, have to be adjusted upward or downward without necessarily changing their direction. This indicates a continuing need for management to exercise its best judgment in interpreting its charts.

ASSET ALLOCATION

Many banks have approached the problem of determining their liquidity requirements through procedures which are variously referred to as an "allocation of assets" or a "conversion of funds." [3] These plans start with a classification of the liability accounts into various categories of deposits and capital funds. The banker then establishes for his own guidance the percentage of each class of liability he would like to hold in various categories of assets. Liquidity is provided by assigning fixed percentages of cash and other liquid assets to each category of liability. Table 9 shows a typical plan.[4]

Thoughtful students of bank liquidity have long recognized the rigidities and inadequacies of such an approach.[5]

The analysis presented in the previous section stressed the fact that liquidity needs, even for specific categories of liabilities, vary over time as funds flow into and out of the bank. It is illogical, for example, to hold the same percentage of the Tax and Loan Account in cash and bank balances when it is at a temporary peak following

---

[3] *Cf.*, Harold E. Zarker, *The Allocation of Bank Assets* (Boston: Bankers Publishing Company, 1957).

[4] Alvin L. Kuehn, "How Much Liquidity?", *Bankers Monthly*, LXXII, No. 7 (July 1955), 32.

[5] Robinson, *op. cit.*, pp. 18–19, states: "The logic of conversion has not been followed here because it is believed to be unworkable. To some extent banks control the way in which they use their funds, but the degree of control varies and recently seems to be declining. Banks often have to employ their funds, not as they would want to, but as they can. Thus a bank conversion scheme may become literally impossible."

LIQUIDITY TABLE (AS OF JUNE 14, 1955)

LIABILITIES	TOTAL	CASH & DUE FROM BANKS	BONDS — U.S. Treas. Obligations		Tax Free & Corp.	LOANS — Indust. & Comm.	Cons.	Real Est. Mortgages	Comm. Paper	Fixed Assets & Accrued Interest
			Under 1 Year	Over 1 Year						
DEPOSITS										
Treas. Tax & Loan	$1,000M	250 25%	750 75%							
State Funds	1,000M	140 14%	240 24%	120 12%			250 25%		250 25%	
15 Largest Accts. and	8,000M	2,070 23%	3,240 36%	2,340 26%	450 5%	900 10%	2,300 23%			
3 Largest Public Funds	1,000									
All Other Demand	10,000M	1,500 15%	1,400 14%	1,000 10%	800 8%	3,000 30%				
Savings	6,000M	420 7%	660 11%	720 12%	600 10%			3,600 60%		
Savings Certificates	600M	42 7%	48 8%	30 5%			120 20%	360 60%		
CAPITAL										
Capital Stock	800M									800 100%
Undivided Profits, Surplus & Reserves	1,200M					600 50%	300 25%		300 25%	
Other Liabilities	400M		80 20%	320 80%						
TOTAL DESIRED DISTRIBUTION	$30,000M	4,422M	6,418M	4,530M	1,850M	4,500M	2,970M	3,960M	550M	800M
ACTUAL ASSET DISTRIBUTION	30,000M	5,000M	6,000M	5,000M	2,500M	4,200M	3,000M	4,000M	–0–	300M
DIFFERENCE: OVER (UNDER)		578M	(418M)	470M	650M	(300M)	30M	40M	(550M)	(500M)

TABLE 9

143

a heavy bond subscription, as when it is at a low point following several Treasury calls. Adequate liquidity will be a different percentage of the various liability categories at different times.

Despite this logic the lure of asset allocation still persists. It seems to have an attractive neatness. In a recent publication [6] the New York State Bankers Association, although accepting the approach to deposit volatility outlined in the preceding section, goes on to allocate the remaining assets.

Beyond the fact that varying degrees of liquidity will be appropriate at different times, there is another basic objection to allocation of even stable or nonvolatile deposits. Given adequate liquidity (and adequate capital) a bank will tend to make the kinds of loans its community needs. It will tend to make *all* the local loans it safely can, and to invest only those funds that cannot be appropriately loaned to local borrowers. It is little more than a statistical exercise to allocate, let us say, 60 per cent of savings deposits to residential mortgages in a stable farm community where few new homes have been built in the past decade and where the active demand for credit is for farm machinery purchases and crop loans.

Nevertheless, asset allocation has a place in the thinking and planning of a well-run bank. It should start, however, with the assets which are available to the individual bank. These assets can then be allocated to those categories of liability for which a bank wishes to determine earnings, cost and profitability. This procedure was followed in the simplified allocation of assets in Step IV of the Functional Analysis of Bank Income and Costs described in Chapter V. There, primary reserves, secondary reserves, and portfolio assets were separately allocated to demand and time deposits and to capital funds. A more detailed allocation of portfolio assets (together with attendant costs and capital protection) to demand and time deposits or to savings deposits as distinct from "other time" deposits, is not only possible but contains a certain useful logic. Many bankers feel that longer-term assets such as mortgages and consumer credit, and perhaps commercial term loans, are more properly extended out of the more stable or longer-term deposits which represent the savings rather than the working balances of the community. Such relationships, as was previously pointed out,

---

[6] *A Report of the Committee on Asset Allocation* (New York: New York State Bankers Association, 1960).

seem to be more psychological than real but they do no particular harm.

The fact of the matter is that an asset allocation plan is just another name for *policy* with respect to the distribution of a bank's assets among the various kinds and maturities of loans and investments which are legally and practically available to a particular bank. The directors cannot intelligently direct a bank's affairs unless they formulate some fairly clear-cut ideas of the direction in which they want the bank to go. Each bank's asset allocation plan should, therefore, be the directors' concept of the ideal bank in their particular community. This function of asset allocation is still a pertinent one. It should serve as a guide to policy and not be a strait jacket.

LOAN AND DEPOSIT FORECASTING

It was noted previously that over time the demands for funds which individual banks experience will be the net of loan increases less deposit growth. If deposits are increasing more rapidly than loans there will be no problem in finding funds to meet the credit needs of the community. If loan demands exceed deposit growth, future liquidity needs will exceed those calculated at any given moment. It was for this reason that the suggested form for estimating liquidity requirements includes a provision for an estimate of future loan growth in relation to future deposit increases.

The simplest method for making such an estimate is to assume that history will repeat itself; that seasonal patterns will not vary widely from year to year and that secular trends will continue. The application of this method of estimating liquidity requirements to several hundred banks over a three-year period [7] has indicated that this is a reasonable assumption much of the time. It is an assumption, however, that needs at all times to be tempered with managerial judgment and foresight.

Loan and deposit trends and fluctuations are both affected by

---

[7] The Bank Examinations Department of the Federal Reserve Bank of New York has used a simplified version of this approach to liquidity needs in connection with its examinations of state member banks since 1956. The majority of banks examined could meet the requirements thus calculated; those which did not, in many cases, had to resort to borrowing in larger amounts and for longer periods than the examiners considered appropriate.

circumstances occurring in particular communities and by the cyclical swings in the economy in general. Management should have both in mind as it studies its charts and plans its liquidity provisions.

CYCLICAL INFLUENCES

Loan demands tend to rise above the normal trend line in times of high business activity and to fall below expectations when the economy as a whole experiences a recession or slack period. The forecasts of loan officers, therefore, need to be tempered by the predictions of the economists. Demand deposits, on the other hand, tend to rise (for all banks) in times of business slack because the Federal Reserve System makes reserves more freely available to encourage credit use and to stimulate an increase in the money supply. In times of high level business activity demand deposits tend to increase more slowly as the Reserve System pursues more restrictive policies.

Time and savings deposits follow trends of their own. Competitive rates of interest play a vital role in determining these trends for the individual bank. A strong local demand for loans has often been the determining factor in persuading bank management to increase the rate of interest paid, within the limitations imposed by law and regulation. But in the economy at large, savings tend to rise in the early stages of a recession and to taper off in boom times when consumers generally expect a continuation of a high level of income and fear the possibility of further price increases.

In assessing the liquidity needs of a particular bank, management must take these broad economic factors into consideration along with, and in the light of, its intimate knowledge of the community.

THE LOCAL SITUATION

Deposit forecasting can perhaps rely somewhat more heavily on past experience than loan forecasting but both involve a current knowledge of the business of the bank's larger customers and a constant awareness of the economic events which may be shaping up in the community or markets a bank serves. This knowledge is not only the essential ingredient of operational budgeting, as discussed in Chapter V, but is equally necessary for liquidity budgeting. In large banks the immediate responsibility for "knowing what is going on" lies with the area officer, department head, or branch manager, whoever is closest to the "territory" or market area being served. In relatively small communities, this knowledge should be at the fingertips of the chief operating officer.

The basic techniques of acquiring such knowledge are simple enough. What is primarily involved is asking the bank's larger customers to help forecast their credit needs in the process of reviewing their annual or interim statements, or in connection with visits to their places of business. Too often officers of large banks are reluctant to "pry into the affairs" of their larger depositors, and officers of small banks are "too busy." Both of these are short-sighted attitudes. The expansion plans of business customers, municipal authorities, or local real estate developers are not made overnight. It is the job of the alert bank officer to be aware of what is going on in his community, or the segment of the credit market he is serving, before predictable events present him with unexpected problems.

The banker who is not aware of the community's plans for a new school until the bond issue is presented to the voters, or who waits until the building permits have been issued before seeking to learn the financing needs of an important local builder, or who remains unaware of a large manufacturer-customer's new product which will require an increased use of credit, is simply not performing his job adequately. Many bankers have this kind of knowledge in the back of their heads but do not organize it systematically. They do not add up all they know, as it were, and put it down on paper. As a result, vital decisions may be too long postponed.

Loan forecasting is at best an approximate science but the approximation will be closer to actuality if it is consciously and conscientiously undertaken. It is suggested, therefore, that comments on past and potential use of credit be made a separate part of the credit files maintained on each large customer. Well-maintained files usually record the date and amount of peak borrowings and a record of the balances maintained. In addition, they should contain the responsible officer's comments on probable credit needs and his prediction with respect to the level of deposit balances likely to be maintained for some period in the future. These comments and predictions, of course, will be meaningful only if the officer in ques-

tion has made an effort to find out the information he needs by calling on the customer, reviewing his financial position, analyzing his
flow of funds, and reviewing his estimate of future business as indicated by unfilled orders, expansion plans, new product development,
etc. The accuracy of the officer's predictions will depend heavily
on the caliber and cooperativeness of the financial officer of the
borrower, as well as on the bank officer's ability to ask the right
questions.

However, the effort in itself will probably be appreciated by the
customers, many of whom look to their banks for just this kind of
financial analysis and guidance.

At least semi-annually the information in the files should be
brought up to date and recapitulated as a formal loan and deposit
forecast. The anticipated net demand for funds, or supply of funds
can then be related intelligently to the bank's other liquidity needs.
Periodically, the projections can be compared with actual results
and the forecaster's skill can be sharpened through an analysis of
past errors. Without such a program for systematically looking
ahead, no bank, no matter how large or small, can adequately plan
for its liquidity needs or intelligently manage its investment portfolio.

MANAGING THE MONEY POSITION

A bank's money position, as stated in the previous chapter, is the
amount of coin and currency and demand balances due from domestic banks it holds primarily to comply with its legal reserve requirements. The amount of these holdings is affected daily by all
the transactions through which payments flow into and out of the
bank. Among these are payments for checks presented to the
bank, the proceeds of checks and other collection items forwarded
by it to other banks, purchases and sales of securities, receipts and
disbursements of cash, and transfers of balances by mail or telegraph, together with other direct charges to its reserve balances.

Because money yields no income, the well-managed bank, large
or small, will attempt to avoid holding any more of it than is necessary. In order to accomplish this worthy purpose, the position
manager must know at all times approximately what his reserve
requirements and holdings of money are. He must therefore start

each day with a knowledge of his position, both as of the opening of business and with respect to the accumulated average for that portion of the reserve-computation period which has already elapsed. Federal Reserve regulations provide that the amount of reserve requirements which must be held at the close of a business day shall be computed on the basis of opening deposit balances. Thus the position manager has a day in which to make the necessary adjustments. However, this leeway does not greatly simplify the problem since the balances themselves are subject to change during the day. Having determined the bank's requirement at the opening of business, it is the money-position manager's task to keep track of all the important transactions which affect his reserve balance during the day and to take steps to counteract their adverse effects, if any.

The principles of managing the money position are virtually the same in large and small banks; it is the number rather than the nature of the transactions which greatly complicates the task for the larger banks in the money centers. For the latter, especially for the banks serving the New York City money and securities markets, the management of reserve positions is not only a daily but an hourly or virtually continuous task. The rapidity with which funds flow through the money market banks reflects the payment for most of the nation's security transactions as well as the financing of brokers and dealers. It results from the high degree to which national corporations have consolidated their balances in the money centers as well as how fully they keep them invested. And, finally, the balancing adjustments of all of the country banks and the settlement of the Federal funds markets are made on the books of the banks in the money centers.[8]

The basic problems involved in managing a money position can be more readily seen in the analysis of procedures which are adequate to a moderate-sized bank, not located in a financial center, and having no correspondent balances among its deposits. The basic figures for such a bank are shown in the following work sheet for the first week of its two-week computation period. The form is one supplied by Federal Reserve Banks to their members but simi-

---

[8] William E. Bachert, *The Commercial Bank Money Position.* Thesis submitted in partial fulfillment of the requirements of the Graduate School of Banking, Rutgers University, New Brunswick, June 1950. Bachert's discussion of this problem is centered on the New York City banks.

lar forms, adjusted to the requirements of state law, can be readily devised for nonmember banks.

A glance at the final column of the work sheet will tell the person responsible for the bank's money position just where he stands at the opening of business each day. For small banks, with only moderate deposit fluctuations, not much more is needed. For larger banks, seeking to keep excess reserves to the barest minimum, a closer scrutiny of daily transactions will be necessary.

The final column of the work sheet shows an accumulated excess of $635,000 after seven days of the reserve computation period have elapsed. Calculation of the current position, however, shows a current reserve deficit of $612,000 as of the opening of business on the eighth day. The position manager's next step is to calculate the effects of the debits and credits he knows will be posted to his reserve account during the day. He is then in a position to project his balance, both on a current and accumulated basis, as of the close of business the same day. On the basis of this projection he can make a decision regarding what actions, if any, will be necessary to keep his position in reasonable balance. A suggested form for making these calculations is reproduced below.[9] It will be seen that the day's transactions would have further increased the current deficit and resulted in an accumulated deficiency, had not the bank transferred a sizable sum from its correspondent banks to its reserve account.

The bulk of the credits and debits affecting the reserve accounts of banks not located in the money centers are usually evident in the clearings figures each morning (checks presented to it and checks forwarded by it for collection), or are the result of transactions, such as securities purchases and sales, which it has itself originated. This is in sharp contrast to the banks which operate in the money centers or which carry substantial amounts of "due to bank" balances. During the course of each day, the latter are subject to immediate and unpredictable demands in the form of interbank transfers and other payments arranged in Federal funds by their depositors.[10]

---

[9] This form is designed for a Reserve member bank which sends its out-of-town checks for collection to its Reserve Bank and which pays for items presented to it by authorization to charge its reserve account.

[10] The Board of Governors of the Federal Reserve System, *The Federal Funds Market, op. cit.*, p. 17, indicates that the practice of settling transactions in Federal funds is one which has grown steadily in recent years.

WORK SHEET FOR COMPUTING RESERVE POSITION

PERIOD: FROM 8/4 TO 8/18

DAY	DEMAND DEPOSITS 1 DUE TO BANKS	2 U.S. GOVT DEMAND DEPOSITS	3 OTHER DEMAND DEPOSITS	Deductions From Demand Deposits 4 CASH ITEMS IN PROCESS OF COLLECTION	5 DEMAND BALANCES DUE FROM BANKS	6 NET DEMAND DEPOSITS Columns 1,2&3 Minus 4&5	7 TIME DEPOSITS	8 REQUIRED RESERVES 12% OF COL 6 AND ∑% OF COL 7	9 CURRENCY AND COIN	10 CLOSING BALANCE WITH FED. RES. BANK	11 TOTAL RESERVE MAINTAINED COL 9 + 10	12 EXCESS + OR DEFICIENCY − COL 11 MINUS COL 8
Thurs.		1,829	29,641	2,665	3,186	25,619	9,920	3,573	826	3,480	4,306	733 +
Fri.		1,822	29,542	2,252	3,672	25,440	9,969		575	3,260		
Cum.						51,059	19,939	7,124	1,401	6,740	8,141	1,017 +
Sat.		1,742	31,446	2,033	4,697	26,458	9,975		560	3,260		
Sun.		1,742	31,446	2,033	4,697	26,458	9,975		560	3,260		
Cum.						103,975	39,889	14,471	2,521	13,240	15,761	1,310 +
Mon.		1,742	31,446	2,033	4,697	26,458	9,975		560	3,200		
Cum.						130,433	49,864	18,145	3,081	16,460	19,541	396 +
Tues.		1,703	30,461	2,280	3,263	26,621	9,985		685	2,460		
Cum.						157,054	59,849	21,839	3,766	19,320	23,086	1,247 +
Wed.		2,135	31,822	3,504	3,233	27,220	9,997		554	2,600		
Cum.						184,274	69,846	25,605	4,320	21,920	26,240	635 +
Thurs.		1,925	30,939	2,413	3,476	26,975	9,991		525			
Cum.						211,249	79,837	29,345	4,845			
Fri.												

Wed.												
Period Totals												
Averages												

★ Figures in these columns are to be calculated daily only from the cumulative (Cum.) totals shown in the columns indicated.

151

MONEY POSITION

Thursday (8/12)
(Amounts in thousands)

	Current	Accumulated (7 days)
Requirement as of last night's closing deposits	3,737	
Less cash on hand at opening	525	
Required reserve tonight	3,212	
Reserve balance collected (our books)	2,600	
Excess or deficit at opening	(−)612	(+)635

❈ ❈ ❈ ❈ ❈

Known Transactions Affecting Reserves Today

Credits

Yesterday's immediate cash letter		1,181
Deferred items available today		685
Security sales available today		—
Currency and coin in transit		100
Credit in local clearings		—
Other		—
Total credits		1,966

Debits

Remittance charged today	2,206	
Securities purchased charged today	—	
Notes due today	—	
Tax and loan call	100	
Currency and coin orders	—	
Debit in local clearings	55	
Other	—	2,361
Projected excess or deficit tonight	(−)1,007	(−)372

❈ ❈ ❈ ❈ ❈

Adjustments today

Credits

Transfers from bank accounts		560
Borrowings		—
Securities sold for "cash"		—
Total credits		560

Debits

Transfers from reserve account	—	—
Funds sold	—	—
Net adjustments		560
Adjusted balances		(−)447	(+)188

Nevertheless, even for country banks, the unpredictable can loom large in the management of its reserve position. The volatility of large deposit accounts can cause management of the money position to go awry as the result of unexpectedly large withdrawals or even large deposits which cannot be put to use. Alert money management, therefore, will attempt to keep a close watch over the larger depositors, and will take into cognizance the transactions which may affect the reserve position, not only on a particular day, but later in the reserve-computation period as well. Large deposits and withdrawals can be scanned daily for clues to future deposit swings and an attempt can be made to get advance notice of future transactions from the financial officers of important corporate customers. At the same time, a calendar of maturing securities and large loan repayments should be maintained and taken into consideration in the daily adjustments of the reserve position. The money-position manager should also have before him each day a brief memorandum of the sources of funds available to him and a list of correspondent balances and liquidity instruments.

For the great majority of relatively small banks with total resources under $10 million, the full investment of volatile deposits is difficult. It is for this reason that excess reserves tend to accumulate in country member banks at times when the Federal Reserve System is making credit freely available. There are several reasons for this. In the first place, Federal funds transactions of less than $500,000, as previously stated, are rare. Secondly, banks are limited in the selling of Federal funds by the size of their reserve accounts. They are not expected to incur substantial reserve deficiencies even for one day. Thirdly, national banks are limited in the amount of funds they may buy (borrow) to an amount not in excess of the aggregate of book capital and 50 per cent of surplus. Finally, the amount to be earned on the full investment of the excess reserves of these smaller banks is hardly enough to make the effort worth while when all of the costs are taken into consideration.

Adjustments, of course, do not have to be made daily because reserve requirements and reserve balances can be averaged over the computation period. Even for banks with total resources well above $10 million, daily adjustments may be impractical. Thus, a bank with an average daily requirement of $2 million may find that its reserves are running roughly $250,000 daily in excess of requirements for the first six days of the computation period. This will represent a cumulative excess of $1,500,000 for *one* day. But to sell this much in Federal funds for a day would virtually deplete its reserve account. At best it can sell the minimum of $500,000 for three or four days.

At times when Federal funds are quite freely available, even though at rates above rates on 91-day bills, it may be easier to maintain an over-invested position and buy funds to balance out to the requirements over the period than to accumulate an excess and try to sell it. This is, in fact, what the larger money-market banks try to do when Federal funds rates are below those at which they can lend or invest for short periods. Thus to keep over-invested is about the only way in which the smaller bank can keep itself fully invested. Even such an approach is not open to very small banks.

The following hypothetical case of a bank slightly under $10 million in resources, illustrates the point.

HYPOTHETICAL BANK

Assets		Liabilities	
Cash	$ 30,000	Demand deposits	$4,080,000
Reserve balance	770,000	Time deposits	5,000,000
Due from banks	80,000	Capital	300,000
		Surplus	400,000
Loans, investments and		Undivided profits and	
other assets	9,000,000	reserve	100,000
	$9,880,000		$9,880,000

Reserve requirements		
12% of net demand	$480,000	
5% of time	250,000	
	$730,000	
Less cash in vault	30,000	
Required reserves	$700,000	
Reserve balance	770,000	
Average daily excess	$ 70,000	
Accumulated (14 days)	$980,000	

Such a bank is limited in selling funds both by the predilection of the market for amounts of no less than $500,000, and by the unwisdom of depleting its reserve account by more than, say, $300,000 on any one day. It can, however, adjust its reserve position by over-investing and creating a modest daily deficiency which usually can be covered by a one-day borrowing. For example, the bank shown above may use $100,000 of its reserve account to acquire Treasury bills which, let us say, yield 2½ per cent.[11] Its reserve position would then be as follows:

Required reserves	$700,000
Reserve balance	670,000
Average daily deficit	30,000
Accumulated (14 days)	420,000

Under the circumstances thus illustrated, the purchase of $500,000 of Federal funds for one day, on any one of the 14 days of the reserve computation period, would have enabled the bank to meet its reserve requirements on average and to make a modest net profit as follows:

PROFIT CALCULATION

Income on $100,000 Treasury bills at 2½% for 14 days		$ 95.90
Cost of $500,000 Federal funds at 3% for one day	$41.10	
Cost of instructions	4.00	45.10
Net gain		$ 51.80
Net gain on annual basis		$1,346.80

This example demonstrates clearly that the investment of even relatively small reserve excesses can be accomplished profitably provided the bank in question is over a minimum size. Such close reserve management, however, requires careful attention to the daily reserve position and the transactions, actual and prospective, which may affect it. The officers of many banks in this size range would not think the profit possibilities worth the effort. But as banks grow larger, the profitability of careful money position management increases proportionately.

One last factor should be noted. Under the regulations of the Board of Governors of the Federal Reserve System,[12] member banks not only have an entire reserve computation period in which to average reserves but are permitted, when occasion demands, to carry

---

[11] Approximate rates prevailing in the spring of 1961.

[12] Federal Reserve Bank of New York, "Reserves of Member Banks," *Operating Circular No. 2*, May 19, 1960.

forward from one reserve computation period to the next, a deficiency not exceeding 2 per cent of requirements without penalty. A deficiency thus carried forward, however, has to be made up in the successive period and may not be carried forward to a third. This safety factor allows for unexpected or unpredictable developments toward the close of a reserve computation period, but banks are not expected to use this privilege deliberately nor too frequently.

IX

CAPITAL ADEQUACY

The ultimate strength of a bank lies in its net worth or capital funds. Such is the consensus of writers on banking, and of bank supervisors. But the problem of bank capital is not quite that simple. It is not merely a question of "the more capital the better"; rather it is how much, and for what reasons or purposes. The bank depositor (and the supervisor as his representative) may favor the maximum amount of capital as protection against the risks inherent in the banking business. The bank stockholder (or bank management as his representative) may, from the short-range viewpoint of maximizing profits, wish to operate with as little capital as possible to gain the greatest leverage in earnings from the employment of deposits. The apparent conflict between the interests of the stockholder and the public, however, is not as sharp as it might appear.

There is an element of public interest in the profitability as well as the safety of banks because the public expects the stockholder to assume all the risk. Without profits there would be no incentive for this risk-taking. By the same token, it is in the interest of the shareholder to combine profitability with safety because, in the longer run, his investment will remain profitable only as long as the bank stays in business. Closed banks pay no dividends. Adequacy of capital, therefore, will be found in some balance between these related but partly conflicting considerations.

THE FUNCTION OF BANK CAPITAL

It has often been said that the primary function of bank capital is to protect the depositor against loss. Although such statements contain an element of truth, they are not complete, nor do they adequately express the true nature of the protective function of bank capital funds. In previous chapters various banking risks have been examined, and it has been shown that each kind of risk has its own first line of protective policy or action. It was shown, for example, that current earnings, not capital, absorb a major portion of bank losses. Most weak-looking bank assets, in fact, can be worked out with relatively little loss, given sufficient time, competent management, reasonable earnings, and the workings of the business cycle. Even the staggering losses of the 1930s were ultimately absorbed out of earnings when banks were not forced into liquidation. This is not to say that losses were not charged to capital funds in the short run; they were. But if too many losses are charged to capital the bank's doors will inevitably be closed.

In the sense in which capital is described as a protection against loss it is the ultimate or final protection. Capital funds will serve to protect the depositor when the bank is closed, but, if a bank had poor earnings, loose internal controls, and a large quantity of risky or speculative assets, the bank supervisor would step in long before the capital funds, as such, were severely impaired.

It is more meaningful, therefore, to look on the function of bank capital funds not as a "cushion of excess assets with which to absorb losses and still remain solvent" [1] but rather as a factor, perhaps the most important factor, in maintaining the confidence a bank must enjoy to *continue* in business and prosper. The essential function of bank capital, in other words, is to keep the bank open and operating so that time and earnings can absorb losses; to inspire sufficient confidence in the bank on the part of depositors and the supervisor so that it will not be faced with costly liquidation. In this sense, capital serves to protect the stockholder as much as, if not more than, the depositor.

The fact that confidence is the vital ingredient of a bank's success

---

[1] Gaylord A. Freeman, Jr., *The Problems of Adequate Bank Capital*, An Analysis Prepared for the Illinois Bankers Association, May 23, 1952, p. 10.

should be self-evident. Depositors must be confident that their money is safe and borrowers must be confident that the bank will be in a position to give constructive consideration to their credit needs in bad times as well as good. Above all, under the closely-supervised private banking system of the United States, the continuing confidence of the bank supervisor is essential to a bank's continued existence.

Even the general public, which pays too little attention to bank statements, has a vague idea that the strength of a bank is somehow related to the amount of its capital funds. Most banks, recognizing this awareness, proudly publicize not only the amount of their capital and surplus, but additions to them as well. The smaller segment of the public which understands and carefully reviews bank statements and annual reports pays considerable attention to capital. The corporate treasurer, in particular, focuses on this aspect of a bank's statement. In the past some of them have devised their own methods of analyzing the adequacy of a bank's capital, although nowadays many of them use one or more of several bank supervisory approaches. These will be discussed a little later. If they happen to be important depositors, they may insist that the bank furnish them with the requisite information even though it is not otherwise published.

It is the bank supervisor, however, who, above all, places reliance on the adequacy of capital as a factor in determining the degree of his confidence in a particular bank. This fact was never more clearly evident than immediately following the bank holiday in 1933 when every bank in the country came before the bar of supervisory judgment. It was the supervisor's appraisal of capital adequacy, more than any other factor, that determined whether and under what conditions a bank might be permitted to reopen. Where conditions were imposed, moreover, they involved in nearly every case some new injection of capital funds either by the stockholders, directors, depositors, or the Reconstruction Finance Corporation.[2]

The primary function of bank capital funds, therefore, is to reassure both the public and the bank supervisor (especially the latter) that the bank is in a position to withstand whatever strains may be

---

[2] A government agency, organized in 1932 to render emergency financial assistance to American industries (including banks) during the depression years. It was liquidated in 1954.

placed upon it. Adequate capital, together with other factors of confidence which will be discussed later, serves to keep banks open so that they may be able to absorb losses out of future earnings rather than out of capital funds themselves.

Bank capital, of course, has other functions. As in any business a part of the capital is needed to supply the working tools of the enterprise. This function is immediately evident in the organization of a new bank where the first expenditure of funds supplied by the stockholders goes for banking quarters and the equipment needed to begin operations.[3] The provision of working tools is a continuing function of bank capital, a responsibility of the stockholder. One cannot expect the depositor to supply the funds for new branch buildings or drive-in facilities. One of the problems to be considered in a subsequent discussion of how adequacy of bank capital may be measured, will be the extent to which it may be available to serve the other purposes and functions of capital funds even though invested in bricks and mortar.

Another important function of capital is the representation of private ownership of commercial banks. The very existence of capital stock distinguishes commercial banks from mutual savings banks and the savings and loan associations which compete with commercial banks for savings. This structural difference entails a number of problems such as tax treatment and reserve requirements which have been in the forefront of public policy discussions for a number of years.

The question of who owns commercial banks is more important than the ownership of other business enterprises because banking is deeply tinged with public necessity. For this reason commercial banks have been "nationalized" in many countries or actually organized by governments. One may well speak of the "adequacy" of the distribution of a bank's capital as well as its amount. Is ownership widely distributed or is it concentrated in the hands of a few? The answers to these questions have a good deal to do with the character of an individual bank and, at times, with the confidence the public may have in it.

A function of bank capital which is closely related to its confi-

---

[3] This function of capital is recognized in Section 24(A) of the Federal Reserve Act (U.S.C. Title 12, sec. 371) which limits the amount of a member bank's investment in bank premises to the amount of its stated capital unless specific permission is obtained to exceed this amount.

dence-inspiring role is that of supporting the credit risks a bank is called upon to assume in its normal business lending. The laws of most states and the National Banking Law relate the maximum amount a bank can advance to any one borrower to a percentage of its capital and surplus. The desire for larger lending limits has inspired many banks to seek additional capital through the sale of stock or even through mergers with other institutions. Even more important, part of the confidence a bank's capital funds inspire is the assurance that it will be able to extend the credit which its community needs and to safely assume the risks involved.[4]

OTHER FACTORS OF CONFIDENCE

Although capital funds may constitute the primary factor of confidence in banking, it is by no means the only one. Both the general public and the bank supervisor take other factors very much into consideration. Some of these elements are general in character; others pertain specifically to individual banks. To the extent that confidence in banks generally increases, the level or standard of capital adequacy for all banks may perhaps be reduced. To the extent that individual factors favorably impress the bank supervisor, a specific bank may be permitted to operate with a relatively smaller amount of capital.

People today certainly have more confidence in banks than they did forty years ago. The bank holiday of 1933 was in essence a lack-of-confidence crisis or panic which swept the country, closing good banks as well as bad. The panic was definitely accentuated by the public's long experience with bank failures even in times of general economic prosperity. As a result of the bitter experience of the 1930's banking laws were substantially strengthened. Federal deposit insurance was inaugurated, and bank examining effort was greatly increased.[5]

The man in the street is probably not fully cognizant of the far-reaching implications of all of the legislative and supervisory buttressing of the banking structure which stemmed from the troubles

---

[4] "To move against the ebb of depression takes great courage; it also takes capital." Freeman, *op. cit.*, p. 10.

[5] For example, the bank examining staff of the Federal Reserve Bank of New York in 1930 consisted of one examiner for each 360MM of member bank loans; today there is an examiner for each 60MM of loans.

of the 1930s, but he is very much aware of deposit insurance. There have been few, if any, panic "runs" on insured banks since its inauguration, even when large defalcations have come to light. However, the informed public and the bank supervisor are much more cognizant of all that has taken place to strengthen banks generally since 1933. In a subsequent evaluation of the various measures of capital adequacy, the importance of these factors will be examined in detail.

As for the factors affecting individual banks, bank supervisors, generally, are in a better position to evaluate them than is the public.[6] Safeguards against risk, above-average earnings, effective operations and cost control, a well-maintained audit program, and sound lending and investing policies are all factors which tend to inspire confidence in a specific bank and in the ability of its management.[7] The supervisor's opinion of the latter, on which a major portion of his confidence is founded, is based fundamentally on his appraisal of how well management has formulated and put into practice the policies which are the subject of this book.

No matter how much confidence one may have in the banking structure, however, or how much faith one may place in the management of a particular bank, the clear lesson of history is that conditions change and that managements age and are replaced. A thin column of steel may support a greater weight than a thick masonry wall, but the strength of the support is still necessary and cannot be safely diminished. Bank capital supports confidence in banks in a very real sense; the quantity needed may be reduced by the improvement in tensile strength resulting from sound management policies, but the basic necessity for adequate capital support cannot be eliminated and should not be minimized.

LEGAL BASIS FOR CAPITAL ADEQUACY

Federal law as well as state law generally prescribes minimum amounts of capital required for the organization of a new bank. This minimum amount is usually related to the population of the

---

[6] Annual reports to shareholders, even when rendered in considerable detail, cannot show comparisons with other banks.

[7] Most banks seek prominent people as directors and advertise their directorate prominently hoping that public confidence in the character and success of the directors will be reflected in confidence in the bank and its management.

place in which the bank will be located. In recent years, as a matter of practical policy, supervisory authorities have usually required new banks to start with more than the legal minimum of capital.

Both Federal and state laws also have minimum capital requirements for the establishment of branches (in states where they are permitted). These legal requirements, however, have little real significance for banking today. They were enacted at a time when banks generally were much smaller. They have not been revised upward largely because the determination of capital adequacy has, in fact, become a matter of administrative judgment rather than definitive law.

With respect to member banks of the Federal Reserve System, the basis of the supervisory authority is laid in Section 9 of the Federal Reserve Act and Regulation H of the Board of Governors. The regulation requires that the net capital and surplus of a member bank "shall be adequate in relation to the character and condition of its assets and to its deposit liabilities and other corporate responsibilities." [8] The relationship of capital adequacy to the character and condition of a bank's assets is clearly established. What this relationship should be, however, is left to the judgment of the bank supervisor and bank management. The remainder of this chapter will be concerned with some of the considerations involved in arriving at such a judgment.

CAPITAL RELATIONSHIPS

Regulation H, as noted above, refers to the relationship of capital funds to both assets and deposits. Historically the ratio of capital funds to deposits has had the longest and widest public acceptance. Early in the twentieth century a rule of thumb developed that a bank should have capital funds equal to at least 10 per cent of its deposit liabilities. This rough rule was enacted into the laws of some states and received a kind of official sanction in 1914 when the Comptroller of the Currency suggested this 10 per cent ratio as the minimum for national banks.

The 10 per cent ratio was generally accepted and widely used

---

[8] Nonmember insured banks must agree to maintain "adequate capital" as a condition of deposit insurance.

until the years of World War II. During that period bank deposits expanded rapidly as the result of bank purchases of government securities. To have maintained the 10 per cent capital-to-deposit ratio in the face of ballooning deposits which were largely created by government security purchases would have seriously impeded the financing of the war. It became quickly evident, therefore, that capital adequacy should be related to the risk factors in a bank's assets and that the risks involved in holdings of U. S. government securities, the country's prime credit, were obviously different from other more normal banking risks.

A new concept of capital adequacy gradually evolved which became known as the "risk-asset" ratio.[9] This was conceived as the ratio of capital funds to total assets less cash, bank balances, and U. S. government securities. A ratio of $1 of capital to $5 of risk assets, or a risk-asset ratio of 20 per cent, was originally considered sufficient.

If capital is the ultimate protection against risk, it is indeed logical that it be related to assets because it is in a bank's assets, its loans, and investments, that risk is found. Deposits, in themselves, contain no risk until they are used to make loans and investments, and the degree of risk will vary with the character of the assets into which deposits are converted. Obviously this risk is not the same for all kinds of loans and investments.

---

[9] *Annual Report of the Comptroller of the Currency for the year 1948*, p. 4. "For these reasons, our bureau in recent years has placed less stress upon the relationship between capital structure and deposits, emphasizing instead adequacy of capital in relation to several factors, particularly competence of management, and volume and quality of assets which necessarily involve some element of uncertainty, however slight. In order to expedite our procedures and perform our duties as efficiently as possible, we have adopted certain rules-of-thumb for preliminary screening. One of the most useful of these is a ratio of capital funds to loans and investments other than United States government securities. When the capitalization of a particular bank, checked in this manner, apparently falls far short of the average, this is a signal for close analysis of relevant factors, such as the character of the loans and investments, the ability of management, local and regional economic conditions and trends, and the like. Even if loans and investments appear high in relation to capital structure at first glance, no criticism or corrective action will follow if it is ascertained that loans and investments are of high quality under the supervision of careful and intelligent management, and appropriate in the economic situation in which the particular bank is operating."

CAPITAL ADEQUACY FORMULAS

The ratio of capital to deposits had the virtue of simplicity and for this reason it is still frequently used as a first quick test of adequacy. A ratio of capital to total assets has the same virtue but escapes the logical flaw of relating risk to deposits. Such a ratio was used for many years by the Federal Deposit Insurance Corporation and the average ratio of capital funds to assets for all banks was taken as a standard.[10] Obviously, as the weaker banks improved their position the standard rose. This application has its own lack of logic.

Relating capital to "risk assets" recognized the difference between cash and government securities and other kinds of assets. It was not long before students of the subject saw that the risks in the latter were not uniform. Some of them closely approximated the riskless character of government obligations, others contained more than normal risk. A number of more or less "scientific" methods of analysis subsequently appeared, each of which was inspired by an attempt to evaluate banking risks more accurately.

NEW YORK STATE BANKERS

One of the earlier attempts to devise an improved approach to capital adequacy was that of a special committee of the New York State Bankers Association appointed to study risk asset ratios. The committee published a Report in March 1952 [11] which recommended a 20 per cent ratio of book capital funds to deposits less cash and government securities. A secondary calculation was also suggested for banks which did not measure up to this standard on the initial screening. In the secondary test other "riskless assets" including obligations guaranteed by the United States government, obligations of United States government agencies, short-term obli-

---

[10] *Annual Report of the Federal Deposit Insurance Corporation* for the year ended December 31, 1947, Washington, D. C., Table 22, p. 49. In this and subsequent reports capital funds are related to "total assets" and to "assets other than cash and United States government obligations."

[11] New York State Bankers Association, *A Report of the Committee on Risk Asset Ratio Study*, March 1952.

gations of New York State, and loans secured by these assets as well as loans secured by cash surrender value of life insurance were deducted from deposits.

The report pointed out that the suggested ratio was a net worth-to-debt ratio, similar to the ratios which banks use in appraising the business risks of their own customers. The committee found it illogical to relate capital to assets because the assets included those in which capital funds themselves were invested. Consistent with this viewpoint, the committee took a strong stand against the deduction of fixed assets from capital funds for the purpose of determining net capital available for risk-taking.

The error of this approach can best be illustrated by taking an extreme example. If two banks were imagined with exactly equal amounts of deposits and capital funds, and with identical portfolios of loans and investments except that one bank had written its bank premises down to $1 and had an extra $500,000 in Treasury bills whereas the other bank carried a new bank building on its books for the same amount, it seems obvious that the first bank would be in a better position to "liquidate" its capital funds and to make them available to absorb potential losses. Depositors cannot be paid in bricks and mortar and, even if the bank premises were sold at full value (unlikely in a serious depression), a bank cannot operate without banking quarters.[12]

ILLINOIS BANKERS ASSOCIATION

At about the same time as the New York Bankers Association study, the Illinois Bankers Association also authorized Gaylord Freeman of the First National Bank of Chicago to study "problems of capital adequacy," [13] the results of which were published under that title in May 1952. This study found that "The amount of capital required depends upon (i) the amount of assets subject to risk, and (ii) the degree of risk." [14] It declared that the amount of capital

---

[12] Bank premises can, of course, be sold and leased back. This frees capital funds for investment in other assets but obligates the bank to additional fixed charges—a drain on earnings.

[13] Freeman, *op. cit.*

[14] *Ibid.*, p. 11.

bears no relationship to the amount of deposits and that there is no uniform degree of risk in relation to deposits. It suggested that each bank review its experience with various kinds of assets during the depression of the 1930s and, on the basis of that experience, establish percentages of capital required for each classification of assets. The report admonishes, "That calculation isn't easy. You can't do it simply by applying any arbitrary factor to all assets. It requires a careful, time-consuming analysis of each asset." [15]

The Adjusted Risk-Asset Ratio

The "Freeman" approach would perhaps be ideal for the individual bank if management and directors would make the effort to prepare the necessary analyses.[16] It is somewhat complex, however, for practical use by most banks and by bank supervisors. It does not provide a standard which would be generally applicable to all banks since each bank's evaluation of its risks would probably differ. For comparative purposes the supervisor needs a standard which can be easily computed and impartially applied.

The simplest form of such an approach is the "adjusted" risk-asset ratio. It relates capital funds to risk assets but, like the New York State Bankers Report, it includes a "secondary calculation" in which assets close to cash and government securities in their "riskless" nature are also deducted from total assets for the purpose of determining "risk assets."

This calculation of capital to "adjusted risk assets" is widely used by supervisory authorities as at least one of the capital tests they regularly apply. The standard usually applied is $1 of capital funds to $6 of risk assets. Slightly higher percentages of risk assets are tolerated if all other factors are favorable. This calculation in the form in which it appears in National and Federal Reserve examination reports is reproduced below:

---

[15] *Ibid.,* p. 33.

[16] Some banks follow such procedures. The Simsbury Bank and Trust Company, Simsbury, Conn., for example, assigns a credit rating to each loan as it is made and has established a capital requirement for each rating. George H. Stebbins, "How Much Capital," *Address* Nineteenth Annual Study Conference, Michigan Bankers Association, Ann Arbor, September 1958.

Risk-Asset Ratio

Total assets $_____

Add:

    Total reserve for bad debts and un-
allocated charge-offs and valuation reserves on loans   _____

    Unallocated charge-offs and valu-
ation reserves on securities   _____ $_____

Deduct:

    Total estimated losses $_____

    50% of assets classified as doubtful   _____

    Cash and due from banks   _____

    U.S. government obligations direct
and guaranteed   _____

    Federal corporation obligations   _____

    Commodity Credit Corporation loans   _____

    New Housing Authority bonds   _____

    Loans or portions of loans—

      . Secured by obligations of U.S.
government and Federal corporation   _____

      Insured under Title I of National
Housing Act   _____

      Insured under Titles II and VI
of National Housing Act   _____

      Guaranteed under Servicemen's
Readjustment Act   _____

      Secured by hypothecated deposits   _____

      Secured by dealers' reserves re-
quired by agreement   _____

    Loans made under Exceptions 10,
11, and 12 of Section 5200, Revised Statutes   _____

    Federal Reserve Bank stock   _____

    Income collected, not earned   _____

                              Risk Assets $_____

THE RATIO OF CAPITAL TO RISK ASSETS IS 1 TO _____

This simplified approach includes in riskless assets some in which the risk, while small, is nevertheless present. There is market risk even in government securities, particularly in the longer maturities, and there is some risk in every loan, no matter how well secured; risk, for example that the collateral has not been properly endorsed or hypothecated. In addition the risk in "risk assets" is not uniform. The risk asset formula makes no distinction between a seasoned amortizing residential mortgage and the bank's investment in fixed assets.

New York Reserve Bank Method of Analysis

To meet these objections the Federal Reserve Bank of New York devised a capital adequacy analysis approach [17] which attempted to indicate the dollar amount of the minimum capital funds required by an individual bank on the basis of its own asset distribution. The amount of capital funds thus computed would be the *minimum* for a bank in which all other factors were favorable. The area of supervisory judgment would involve how much *more* capital than the minimum an individual bank might need because of its peculiar circumstances. This approach to the capital problem is less detailed than the "Freeman method" but is more selective than a straight risk-asset ratio.

For the purpose of this analysis, bank assets are divided into six rough groupings. These, of course, do not accurately reflect all of the various shades or degrees of risk, but they appear to be the smallest number of major categories into which bank assets normally fall and they provide a more selective basis than the simple distinction between "risk" and "non-risk" used in the risk-asset approach.

To each of these six categories is assigned a specific capital percentage requirement. Although these allocations are necessarily arbitrary they are generally consistent with traditional banking and supervisory thought. They are designed to be large enough not only to absorb probable losses in each category of assets but to provide enough additional capital to maintain supervisory confidence and keep the bank open. Just as bank credit men look to find various capital ratios in different kinds of commercial enterprises, so different kinds of banking business can be said, on the average, to require varying degrees of capital protection.

The first of these six asset categories consists of what may be

---

[17] Federal Reserve Bank of New York, "A Measure of Minimum Capital Adequacy," December 12, 1952. This formula was devised by the author, then Assistant Vice President in charge of Bank Supervision. It has been widely distributed through the Stonier Graduate School of Banking and was entered as Exhibit 178 in the hearings "In the Matter of the Continental Bank and Trust Company, Salt Lake City" before the Board of Governors of the Federal Reserve System.

called a bank's primary and secondary reserves. These include cash on hand, bank balances, and U. S. government securities maturing within five years. Other assets of comparable quality and very short maturity, such as bankers' acceptances and federal funds sold, also belong in this category.

Against these virtually riskless assets no capital is required. There is, of course, some market risk even in short-term government securities but ordinarily it is small enough to be readily absorbed out of earnings.

The second category may be designated as "minimum risk" assets. These are loans and investments generally recognized as having less than normal credit risk or as being readily pledgeable or saleable, although sometimes at a discount from face value. In this category are government securities with maturities over five years, government-guaranteed loans and securities of government agencies, loans secured by similar assets and by savings pass books and cash value of life insurance, prime commercial paper, brokers loans and other assets of similar quality.

Against these minimum risk assets a minimum capital requirement of 5 per cent is suggested. It will be seen that the assets included in this category are, for the most part, those which are considered "riskless" in the secondary computation used in the risk-asset ratio. Although the credit risk in such assets is minimal, they are not entirely riskless. Banks themselves would not generally lend money to any enterprise the current liabilities of which exceed twenty times its net worth no matter how free from risk its operations might appear. Some minimum capital protection is advisable for all but those assets which are essentially cash or its equivalent.

The third general category is designated as "portfolio" assets. These represent normal or usual banking risks. They include all of the remaining loan portfolio not adversely *"classified"* by the examiners, and the rest of the investment-grade securities (other than U. S. governments) maturing in over five years.

Against these normal risk assets a capital requirement of 12 per cent is suggested. The actual degree of risk, of course, will vary considerably among these "portfolio assets." The risk factor may not be identical for the same type of loan in two different banks because of variations in the skill with which loans are made or the forcefulness with which they are collected. "Mortgages" in one institution may be all conservatively made on one-family dwellings; in another bank the same caption might include perhaps a preponderance of loans against commercial or specialty properties. The 12 per cent requirement is considered to be a minimum capital protection against the average or normal portfolio mix. It assumes that loans containing more than normal credit risk will be "listed" in the examination report. Bank examiners classify as "substandard" those assets "which involve more than a normal banking risk due to the financial condition or unfavorable record of the obligor, insufficiency of security, or other factors noted. . . ." They list for "special mention" loans or assets which are not quite "substandard" but which nevertheless contain some credit weakness. Assets which appear to contain some loss potential are classified as "doubtful" and where loss has been determined or appears inevitable the asset is classified by the examiner as "loss."

Against assets classified by the examiner as "substandard" or listed by him for special mention, a 20 per cent capital allocation is suggested. Such assets do not necessarily contain an element of loss. Even the best-run bank will occasionally make loans which involve more than normal risk. But riskier business requires somewhat higher capital protection.

The fifth grouping consists of "work-out" assets. These include stocks, defaulted bonds, and other real estate, assets which banks may not legally acquire except by foreclosure in satisfaction of debts previously contracted. Bank supervisors generally expect that such assets will be disposed of promptly.

With respect to work-out assets a 50 per cent capital requirement is considered reasonable. A few state-chartered banks still legally hold common stocks often written down to 1933 prices. Market appreciation on such stocks is allowed, in effect, as capital protection against the remaining book value.

The final category consists of bank premises and furniture and fixtures. These are not considered bank investments in a true sense. Rather they are regarded as the working tools of the banking business which should be provided by the stockholders. Costly and elaborate premises may attract business but they provide little protection for the depositor. Bank buildings can be disposed of only when a bank goes into liquidation and, if this occurs in a serious depression, the real estate will be least readily saleable. From the viewpoint of the bank as a going concern, and as protection for depositors, the bank supervisor is chiefly concerned with the amount of capital a bank has in excess of its fixed assets.[18]   Therefore a full 100 per cent allocation of capital is suggested against fixed assets.

If banks occupy only a portion of their premises and rent the remainder to others, the New York Reserve Bank method permits the capitalization of rental income (arbitrarily calculated at five times gross rentals) and the treatment of the rented portion as other real estate subject to a 50 per cent capital allocation.

This analytical approach is summarized below:

	Capital Requirement
ASET CLASSIFICATION	
Primary and Secondary Reserve Assets	–0–
Cash and due from banks	
Government securities due under 5 years	
Other comparable assets	
Minimum Risk Assets	5%
Government securities due 5 years or more	
Other investment grade securities due within 5 years	
F.H.A. insured and guaranteed portion V.A. mortgages	
Insured modernization loans	
Loans secured by passbooks	
Loans secured by U.S. government securities	
Loans secured by cash value of life insurance	
Short-term loans to municipalities	
Money market loans (brokers' loans, commercial paper, short-term commodity loans, etc.)	
Other comparable assets	
Portfolio Assets	12%
Investments, except those included above and stocks or defaulted bonds	
Loans other than those included above or loans classified substandard, doubtful or loss	
Substandard and Specially Mentioned Assets	20%
Loans and other assets so classified except real estate, stocks and defaulted bonds	
Workout Assets	50%
Real estate not used for bank premises	
Stocks and defaulted bonds	

---

[18] However,, in reopening banks in 1933, bank supervisory authorities often gave nearly full value to bank premises.   One bank was reopened with "sound capital funds" of $1 million which included a bank building carried at $900,000.

ASSET CLASSIFICATION	Capital Requirement
Fixed Assets	100%
Bank premises	
Furniture and fixtures	

Against the capital requirement thus computed is measured the bank's good capital funds. These consist of book capital funds and all capital or "bad debt" reserves,[19] less assets classified as loss and one-half of the assets classified as "doubtful." In accordance with the general agreement among supervisory authorities arrived at in 1938, neither appreciation nor depreciation in investment grade securities is considered in the calculation of capital funds. The analysis, by requiring a higher percentage of capital against longer-term securities, makes some provision for the greater risk of market fluctuation. The method was designed to permit a range of supervisory judgment between the 100 per cent minimum for the rare bank in which all other factors are favorable and 125 per cent of minimum above which capital adequacy, as such, would seldom be questioned.

BOARD OF GOVERNORS' FORM OF ANALYSIS

A somewhat more complex approach to capital adequacy was subsequently developed by a staff group of the Board of Governors of the Federal Reserve System.[20] It combines a capital adequacy test with a liquidity test, requiring more capital for banks which are less liquid. This form is reproduced on pages 176–177. The following explanatory notes are pertinent:

A thorough appraisal of the capital needs of a particular bank must take due account of all relevant factors affecting the bank. These include the characteristics of its assets, its liabilities, and its management—as well as the history and prospects of the bank, its customers, and its community. The complexity of the problem requires a consid-

---

[19] Reserve for bad debts established from pre-tax income in accordance with a formula permitted by the Internal Revenue Service. (Coll. No. 54–55, April 8, 1954.)

[20] "Form for Analyzing Bank Capital," April 1956, Entered as Exhibit No. 154 in the Hearings before the Board of Governors, in the matter of the Continental Bank and Trust Company, Salt Lake City.

erable exercise of judgment. The groupings and percentages suggested in the Form for Analyzing Bank Capital can necessarily be no
more than aids to the exercise of judgment.

The requirements indicated by the various items of the form are
essentially "norms" and can provide no more than an initial presumption as the actual capital required by a particular bank. These
"norms" are entitled to considerable weight, but various upward and
downward adjustments could be made individually as the requirements are entered for each group of assets; but it is usually preferable,
particularly for future reference, to combine them and enter them as
a single adjustment under Item 8, indicating on the Analysis Form or
on an attached page the specific basis for each adjustment.

The requirements suggested in the Analysis Form assume that the
bank has adequate safeguards and insurance coverage against fire,
defalcation, burglary, etc.   Lack of such safeguards or coverage would
place upon the bank's capital risks which it should not be called upon
to bear.

It should be noted that this form requires a higher capital requirement for the first $500,000 of portfolio assets, in effect requir-
ing relatively more capital of small banks.   The reasons for this are:

The extra requirement of 15 per cent of the first $100,000 of port-
folio, 10 per cent of the next $100,000, and 5 per cent of the next
$300,000, as specified in Item 4, is a rough approximation of the con-
centration of risk (lack of diversification) which is likely in a smaller
portfolio, and which is usually reflected in the somewhat larger proportion of capital shown by most banks with smaller portfolios.   This
requirement is applied to all banks, but it is naturally a larger portion
of the total capital requirements of banks with smaller portfolios.
However, a particular portfolio, whatever its size, may in fact have
either more or less concentration of risk than other portfolios of similar
size.   If there is in fact greater or lesser concentration of risk in the
portfolio assets of a particular bank—as for example dependence upon
a smaller or larger number of economic activities—it would be appropriate to increase or decrease the requirements correspondingly.

Like the New York Reserve Bank analysis, the Board of Governors' form requires a 100 per cent capital allocation against fixed
assets but allows an adjustment for "rental properties."   The explanatory notes state:

Bank premises, furniture and fixtures, and other real estate are assigned a 100 per cent requirement as a first approximation, since these
assets are usually not available to pay depositors unless the bank goes

into liquidation, and even then they usually can be turned into cash only at a substantial sacrifice. However, some properties which bring in independent income, such as bank premises largely rented to others, may be more readily converted into cash by selling or borrowing on them, and in such situations it may be appropriate to reduce the 100 per cent requirement by an amount equal to the assumed "sacrifice" value, such as, say, two or three times the gross annual independent income.

The most unusual feature of the Board of Governors' form is the provision for a "liquidity calculation" and for additional capital requirements, for those banks which do not meet the liquidity test. This additional requirement is based on the theory that perfectly sound assets are subject to shrinkage if they have to be sold in an adverse market or forcibly collected. The liquidity calculation is explained as follows:

The provision for 47 per cent liquidity for demand deposits of individuals, partnerships and corporations actually represents 33⅓ per cent possible shrinkage in deposits, plus 20 per cent of the remaining 66⅔ per cent. Thirty-six per cent of time deposits I.P.C. represents 20 per cent shrinkage, plus 20 per cent of the remaining 80 per cent. In both instances, the provision for 20 per cent liquidity for remaining deposits is to help the bank continue as a going concern even after suffering substantial deposit shrinkage.

Among possible special factors to be considered in connection with the liquidity calculation would be concentration or diversification of risk among deposits. This might be due to such things as dependence upon a smaller or larger number of economic activities, or preponderance of small or large deposits—large deposits usually being more volatile.

Liquidity available for primary and secondary reserve assets is assumed to equal the amount of those assets less only the regular capital required thereon, since the regular capital specified for these assets assumes forced liquidation. However, the regular capital specified for other assets (*i.e.*, those in Groups 2–4) is only a portion (approximately 40 per cent) of that required for forced liquidation. Therefore, in determining the liquidity available from such other assets, the amount of such other assets must be reduced by more than the regular specified capital.

This extra capital required is to cover possible losses in forced liquidation of assets other than primary and secondary reserves in case they had to be used to provide liquidity. The 4 per cent indicated for Line E amounts to an automatic addition to the 6.5 per cent that has already been applied to Line C, and results in a total extra require-

FORM FOR ANALYZING BANK CAPITAL
(See Notes on Reverse Side)

April 1956

BANK: _____

LOCATION: _____

BASED ON REPORT OF EXAMINATION AS OF _____. DISTRICT NO. _____

(Dollar Amounts in Thousands)

	AMOUNT OUTSTANDING	CAPITAL REQUIREMENT		LIQUIDITY CALCULATION	
		Per Cent	Amount		
(1) PRIMARY AND SECONDARY RESERVE				47% of Demand Deposits i.p.c.	$ _____
Cash Assets	$ _____	0%		36% of Time Deposits i.p.c.	_____
Guar. Portion of CCC or V-loans	_____			100% of Deposits of Banks	_____
Comm. Paper, Bnk Accept. & Brks' Lns	_____			100% of Other Deposits	_____
U.S. Govt. Secs:		0.5%	$ _____	100% of Borrowings	_____
Bills	_____			Allow. for spec. factors, if info. available (+ or −)	_____
Certificates, etc. (to 1 yr.)	_____				
Other (1-5 yrs.) (Incl. Treas Inv. Series A & B)	_____			A. Total Provision for Liquidity	_____
Other Secs. Inv. Rtngs 1 & 2 or Equiv. (to 3 yrs.)	_____	4.0%	_____	B. Liquidity available from Prim. and Secondary Res. ("amt. outstanding" less cap. required thereon)	_____
TOTAL	$ _____				
(2) MINIMUM RISK ASSETS				C. Liquidity to be provided from assets in Groups 2, 3 or 4 (zero if B equals or exceeds A, otherwise A less B)	_____
U.S. Govt. Secs. (5-10 yrs.)	_____				
Ins. Portion FHA Rep. & Modr'n Loans	_____				
Loans on Passb'ks, U.S. Secs. or CSV Life ins.	_____			D. Liquidity available from Min. Risk Assets (90% of "amt. outstanding" in line 2)	_____
Short-term Municipal Loans	_____				
TOTAL	$ _____	4%	_____		
(3) INTERMEDIATE ASSETS				E. Liquidity to be provided from assets in Groups 3 or 4 (zero if D equals or exceeds C, otherwise C less D)	_____
U.S. Govt. Secs. (Over 10 yrs.)	_____				
FHA and VA Loans	_____			F. Liquidity available from Intermediate Assets (85% of "amt. outstanding" in line 3)	_____
TOTAL	$ _____	6%	_____		
(4) PORTFOLIO ASSETS (Gross of Res.)				G. Liquidity to be provided from Portfolio Assets (zero if F equals or exceeds E, otherwise E less F)	_____
Investments (not listed elsewhere)	_____				
Loans (not listed elsewhere)	_____				
TOTAL	$ _____	10%*	_____		

*Plus 15% of 1st $100,000 of portfolio, 10% of next $100,000 and 5% of next $300,000.

• • • • • • • • • • • •

	AMOUNT OUTSTANDING	Per Cent	Amount		
(5) FIXED, CLASSIFIED & OTHER ASSETS				Extra Capital Required on Any Assets in Groups 2-4 Used for Liquidity	
Bk Prem., Furn. & Fixt., Other Real Est.	_____				
Stocks & Defaulted Secs.	_____	100%	_____		
Assets Classified as "Loss"	_____				
Assets Classified as "Doubtful"	_____	50%	_____		
Assets Classified as "Substandard"	_____	20%	_____	6.5% of line C	_____
Accruals, Fed. Res. Bk. Stock, Prep. Expen.	_____	0%	_____	4.0% of line E	_____
TOTAL ASSETS	$ _____			9.5% of line G	_____

(6) ALLOWANCE FOR TRUST DEPT. (Amt. equal to 300% of annual gross earnings of Department) _____

(7) EXTRA CAP. REQD. IF ANY ASSETS IN GROUPS 2-4 USED FOR LIQUIDITY (zero if line C in Liquidity Calculation is zero, otherwise Total in line H) _____   ◄─ H. Total Extra Cap. Req. $ _____

(8) ALLOW. FOR SPEC. OR ADDIT. FACTORS, IF INFO. AVAILABLE (+ or −) (see notes on reverse side) _____

(9) TOTAL CAPITAL REQUIREMENT (1 thru 8) $ _____

(10) ACTUAL CAP., ETC. (Sum of Cap. Stock, Surplus, Undiv. Profits, Res. for Conting., Loan Valuation Res., Net unapplied Sec. Valuation Res., Unallocated Charge-offs, and any comparable items) (Exclude Depreciation and Amortization Reserves) $ _____

(11) AMOUNT BY WHICH ACTUAL IS: { MORE than requirement (10 minus 9) _____ + $ _____
       or
       LESS than requirement (9 minus 10) _____ − $ _____ }

(12) RATIO OF ACTUAL CAPITAL, ETC. TO REQUIREMENT (10 divided by 9) _____   %

NOTES REGARDING FORM FOR ANALYZING BANK CAPITAL

A thorough appraisal of the capital needs of a particular bank must take due account of all relevant factors affecting the bank. These include the characteristics of its assets, its liabilities, its trust or other corporate responsibilities, and its management--as well as the history and prospects of the bank, its customers and its community. The complexity of the problem requires a considerable exercise of judgment. The groupings and percentages suggested in the Form For Analyzing Bank Capital can necessarily be no more than aids to the exercise of judgment.

The requirements indicated by the various items on the form are essentially "norms" and can provide no more than an initial presumption as to the actual capital required by a particular bank. These "norms" are entitled to considerable weight, but various upward or downward adjustments in requirements may be appropriate for a particular bank if special or unusual circumstances are in fact present in the specific situation. Such adjustments could be made individually as the requirements are entered for each group of assets; but it usually is preferable, particularly for future reference, to combine them and enter them as a single adjustment under Item 8, indicating on the Analysis Form or an attached page the specific basis for each adjustment.

The requirements suggested in the Analysis Form assume that the bank has adequate safeguards and insurance coverage against fire, defalcation, burglary, etc. Lack of such safeguards or coverage would place upon the bank's capital risks which it should not be called upon to bear.

ITEM (4) — PORTFOLIO ASSETS

Concentration or Diversification. — The extra requirement of 15% of the first $100,000 of portfolio, 10% of the next $100,000, and 5% of the next $300,000, as specified in item 4, is a rough approximation of the concentration of risk (lack of diversification) which is likely in a smaller portfolio, and which is usually reflected in the somewhat larger proportion of capital shown by most banks with smaller portfolios. This requirement is applied to all banks, but is naturally a larger portion of the total capital requirements of banks with smaller portfolios. However, a particular portfolio, whatever its size, may in fact have either more or less concentration of risk than other portfolios of similar size. If there is in fact substantially greater or lesser concentration of risk in the portfolio assets of the particular bank--as for example dependence upon a smaller or larger number of economic activities--it would be appropriate to increase or decrease requirements correspondingly.

Drafts Accepted By Bank. — When drafts have been accepted by the bank, ordinarily the customers' liability to the bank should be treated as Portfolio Assets if the acceptances are outstanding, or the acceptances themselves should be so treated if held by the bank.

ITEM (5) — FIXED, CLASSIFIED, AND OTHER ASSETS

Rental Properties. — Bank premises, furniture and fixtures, and other real estate are assigned a 100% requirement as a first approximation, since these assets usually are not available to pay depositors unless the bank goes into liquidation, and even then they usually can be turned into cash only at substantial sacrifice. However, some properties which bring in independent income, such as bank premises largely rented to others, may be more readily convertible into cash by selling or borrowing on them, and in such situations it may be appropriate to reduce the 100% requirement by an amount equal to an assumed "sacrifice" value, such as, say, two or three times the gross annual independent income.

Stocks. — In the case of stocks, their wide fluctuations in price suggest a 100% requirement as a first approximation. However, in some cases it may be appropriate to reduce the 100% requirement against a stock by an amount equal to an assumed "sacrifice" value, such as the lowest market value reached by the stock in, say, the preceding 36 or 48 months.

Hidden Assets. — In some cases assets may be carried at book values which appear to be below their actual value, and may thus appear to provide hidden strength. However, any allowance for such a situation should be made with great caution, and only after taking full account of possible declines in values and the great difficulty of liquidating assets in distress circumstances.

ITEM (6) — ALLOWANCE FOR TRUST DEPARTMENT

Deposited Securities. — The requirement for the trust department should in no event be less than the amount of any securities deposited with the State authorities for the protection of private or court trusts, since such securities are not available in ordinary circumstances to protect the bank's depositors.

LIQUIDITY CALCULATION

Percentages of Deposits. — The provision for 47% liquidity for demand deposits of individuals, partnerships and corporations actually represents 33-1/3% possible shrinkage in deposits, plus 20% of the remaining 66-2/3%. 36% of time deposits i.p.c. represents 20% shrinkage, plus 20% of the remaining 80%. In both instances, the provision for 20% liquidity for remaining deposits is to help the bank continue as a going concern even after suffering substantial deposit shrinkage.

Among possible special factors to be considered in connection with the liquidity calculation would be concentration or diversification of risk among deposits. This might be due to such things as dependence upon a smaller or larger number of economic activities, or preponderance of large or small deposits--large deposits usually being more volatile.

Liquidity Available from Assets. — Liquidity available from primary and secondary reserves is assumed to equal the amount of those assets less only the regular capital required thereon, since the regular capital specified for these assets assumes forced liquidation. However, the regular capital specified for other assets (i.e., those in Groups 2-4) is only a portion (approximately 40%) of that required for forced liquidation. Therefore, in determining the liquidity available from such other assets, the amount of such other assets must be reduced by more than the regular specified capital.

Extra Capital Required. — This extra capital is to cover possible losses in forced liquidation of assets other than primary and secondary reserves in case they had to be used to provide liquidity. The 4% indicated for Line E amounts to an automatic addition to the 6.5% that has already been applied to Line C, and results in a total extra requirement of 10.5% of the liquidity to be provided from Intermediate Assets. Similarly, the total extra requirement on the liquidity to be provided from Portfolio Assets is 20%. If the same amounts of extra capital were stated as percentages of the assets to be liquidated rather than of the liquidity to be provided, the percentages would be smaller, namely, 6% of Minimum Risk Assets, 9% of Intermediate Assets, and 15% of Portfolio Assets.

ment of 10.5 per cent of the liquidity to be provided from Intermediate Assets. Similarly, the total extra requirement on the liquidity to be provided from Portfolio Assets is 20 per cent. If the same amount of extra capital were to be stated as percentages of the assets to be liquidated rather than of the liquidity to be provided, the percentages would be smaller, namely, 6 per cent of Minimum Risk Assets, 9 per cent of Intermediate Assets, and 15 per cent of Portfolio Assets.

The liquidity calculation used in the above analysis is based on uniform estimates of liquidity needs similar to the "asset allocation" plans reviewed in Chapter VIII. It stipulates (as a first approximation at least) a degree of liquidity roughly equal to the amount by which bank deposits shrank on the average during the depression of the 1930s. Most informed persons would argue that this requirement is high in the light of Federal deposit insurance and the other factors which have strengthened banks and supervisory confidence in them. A more specific objection to this blanket approach (if not used judiciously) is the fact that, for the individual bank, liquidity needs (and therefore an adequate portfolio of liquid assets) vary throughout the year in response to seasonal or other periodical changes in the demand for and supply of funds. As a result, banks which may fully meet the liquidity tests of the Board of Governors' form of analysis at one period of the year may be deficient at another but still meet fully the liquidity test suggested in Chapter VIII at both times.

A unique feature of the Board of Governors' formula is its capital requirement for potential liabilities in connection with trust activities. Because trust assets are carried on the books of banks in many different ways (inventory cost, unit cost, etc.) the aggregate of trust assets is a poor measure of the risks involved. Trust fees, on the other hand, are roughly uniform and provide a reasonably comparable measure of trust activity and therefore of potential liability.

The provision of capital to the extent of three times gross income from all trust activities is admittedly an arbitrary requirement. Unquestionably the operation of a trust department involves a bank in risk of loss; not only the risk of surcharge but also the risk of costly litigation and the uncertainties and possible unfavorable publicity involved in being sued for large sums whether or not the suits are successful. The risk of loss in trust operations is probably greater in connection with personal trusts than with agency and corporate trust accounts in many of which discretion is limited or clearly defined. Just how great the actual risk may be is virtually impossible to determine because available records do not go back far enough to provide a factual basis of experience.[21] The Board of Governors' requirement coincides closely with the amount of capital held on the average by a number of large institutions which conduct only a trust business except for a minor amount of incidental deposit banking.

COMPARISON OF ANALYTICAL APPROACHES TO CAPITAL ADEQUACY

Analytical or statistical methods of computing capital adequacy represent attempts to standardize or systematize the more or less intuitive judgment of bank supervisors. Many supervisors would claim that they can gauge the adequacy of capital without benefit of such formulas and, in fact, use the formulas only as a starting place for the exercise of judgment based on experience. Even experienced supervisors, however, find it difficult to convince bank management or directors, on occasion, of the soundness of their sometimes quite subjective views. They resort to statistical forms of analysis, using them as tools to demonstrate the objectivity of their judgment, because a formula will convince bank mangement that its special situation is receiving comparable treatment and equitable consideration.

Generally, the different analytical approaches described above provide roughly comparable answers; in individual cases, however, the computed requirement may differ quite widely. A random sample of fifty banks was analyzed using each of the three principal methods, and the ratios computed. The first column in Table 10 shows the average of each ratio for all fifty banks. The sample compares closely with national averages.

In Column 2 the capital of each of the fifty banks was theoret-

---

21 The experience of the Bank Examinations Department of the Federal Reserve Bank of New York over the past 10 years is that few trust departments have had cash settlements or surcharges in excess of 1½ per cent of gross commissions in any year. This, however, is admittedly short-range experience under generally favorable economic conditions.

ically increased or decreased to exactly the minimum requirement of the New York Federal Reserve formula and the other two ratios recomputed to show a comparison at the "minimum" level. Column 3 shows the range of individual banks at this average "minimum."

TABLE 10

COMPARISON OF CAPITAL FORMULAS

	1 *Actual*	2 *Theoretical*	3 *Range*
New York formula	128%	100%	—
Board formula	116	91	68%–118%
Risk-asset ratio	1/6	1/7.4	1/3.4, 1/12.7

Both the adjusted risk-asset approach and the Board form of analysis require, on the average, somewhat more capital than the bare minimum computed by the New York method. It should be noted, however, that this *is* a minimum and that in actual practice, when all factors are taken into consideration, adequacy under this formula is usually in the range of 115 to 125 per cent of the basic minimum.

In specific cases the risk-asset ratio favors the bank with a relatively high investment in fixed assets. The Board of Governors' analysis form penalizes the bank which has a relatively small investment in short-term assets (whether it needs them or not). None can authoritatively say that either of the methods is "right" and that is why supervisors insist that, at best, any formula is no more than a "screening device." Many banks and bank supervisors use several of them for this purpose. In the final analysis the intangible factors of confidence will receive a great deal of weight in the ultimate determination of how much capital is adequate.

BASIS OF FORMULAS

Supervisory judgment, of course, underlies the various percentages used in the formulas themselves and determines the standards from which the formulas will measure relative deviation. This judgment is primarily based on experience which, for most people in positions of senior supervisory responsibility today, consists of first-hand knowledge of the condition of banks in the mid-1930s. Although they may sincerely believe that these circumstances will not recur in their lifetime, they are not convinced that other circumstances, unforeseen but equally disastrous, may not. "Capital adequacy," therefore, tends to mean enough capital to see a bank through another period of equal strain. How much capital was that?

To shed some light on this specific question a sample of fifty banks (which survived the depression of the 1930s) was chosen at random and their loss experience during the ten years from 1929 through 1939 subjected to careful analysis. Nineteen of the fifty banks went through this period without having to obtain additional capital. The other thirty-one did obtain additional capital in one way or another; through deposit waivers, stockholder assessments, sale of preferred stock to the R.F.C. or others, or by other devices.

Available statistics permit the evaluation of the capital position of these banks only on the basis of an unadjusted risk-asset ratio: the ratio of capital funds to total assets less cash and government securities. On this basis, book capital position was measured as of mid-1929 (condition report data) and as of the examination made in 1933 on the basis of which many of these banks were recapitalized and reopened. All of these banks were closed at least briefly during the bank holiday and their reopening was a practical test of how much capital was needed at that time to obtain or regain supervisory confidence.

Not all the banks reopened at the same time. Reorganization took time, especially if additional capital had to be raised. For the purpose of determining how much additional capital a bank required, therefore, the total amount of additional capital funds acquired between 1933 and 1939 was taken into consideration. "Net sound capital" required to reopen in 1933, as that term is used here, includes the book capital funds and reserves of the bank in 1933 plus the additional capital raised through 1939, less estimated losses, security depreciation and assets classified as "doubtful" as shown in the examination report nearest to June 30, 1933. This figure for the fifty banks averaged 21.2 per cent of risk assets. For the banks which were required to raise additional capital, the ratio averaged somewhat higher (22.8) than for the banks which survived the bank holiday unscathed. For the latter the comparable figure was 18.7 per cent, reflecting perhaps the more favorable supervisory judgment with respect to the ability of management or the quality of the assets.

These figures support, or at least explain, the general feeling among bank supervisors that a 20 per cent primary risk-asset ratio is "about right." Nor is this the whole story. By 1933 these fifty banks collectively had been through a substantial liquidation. Their risk assets had shrunk from an aggregate of $373 million on June 30, 1929 to $259 million as of the examination date in 1933, a decline of 30 per cent. In the process net losses for the full years 1929–1933 had totalled $35 million or nearly 10 per cent of their 1929 risk assets and, at the 1933 examination, the total of assets classified as loss or doubtful totalled another $38 million. The two together thus aggregated almost exactly 20 per cent of 1929 risk assets.

Another way of looking at it would be to ask "How much capital would these banks have needed in 1929 to survive the depression without raising additional capital funds?" The nineteen banks which accomplished this feat had a risk-asset ratio of 18.4 per cent in 1929. The thirty-one which needed more capital had an average risk-asset ratio of only 15.5 per cent in 1929. If, for these latter banks, the additional capital funds raised between 1933 and 1939 is added to the actual capital funds held in 1929 (the measure of the amount of capital they needed to survive the depression) the ratio in 1929 would have been 23 per cent of risk assets.

These signs, with remarkable unanimity, indicate the approximate sufficiency of a 20 per cent primary or unadjusted risk-asset ratio in relation to the average character and risk of 1929 bank assets, the caliber of 1929 bank management, and the 1929–33 degree of public confidence in banks and the economic future. The bank supervisor may not be entirely convinced that 1933 will never return but the objective student of banking can note many important changes in the banking scene since 1929. The need for capital today can be intelligently discussed in terms of 1929 only if one can appraise the changes which have since taken place in the factors affecting capital adequacy. Some of these are not easy to appraise statistically or objectively.

The Federal Deposit Insurance Corporation has undoubtedly

lessened the chances of wholesale loss of public confidence in banks, but Solomon, in all his wisdom, would have difficulty translating this increased confidence into any given number of percentage points in a risk-asset ratio! Whether management is better today than it was in 1929 is a moot question. Those bank managers who lived through 1933–34 are certainly wiser, but their ranks are rapidly thinning. It is always possible for a "new era" philosophy to creep back into banking if (in some quarters at least) it has not already done so.

When it comes to asset quality the advocates of lower capital requirements are on firmer ground. Fifty-eight per cent of the gross losses incurred between 1929 and 1939 by the fifty banks in the sample studied were on securities, mostly corporate securities which constitute a very minor portion of bank assets today. These securities comprised 20 per cent of risk assets in 1929. Many of them were of a caliber that banks may no longer legally acquire.

Another large portion of bank losses resulted from the foreclosure of mortgage loans and the forced sale of the resultant real estate at sacrifice prices. These were mostly mortgages which had been on the books for years without amortization. Today virtually all mortgages are being amortized. They are also being written for longer terms and frequently refinanced so that the average equity is not so large as one might suppose.

Loans against marketable collateral were another weak spot in the 1929 risk asset portfolio. The margin requirements of the Board of Governors' Regulation U [22] effectively prevent the use of excessive bank credit for purchasing or carrying listed securities, but banks still lend against stocks for other purposes and the market value of those stocks could fall rather sharply.

Consumer credit, a substantial factor in many banks, is still largely untried, at least with respect to 36-month maturities on automobile paper, uninsured home modernization loans, "boat" loans, check credit, and whatever may come along next. Consumer credit has inherent strength deriving from regular monthly payments, but its repayment on schedule in too many cases represents marginal income of debt-burdened individuals and this is an element of weakness.

---

[22] "Loans by Banks for the Purpose of Purchasing or Carrying Registered Stocks" (12 C F R 221).

Thus, despite the strengthening of the banking structure and despite the obvious improvement in the quality of bank assets, it should be clear that all the risk has not been eliminated from the banking business. The formulas used by the various supervisory authorities and their more or less flexible application recognize, to an important degree, the improvement which has taken place.[23] The decision of bank supervisors in 1938, previously noted, not to take depreciation of investment-grade securities into account in computing a bank's capital position is, in itself, a substantial liberalization. In 1957, for example, when the yield on long-term government securities rose above 3½ per cent for the first time in over twenty years, the capital of many banks would have been seriously reduced if banks had been required to mark down to market values their still substantial holdings of government issues bearing only 2½ per cent coupons. The supervisors bravely ignored this situation, despite some inner qualms, as they should have as long as the banks had adequate liquidity.

The public interest in safe banking, however, and the need to avoid forever a recurrence of 1933, require a conservative approach to the problem of capital adequacy. Bank shareholders should be equally interested in providing the assurance that the banks they own will be able to survive whatever adverse circumstances may possibly develop, and history bears abundant witness to the periodic recurrence of the lean years of trial and tribulation.

SIGNIFICANCE FOR BANK POLICY

Whatever formulas the supervisors may use, and however strong their "moral suasion," the fundamental responsibility for capital adequacy rests with the directors of each individual bank.[24] It should be helpful for the directors to understand the basis of the supervisory evaluation and to use one or more of the supervisory formulas as a measure at least, of the trends in their capital positions. Not all banks will wish to go as far as the Illinois Bankers

---

[23] On the average the minimum requirement of the New York Reserve Bank formula would represent a primary or unadjusted risk asset ratio of 11.7 per cent as compared with the original 20 per cent standard.

[24] *Cf.* Research Council, American Bankers Association, *The Adequacy of a Bank's Capital* (A Statement of Principle) New York, October 1954.

Association's recommendation and appraise each asset in terms of its capital needs, but all banks should go farther than the rough groupings, say, of the New York Reserve formula. Within the logical framework of that formula, capital allocations, ranging from perhaps 6 to 16 per cent, could be used to distinguish between types of loans which the directors consider "prime" and those in which they recognize normal or greater risk. Different capital allocations might be made with respect to different groups of securities as well, distinguishing between maturities, credit risks, and breadth of market.[25] Such an evaluation of the risks inherent in the loans and securities of a particular bank, made periodically by its directors with the guidance of management, would be at the very least an instructive exercise and could provide an effective review of lending and investing policies.

Dividend policy (Chapter V) is of course directly related to the capital adequacy problem. From the viewpoint of the stockholder and the profitability of his investment it is just as important not to have too much capital as it is essential, from the viewpoint of safety and growth, to have enough. One small New York State bank comes to mind which has three times the minimum requirements as computed on the New York Reserve Bank formula—a 40 per cent adjusted risk-asset ratio which is 17 per cent of deposits. Despite this wealth of capital funds the directors continue to hoard capital and pay out only half of current earnings in dividends.[26] Because this bank has more capital than it needs the stockholders are earning only 5¼ per cent on the book value of their investment (despite average or better earnings on total assets) and receiving only 2½ per cent as dividends. Another result is that the bank's stock, with a book value of nearly $150, traded in a nominal market at $75.[27] And, as the bank continues to accumulate capital funds, its earning power in relation thereto is further diluted.

Although this is an extreme example, the problem of excess capital is not an uncommon one in small banks. It is clearly the super-

---

[25] *Cf.* Roger A. Lyon, *Investment Portfolio Management in the Commercial Bank* (New Brunswick, N. J.: Rutgers University Press, 1960), pp. 46–55.

[26] The directors (and substantial owners) of this small bank are more interested in absolute safety than in profitability. They still recount with pride how this bank refused to close when it received notice of the "bank holiday" in 1934.

[27] This was in 1960 when most bank stocks sold above their book values.

visor's task to determine how much capital is too little; it is obviously the responsibility of management to avoid having too much.

Just how much capital is enough can perhaps never be fully determined in advance of the hour of need. However, from the viewpoint of management, as well as the supervisor, the risks of having too little exceed the costs of a moderate excess. In the review of the 1929–1934 experience, it is significant, perhaps, that the nineteen banks which survived the depression without having to raise additional capital had, in 1929, a capital ratio only 2.9 per cent higher on the average than the thirty-one which needed recapitalization.

Adequate capital, of course, is not a substitute for sound lending and investing policies; it cannot take the place of experienced and progressive management or a well-conceived program of control, profit planning and audit. It can only provide assurance to the public, the stockholder and the supervisor that the bank has the strength and the wherewithal to survive circumstances and conditions which the best management can never foresee. In a real sense, the provision of adequate capital is the price of the private enterprise banking system in the United States.

MANAGING THE CAPITAL ACCOUNT

Over and above the adequacy of a bank's capital funds there remains the management problem of how the net worth of the bank can best be distributed among the various capital accounts. When a new bank is organized its capital stock is usually sold at a premium to create a paid-in surplus, a reserve for organization expenses, and initial operating losses. As earnings accumulate they are credited to the Undivided Profits account. The national banking law and the laws of most states require that, before paying out Undivided Profits in dividends, some portion of earnings must be carried to Surplus Account until the latter account equals a stated percentage of capital.[28] Most bankers, regardless of legal requirements, like to see the Surplus Account equal at least to the bank's stated Capital Account.

As Surplus and Undivided Profits increase, the book value of

---

[28] U.S.R.S., Section 5199(a) requires national banks to build up Surplus to 100 per cent of Capital (U.S.C., Title 12, section 60).

the shares increases in relation to par value. If there is an active market for the stock the shares will increase proportionately in market price. If management is interested in a fairly wide distribution of the bank's stock, if it wishes to facilitate the transfer of ownership from one generation to the next, so to speak, it will not wish to see the price of the bank's stock rise too high. Reductions in book value, and therefore market price, can be brought about either through the declaration of stock dividends or by reducing the par value of the stock and, accordingly, increasing the number of shares outstanding (stock splits).

A market price somewhere below $100 per share facilitates not only the transfer of outstanding shares but makes the sale of new stock easier. Many banks declare stock dividends preparatory to issuing new shares, partly to make the issuing price more attractive and partly to increase the proportionate share of existing stockholders in future earnings of the bank, should they be unable to exercise their preemptive rights to the new stock.

Aside from building up capital and surplus it is important to accumulate and maintain adequate reserves. Nearly all banks now take advantage of the provisions of the Internal Revenue Code which permit the accumulation of a tax-free reserve against loans in a maximum amount equal to the bank's average loss experience in its twenty worst years multiplied by the total of its outstanding loans.[29] Well-managed banks, in addition, establish valuation reserves (reserves deducted from assets on published statements) against securities as well. Certainly all security profits should be credited to such reserves since they are, in effect, nonrecurring profits resulting from a swing in the level of interest rates which will probably reverse itself.

PREFERRED STOCK AND CAPITAL DEBENTURES

Traditionally banks have issued preferred stock and capital debentures only at times when the sale of common stock was virtually impossible. The sale of senior equity has been considered an emergency measure. Is this sound bank policy? The Financial Institutions Act of 1957, designed to revamp and modernize the

---

[29] Section 166(c) of the Internal Revenue Code of 1954 and Coll. No. 54–55, dated April 8, 1954, covering taxable years beginning December 31, 1952.

banking law, originally contained a provision authorizing the issuance of debt obligations as well as preferred stock.[30] Capital debentures are very attractive from the tax viewpoint because the interest charges are deductible from earnings before taxes. They have also been attractive investments for insurance companies and other institutional investors. In many cases capital debentures were issued by banks in order to refund similar obligations originally issued to the Reconstruction Finance Corporation. In a few cases they were issued to provide additional capital funds at a time when the market for common stock was depressed.

All the Federal supervisory authorities have consistently opposed the issuance of debt obligations by banks (except for the purpose of refinancing obligations due to the R.F.C.) on the grounds that bank capital should be permanent and not subject to retirement at the demand of the holders. The bank argument has been, in effect, that capital debentures represent a means of anticipating the retention of future earnings; that they are a means of obtaining additional and perhaps needed capital protection at relatively low cost; and that they mature and will be paid off only as such capital protection is replaced from earnings. The supervisor replies that future earnings may not, in fact, materialize and that just when capital protection may be needed most all earnings may be required to absorb current losses; thus the maturing debt would only further complicate the problem of a bank's survival. The supervisor, therefore, has been adamant against the use of "debt capital" except in emergency or other extenuating circumstances.[31]

---

[30] Sections 20 and 21, Title I of a tentative bill in the form of a Committee Print, dated January 1, 1957 which was the basis of S 1451, 85th Cong. 1st sess., 1957 (Washington, D. C.: United States Government Printing Office, 1957) p. 14. The Report of the Advisory Committee for the Study of Federal Statutes Governing Financial Institutions and Credit to the Committee of Banking and Currency of the United States Senate, December 17, 1956, had said: "The restrictions of the present law on the acquisition of additional capital by banks are not, in our judgment, reasonable. . . . In some circumstances, preferred stock or debenture issues would offer a better and more feasible means of acquiring additional capital. . . . The use of such securities, therefore, provides a flexible means of adjusting the capital requirements of banks to the needs of the times."

[31] Ray M. Gidney, Comptroller of the Currency, commenting on the provision for capital debentures contained in the draft Financial Institutions Act (*supra*) said: "In the troublesome period of the early thirties, where many reorganizations took place, some of the state banking departments had some-

Preferred stock, on the other hand, is a permanent form of capital without fixed maturity. If preferred stock can be sold at lower cost than common stock should not banks be permitted to use this form of capitalization? During the period from 1935 to 1955, when bank stocks generally were selling below their liquidation value, a great deal of interest in preferred stock was generated. A few banks actually sold preferred stock and others studied the question carefully. As a result of inquiries from at least one large New York City bank, the Superintendent of Banks of the State of New York declared in 1954: [32]

> We regard capital strength as having such vital importance for banking institutions of all types that we have recently, after an extended study, decided to modify our traditional attitude toward sale of preferred stock by commercial banks. In the past, we have tended to be so partial to common stock that we have pretty largely reserved approval of preferred issues to unusual and extraordinary circumstances. Now we have come to the view that preferred capital might be more broadly appropriate and useful than that, and so we would not any longer reject on principle alone any new capital proposal involving preferred stock, a security that has attractions for certain institutional investors that common stock does not have.

Despite supervisory doubts and objections, the Financial Institutions Act of 1957, as it was passed by the Senate, contained a provision permitting national banks to issue preferred stock, with the approval of the Comptroller, when "it is the most practical method of obtaining desired and needed capital." [33] The act, however, was not passed by the House of Representatives and, because of the great improvement in the market for bank common stock

---

thing of an advantage in the matter of the ease with which adjustments could be made. In a really desperate situation I believe these capital notes or debentures could be useful, because in that way it might be possible to have one interested party put in a large sum in capital notes, and thus patch up the situation. But we would take the same position on them as to their being of an emergency character as we would on preferred stock. . . ." *Hearings before a Subcommittee of the Committee on Banking and Currency, United States Senate*, 85th Cong., 1st sess., Part 2, February 11, 1957 (Washington, D. C.: United States Printing Office, 1957), pp. 778–9.

[32] William A. Lyon, *Address* before the annual meeting of the Savings Banks Association of New York, White Sulphur Springs, November 3, 1954.

[33] Report from the Committee of Banking and Currency, United States Senate, to accompany S 1451, 85th Cong., 1st sess., March 4, 1957 (Washington, D. C.: United States Printing Office, 1957), Title I, Section 20, p. 6.

since 1957, the drive to empower banks to issue preferred stock has dwindled. It is an issue, however, which may well be revived if bank earnings do not keep pace with banking growth.

Preferred stock has many advantages under certain circumstances [34] and most of the objections raised by those who opposed it for banks (largely for traditional reasons) could be overcome by legal provisions requiring such preferred stock to be issued in callable and convertible form, to have voting rights only in the event of default, and to be limited to a relatively modest percentage (certainly no more than one-third) of the total outstanding capital. Bank holding companies, like Marine Midland Corporation of New York, have used this method of obtaining additional capital to good advantage even in recent years and there appears to be no logical reason why banks should not be permitted the same degree of flexibility in capital financing.

------

[34] *Cf.* Morris A. Schapiro, "Preferred Capital for Banks Approved." *Address* before the New Haven Chapter of American Institute of Banking, New Haven, Connecticut, November 9, 1954.

X

LENDING POLICIES

Lending is the essence of commercial banking; consequently, the formulation and implementation of sound lending policies are among the most important responsibilities of bank directors and management. Well-conceived lending policies and careful lending practices are essential if a bank is to perform its credit-creating function effectively and minimize the risk inherent in any extension of credit.

Policy decisions are required with respect to the kind and number of loans a bank will make, as well as to whom it will lend and under what circumstances. Lending policies should in every case be reduced to writing since only then will they be clearly and uniformly understood by the officers who grant them and the directors who approve them. Moreover, the very act of formulating a policy and expressing it in words that all agree to will sharpen the issues and make the end product more effective. Once established, even the best of policies needs periodic review in the light of ever-changing conditions in the community.

This chapter will explore some of the considerations which should play a part in the formulation of sound lending policies for all banks.

COMMUNITY NEEDS

The starting point of loan policy should be a knowledge of the legitimate credit needs of the community or credit markets which the bank serves or intends to serve. This is basic. It has long been recognized that it is a fundamental obligation of a bank to serve the credit needs of its community. Which of these needs are "legitimate" is a further matter of policy to be discussed later. For the moment legitimate credit may be conceived of as any use of bank credit which will further the stability or growth of the community, or the economic well-being of its inhabitants.

The credit needs of the community will be served whether commercial banks serve them or not. The American financial scene is cluttered with competitive institutions and government agencies serving credit needs which, originally at least, commercial banks either failed to recognize or were reluctant to provide for. Bankers may complain about this "unfair competition," but the fact remains that commercial banks did not make consumer loans in volume until long after the finance companies had shown the way. Commercial banks generally were not prepared to make the volume or kind of mortgage loans for which the public turned to the savings and loan associations in such large numbers. Even Federally-insured mortgage loans were looked upon with suspicion in the late 1930s by all but a few farsighted bankers.

Commercial banks, of course, cannot appropriately serve *all* of the credit needs of their communities. Some of them, because of their capital or long-term nature, are not eligible for bank credit. The banks, however, should at least be aware of such needs. Even if they cannot fill them directly, banks can do a great deal to facilitate the flow of longer-term or capital funds into their communities, or to meet any excess need for short-term funds, through their relationships with the market, other institutional investors, and their correspondent banks in the money centers. A bank's first step, therefore, in formulating lending policies is to assess the needs of the credit market or community it serves.

The most common way to determine the credit needs of a community is for the bank officer to sit at a desk in the bank's lobby and wait for potential borrowers to come in. Up to a point this is an effective method and is probably typical of most of the country's smaller banks. Borrowers do come in and, if encouraged by constructive consideration of their requests for credit, will bring their friends. The need for credit can then be assessed by the actual demand.

Too frequently, however, because of the lending officers' prejudices or predilections, some segment of the borrowing public gets the impression that it is somewhat less than welcome in a particular bank and promptly searches out competitive sources of credit. It occurs too frequently that a bank located in a residential community and holding virtually no consumer loans seems to think it has amply satisfied all of its community's credit needs. Obviously it hasn't. Bank examiners find many banks with abnormally low loan-to-deposit ratios (particularly very small banks) in communities where government agencies or other financial institutions are supplying a major portion of the credit. Nevertheless the bank officer will always claim he is making all of the "good" loans the community demands.

To know something about the credit market of a community it is necessary to get outside the bank, in thought at least, and find out who is borrowing and where. This outside look need not be a formal "market research" project,[1] particularly in smaller communities where the officers and directors have an intimate knowledge of most of the economic activity. In larger banks and large communities a formal market survey is highly desirable if only as a periodic check on the directors' knowledge. A knowledge of the credit needs of the bank's customers, actual and potential, for the present and the foreseeable future is essential, not only to establish lending policies, but is vital in determining liquidity needs and investment policy as well.

DETERMINING THE SIZE OF THE LOAN PORTFOLIO

Having arrived at a reasonably clear concept of how much credit and what varieties of loans the community needs, the next task of bank management is to appraise its own willingness and ability to meet that demand. In some communities the demand for credit is virtually insatiable. In more fully developed and stable communities management may have to search out opportunities to make sound loans. In any event the limiting factor should be the community needs and the bank's ability to meet those needs, rather than any arbitrary set of ratios representing preconceived ideas of appropriate or average statistical relationships.

If a bank has provided adequate liquidity, and if it has adequate

---

[1] Market Research will be discussed at greater length in Chapter XIV, "Community Relations."

capital, it should make all the sound local loans it can. If its own resources are not sufficient to meet the community's legitimate needs, it should exert every effort to participate or place local loans with correspondent banks or other financial institutions, retaining, if possible, the servicing of the loans and the direct contacts with customers.

In the past some students of banking have been concerned with the diversification of a bank's loan portfolio and have counselled against a complete concentration in local credits particularly in communities economically dependent on a single crop or enterprise. If such diversification can be obtained only at the expense of the legitimate credit needs of the community in question the principal function of commercial banking is negated. The answer lies not in denying local credit needs but in the diversification of the banking structure itself through more extensive branch or holding company banking.

Given adequate liquidity and capital protection, a bank's ability to increase its loans is limited only by the volume of its relatively stable deposits.   Furthermore, the ability and the willingness to lend are the most important factors in creating and maintaining depositor relationships.   This is equally true with respect to both larger business customers and to the small business or individual borrower. Just as the making of loans creates deposits in the banking system as a whole, the making of loans by an individual bank creates depositor relationships, spurs economic activity in the community, and, in the long run, results in higher deposit levels for the bank itself.

DETERMINING THE CHARACTER OF LOANS

A bank's lending policies are, in effect, "screening devices" by which the directors seek to establish the kind and character of loans they think a bank should make. This is particularly the case when loan demand is pressing hard against a bank's available funds. From a policy viewpoint, the character of a loan should take precedence over its form. In other words, it is more important that loans be sound than that they be in the form of mortgage loans, business loans, consumer credit, etc. The form of lending will reflect the demands of the community.

Here again simple statistical relationships, although widely used as rough guidelines, should not be determinative. A bank in a rapidly growing residential community not only will, but *should* have a higher ratio of mortgage loans to total loans than a bank in a stable industrial area. The latter, by the same token, will and *should* have a higher ratio of commercial loans and perhaps of consumer credit. It is desirable for the directors, as a matter of policy, to establish ceilings on the various forms of lending, but they should do so solely for the purpose of distributing available bank credit in proportion to the community's needs to avoid slighting one form of demand by too liberally supplying another.

Some writers on this subject would relate the character of the loan portfolio to the kind of deposits the bank holds. They would counsel, for example, that mortgage loans and term loans should only be made out of more stable or longer-term savings deposits. In discussing liquidity needs in Chapter VII, it was shown that some portion of demand deposits is just as stable as any deposit can be. It is important for liquidity reasons that longer-term loans not exceed stable deposits but, given stability, the fact that such deposits are demand or time makes no real difference.

It is in considering the character of loans that the basis for distinguishing between "legitimate" and other credit demands becomes apparent. Several criteria which should serve as a basis for lending policy will be suggested and analyzed. The two most important are the arrangements made for the repayment of the loan and consideration of the purpose for which it is granted. A third essential criterion, safety or collectibility, is inherent in the other two but involves, as well, technical considerations of credit analysis and loan administration.[2]

Safety, in the view presented here, is not necessarily synonymous with soundness, which is taken in a broader context related both to safety and to the credit needs of the community. A perfectly collectible loan may be made for a speculative or economically unsound purpose. To make such loans in number, however, is not sound banking, especially if it results in turning down (for lack of funds) perhaps riskier loans which would contribute more to the

---

[2] Writers frequently refer to the three C's of Credit: Capital, Capacity, and Character. The three P's of Policy may be said to be: Payment, Purpose and Protection.

economic development of the community and the longer-run growth of the bank itself. Sound lending, it should be remembered, is an art, not a science.

The point is not that banks can ignore risk or sacrifice reasonable safety. A loan which is clearly unsafe cannot be sound. However, absolute safety is neither the *only*, nor even the *best* criterion of soundness, and competent and imaginative lending officers can often make safe loans out of borderline credit situations.

PAYMENT

In discussing the functions of commercial banks in Chapter I it was shown how bank lending bridges the gap, or time lag, between production and consumption. In this connection, it has often been said that credit is the life blood of the economy. If this is true, then credit which ceases to flow through the economy and becomes stagnant (as a substitute for permanent capital, for example) can be said to represent a hardening of the economic arteries.

It should be a basic policy of commercial bank lending, therefore, that money loaned in whatever form should flow back to the bank as the transaction being financed is consummated or liquidated. The terms of repayment, in other words, should be related to the form and nature of the transaction being financed and a definite repayment program should be established with respect to every loan, no matter how well secured.[3]

Another way of stating this principle is to say that a sound bank loan should be collectible from the anticipated income or profits of the borrower rather than from the liquidation of any collateral that may be pledged. Whenever a bank has to foreclose and sell collateral it demonstrates thereby that the extension of credit was unsound in the first place, even though the bank incurs no loss. The borrower usually *does* lose and the community may suffer as well. The latter fact becomes abundantly clear if many banks are forced to liquidate numerous loans and, in the process of disposing of the collateral, depress the market sharply, thus effectively destroying existing values in the entire community. In essence, the

---

[3] Rodkey, *Sound Policies for Bank Management,* p. 98; "Even with loans secured by stock market collateral having clearly adequate margins it is desirable to have some orderly plan of repayment for the benefit both of the borrower and the bank."

collapse of real estate values in the mid-1930s was the direct result of unsound mortgage lending in the 1920s, lending which was unsound precisely because it was based on collateral values rather than on realistic payment schedules.

The proper function of collateral is to minimize the risk of loss to the bank in the event the income or profits of the borrower fail to materialize in sufficient quantity to repay the loan for reasons which neither the bank nor the borrower can foresee. This protective function will be elaborated upon later in this chapter. In most cases capacity to pay, if properly measured, is better security than collateral.

It follows from this discussion that the terms on which various kinds of loans are made will not be uniform because they will be made to finance transactions taking place over differing periods of time. What *is* important is to estimate the rate of repayment and the ultimate final payment date at the time the loan is granted, and to establish a repayment schedule on that basis. Any deviation from a repayment schedule so established will be an automatic signal that something has gone wrong with the original estimates and that the loan may be in need of immediate attention. Even more importantly, such a procedure will provide the bank with a far more realistic picture of the flow of funds through its loan portfolio so that it can more accurately gauge its true liquidity position.

The 90-day note, put on the books with little thought of the length of time for which the funds will really be needed, has long since lost favor with the informed student of banking. It is still widely used by many banks, however, largely as a matter of habit. The same thing may be said of the "demand" loan which, by its very nature, tends to rely too heavily on collateral values. Experienced bankers know that demand loans are often the slowest and longest-term loans in their portfolios. They are seldom appropriate instruments except when used to finance very short-term transactions in highly liquid securities or commodities.

Another aspect of repayment policy in need of careful review is the traditional requirement of an annual "clean-up" or period of time during which the borrower is completely off the bank's books. To require a clean-up from borrowers who have a long-term or semipermanent need for working capital (such as finance companies or dairy farmers) is to delude oneself about the nature of the loan and to encourage the practice of switching loans from one bank to another for no other reason than to comply with an unrealistic tradition. Some bankers argue that the clean-up gives them an opportunity to review the credit before taking it on again. Outstanding loans should be periodically reviewed also, and a bank may be in a better position to work with a weak borrower who is more steadily dependent upon it. If it holds firm against the policy of "throwing good money after bad," it will have essentially the same opportunity to review the credit standing of the borrower when it renews a note as when it originally accepts it.

The principle of relating repayments to the nature of the transaction justifies not only some longer-term loans but even justifies some situations in which a borrower may stay on the books without material reduction for considerable periods of time. Customers whose business is expanding rapidly, for example, may need to use their profits to expand their physical plant and at the same time need additional short-term credit to carry the higher inventory and receivables resulting from their increased but profitable volume. In such cases the bank's credit is related to the increased flow of transactions through the business of the borrower and can be considered sound even though, for a period, the loans are not being repaid.[4]

In summary, it should be a basic premise of a bank's lending policy to consider the means and timing of repayment when a loan is granted, and to make loans only when a borrower agrees in advance to a repayment program related to a realistic appraisal of his ability to repay. The actual period may range from a few weeks (or even days) to ten years or longer (as in mortgage lending) and the longer term will ordinarily require more stringent credit scrutiny or the pledge of collateral. The essential thing for both the bank and the borrower is that there be a payment program.

PURPOSE

The purpose for which the proceeds of a loan is to be used is a less obvious criterion of policy than the prospects of its repayment, but it is, nevertheless, an essential ingredient of soundness in the broader sense. When the author began examining banks some

---

[4] In practice, under such circumstances, a bank will frequently grant new advances while requiring continued repayment on the old, thus preserving the form of continued amortization.

thirty years ago, the purpose of commercial loans could generally be deduced from a comparison of the financial statements of the borrower. The purpose of loans to individuals, however, was seldom, if ever, recorded in the files. Indeed, most bankers reacted with dismay to the suggestion of asking a credit-worthy borrower, or one who had pledged adequate collateral, to what use he intended to put the money.[5]

Some of this attitude reflected a competitive situation in which safe loans, let alone sound ones, were hard to come by, and loan rates, especially in the smaller banks, had not declined to the same extent as yields in the bond market. An offended customer could all too easily take his borrowing to another bank where such questions were never asked.

More importantly, however, this situation evidenced a misunderstanding on the part of both the bank and the borrower concerning the appropriate role of a bank as a supplier of liquid funds to the community. In Chapter I reference was made to a survey conducted by Dun and Bradstreet which indicated that the modern businessman is seeking sound financial advice as well as credit availability from his banker. He obviously cannot expect to receive very sound advice if he keeps his banker in the dark about his affairs. Individuals may not be looking for advice to quite the same extent but it is clear that a banker cannot know whether the money he lends will produce income or profits to repay the loan, and cannot relate the repayment program to the nature of the transaction unless he knows what it is. Purpose and payment are thus seen to be intimately interwoven.

Purpose, moreover, becames even more important when credit is scarce. The whole focus of monetary policy is to restrict the creation of new credit at times when the economy is fully extended in the expectation that the commercial banking system, forced to ration credit, will choose to use its limited resources to finance productive rather than speculative activity. This was explicit in the "Voluntary Credit Restraint" program of 1951–52,[6] and has been

---

[5] As late as 1956 the Board of Governors of the Federal Reserve System dropped a proposal to require a positive statement of purpose in connection with loans secured by stocks and subject to Regulation U because of the widespread objection on the part of member banks to "invading the privacy" of their borrowers.

[6] Federal Reserve Bulletin, Volume 37 (1951) pp. 263, 379.

implicit in the more general monetary restraint of subsequent periods of incipient inflation. At such times, banks may find themselves torn between the objectives of public policy and some of the credit requests of good customers and substantial depositors. Since deposits represent the funds with which loans are made, large depositors occasionally win out.

Nevertheless, in addition to whatever moral responsibility they have to support sound money as such, commercial banks have a vested self-interest in the balanced economic growth of their communities and, when their lending resources are limited, should seek, as a matter of policy if not a matter of course, to employ those resources in ways which will contribute most to the growth of their communities. To do this effectively they must know the purposes for which their credit is used.

When a bank grants a loan, it can control, at best, only the purpose for which the newly created money is first spent. Money, once created, flows through the spending stream into many hands and can be used for numerous purposes not all of which may be productive. But here again purpose and payment are closely linked. When a loan is repaid the bank regains control of purpose. If loans, even though well secured, are allowed to remain outstanding indefinitely, the borrower may in fact use the funds for a number of successive purposes. For example, a bank customer may borrow 50 per cent of the market value of stock exchange collateral for the express purpose of paying his son's college tuition. Within two years he can accumulate enough from his income to repay the bank. Instead, he chooses to purchase additional listed stocks. Legally, under Regulation U [7] and the margin requirements in force at the time, he may be permitted to borrow no more than 25 per cent of the value of stocks to purchase or carry registered stocks. The borrower, in effect, is enabled to evade the law by taking advantage of the bank's failure to relate the original loan to the purpose for which it was granted and require repayment in the light of the borrower's earning capacity.[8] In other words, the bank

---

[7] Board of Governors of the Federal Reserve System, *Regulation U,* (12 C.F.R. 221) governs loans by banks for the purpose of purchasing or carrying registered stocks.

[8] A somewhat similar circumvention of Regulation U can occur when a borrower uses his liquid funds to purchase stocks and subsequently borrows ostensibly for a nonregulated purpose. In June 1959, the Board of Governors

lost control of purpose through failure to insist on scheduled repayment. Sound lending policy requires that purpose be disclosed and that payment be required in a realistic relationship to the income or profits of the borrower and the purpose for which the proceeds are used.

PROTECTION

It could be claimed with considerable justification that if a loan is made for a sound purpose, and if the repayments are realistically scheduled to flow from the liquidation of the transaction being financed, little more is required to make it a "good" loan. Life, however, is uncertain and, as Robert Burns observed many years ago, "The best laid schemes o' mice an' men gang aft a-gley." Because of the responsibilities which a bank owes to its depositors as well as its stockholders, it is incumbent upon bank management to take every possible precaution to the end that if the borrower's affairs "gang a-gley" the bank will not be the loser.

The two principle bulwarks against unforeseeable contingencies are the credit worthiness of the borrower (including that of endorsers and guarantors) and the value of the collateral pledged to secure a loan. To the extent that complete credit worthiness may be questioned, collateral assumes increasing importance—at times perhaps too much.

CREDIT WORTHINESS

A borrower is "worthy" of credit if he can produce unimpeachable evidence of his ability and willingness to repay his loans as agreed. Credit worthiness or credit standing is based to a large extent on character and reputation and, with respect to sizeable loans, on the financial condition of the borrower as shown by his financial state-

---

adopted an amendment to the Regulation which, in effect, defined as being a loan for the purpose of carrying securities (and therefore regulated) any loan to a borrower who owned listed stocks which he had not held free of lien for a continuous period of 1 year. The amendment proved unworkable and was rescinded in March 1960. At the time it was stated, "The Board is concerned with evasive extensions of bank credit for the purpose of carrying registered stocks and expects banks to be alert in detecting and preventing attempts to circumvent the basic purposes of this regulation."

ment and his earning record. Financial statement analysis is a fundamental banking art, the techniques of which are not directly pertinent to this discussion of policy, important as they are.[9] It may be noted, however, that a bank's appraisal of its customers' credit worthiness is not unlike the bank supervisor's appraisal of the soundness of the bank itself.

The relationship of the borrower's net worth to his obligations and to the risk inherent in the business is an essential concept of both. The customer's net worth, like the bank's capital, serves to assure the confidence of the lender that the borrower will be able to meet his obligations. Earning capacity is a vital ingredient of both credit worthiness and supervisory confidence, as is liquidity—the relationship of current assets to current liabilities. And character, which along with capital and capacity is one of the "Three C's of Credit," is as important in the evaluation of the credit worthiness of a commercial enterprise as is the supervisor's appraisal of management in a commercial bank.

From a policy viewpoint the important thing is that the lending officers be provided with adequate tools to appraise credits effectively. To this end policy, as established by the directors, should insist on financial statements and earnings records from all important borrowers no matter how sterling their character may appear or how often the principals in the business play golf with one of the bank's directors. The statements, moreover, should be complete and in sufficient detail to permit effective analysis. Where sizeable amounts are involved, the figures should be audited by a reputable accounting firm.[10]

It is also important that policy insist on a continuing close analysis of the financial position of the borrower. The directors can accomplish this by establishing requirements for periodic reviews of outstanding loans in various size or class categories. Early observation of unfavorable trends will enable the bank to take effective protective measures or render often vital financial guidance which

---

[9] *Cf.* Roger F. Murray, "Evaluating Credit Worthiness," in *Business Loans of American Commercial Banks,* ed. Benjamin Haggott Beckhart (New York: The Ronald Press Company, 1959), Chapter 4.

[10] *Cf.* Murray, *op. cit.,* p. 78: "For precision workmanship, an audited statement is the sharp true blade of analysis; unaudited figures may be a dull, unpredictable tool."

may make the difference not only between repayment or loss, but between the success or failure of the borrower. The larger the loan and the greater the risk factor, the closer the bank's contacts with the borrower should be.

ASSETS PLEDGED TO SECURE BORROWINGS

Some bankers try to obtain a lien on some asset of the borrower to support a loan whenever possible. There is nothing wrong with such policy if it does not lead to overreliance on security to the neglect of the more important credit considerations discussed above.

With respect to business loans, the real significance of collateral or other protective arrangements lies in the fact that such devices enable bank management to make economically desirable loans, or to work out weak credit situations, when such action would not be entirely safe without security. Many loans to small or new enterprises or to businesses that are expanding rapidly could not be justified on the basis of credit worthiness alone. Longer-term loans to the most credit worthy of borrowers also require additional protection because of the greater risk involved in the time factor alone.

Collateral protection for business loans may be arranged in many different ways, [11] depending on the nature of the business and the particular circumstances in each case. In many instances it may take the form of a direct pledge of assets such as liens on fixed assets or the pledge of inventory or receivables. In connection with most longer-term loans, banks require protective covenants in the loan agreement requiring the borrower, for example, to maintain certain minimum balance sheet ratios or to agree not to pledge certain assets as long as the loan is outstanding. Many loan agreements also contain provisions limiting dividend payments, or withdrawals by the principals, and some set ceilings on the salary payments to senior officers.

In connection with loans to small or closely held corporations it is usually desirable to obtain the endorsements of the principals and their wives in order to tie in the real net worth of the corporation as support for the loan. Statements of such businesses frequently

---

[11] *Cf.* H. Felix De C. Pereira, "Risk Protection," in Beckhart *op. cit.*, Chapter 5.

reveal substantial amounts due to the principals. When such debt is formally subordinated to the bank loan, it serves, in effect, as additional capital.

With respect to loans to individuals for more than nominal amounts, experienced lending officers agree that there are few occasions when unsecured loans can be justified unless the individual is engaged in business, or unless the loan is directly related to a specific short-term transaction and is written for an equally short term. No matter how wealthy the individual, no matter how "good" his statement, he should be required to secure his obligations. A firm policy in this regard will avoid the necessity of making many difficult decisions in borderline cases.

This discussion of lending policy has been far from exhaustive of the subject which lies at the very heart of commercial banking operations. Nevertheless, it should be clear that a bank's policies will be sound if the directors lay down firm guide lines concerning the purposes for which the bank's credit may appropriately be used, and relate the bank's repayment requirements to those purposes, making certain, at the same time, that the bank obtains sufficient protection against the risks of the unforeseen.

INTEREST RATE POLICY

The range of rates which a bank may charge on various kinds of loans will be determined to a considerable degree by forces beyond its control, *i.e.*, the level of rates in the market and the forces of competition. To a significant extent, however, the rates established by an individual bank, in the light of these market factors, can be flexibly administered (within limits) to determine the volume and character of the bank's loan portfolio and to bring about changes therein over time. To accomplish this desirable end, a knowledge of the broad implications of interest rates is essential.

The general level of rates, at any given time, is the result of the interplay between the demand for and the supply of funds in the market. Demand increases when business activity rises, and tends to fall when business activity slackens. The supply of funds on the other hand is, in large measure, determined by the credit policy of the Federal Reserve System which, by providing reserves to the banking system, makes possible the creation of credit which feeds not only the commercial banks but, through them, other lenders as well. When funds are plentiful, market rates generally tend to decline, banks seek loans more aggressively, and therefore lower their rates to induce marginal borrowers to come into the market. When funds are scarce banks raise their rates and some potential borrowers may defer the use of credit or seek it elsewhere. By and large, rates are more likely to determine *where* a borrower obtains his funds than *whether* he borrows. High rates will not long deter the borrower who can use the funds profitably, nor will low rates induce borrowing which cannot be put to productive use.

While the level of rates depends on the forces of demand and supply, the cost of lending constitutes a "floor" beneath this level. The rates which banks charge, therefore, must be sufficiently high to cover (1) the cost of the funds loaned, (2) the cost of making and servicing different kinds of loans (including a proportionate share of the overhead expenses of the bank), (3) a cost factor representing the probable losses which may be incurred over time, and (4) a reasonable margin of profit.[12] It is important that bank management be aware of these costs which go far to explain why (at any given level) rates on different kinds of loans may vary quite widely. [13] Banks, quite naturally, tend to set lower rates on loans which cost less to process and on those in which the risk factor is at a minimum. They tend to charge lower rates on large loans than on small ones because the cost per dollar of loan is less. More importantly, large loans are generally made only to borrowers with above-average credit ratings. Collection costs and potential losses are diminished as the responsibility of the borrower increases and as the term of the loan is shortened. By the same token, rates on unsecured loans tend to be lower than those on secured loans because unsecured loans are made primarily to the most credit-worthy borrowers and there is a real cost factor involved in processing, recording, and periodically pricing collateral security.

Above this theoretical "floor," bank lending rates are established in a highly complex and competitive market which includes a variety of other lenders, many of whom are specialists in particular kinds of credit instruments. Large corporations, for example, when

---

[12] Robinson, *Management of Bank Funds,* pp. 116–17.

[13] *Cf.* Mona E. Dingle, "Interest Rates on Business Loans," in Beckhart, *op cit.,* Chapter 13.

in need of capital financing, may either arrange term loans with their banks, private placements with insurance companies, or go to the public capital markets. Their choice will be influenced partly by rate and partly by the various terms imposed by different lenders. For short-term financing, the same corporations (if their credit standing is high) may choose between banks and the commercial paper market. The purchaser of a home who seeks mortgage financing may choose between a commercial bank, a savings bank, a savings and loan association, a life insurance company, or a private lender. Finance companies and credit unions compete with commercial banks for consumer loans, as do various government agencies for farm loans. There is, in short, no lack of competition in most of the broad segments of bank lending.

Despite the prevalence of competition, however, direct rate competition between banks serving the same market is rare. In fact, the more competitive a bank's situation, the more is the likelihood that its lending rates will conform closely with those of its immediate competitors.[14] Such a bank cannot long charge higher rates for *the same kinds of loans* without losing many of its best customers. If it offers lower rates it is likely to receive more applications than it can accommodate. It is this fact which explains the prevalence of the so-called "prime rate"—the rate large banks operating in the national market almost uniformly charge their most desirable customers.[15]

Rate differentials can be maintained within a competitive lending market only when the quality of collateral services or the conditions of the lending arrangements differ. They can also be deliberately maintained either to persuade some borrowers to seek credit elsewhere or, conversely, to attract certain specific borrowers or types of loans. It is in this area that the policy aspects of the establishment of interest rates assumes its greatest importance. It is in the light of the general uniformity of rates for comparable kinds of loans that interest rate differentials operate as an impersonal, semi-automatic control mechanism governing the use of bank credit.

---

[14] It has been frequently pointed out that banking is an enterprise in which there is a minimum of rate competition. *Cf.* Clay J. Anderson, "Competitive Factors in Business Loans," in Beckhart, *op. cit.*, Chapter 11.

[15] *Cf.* M. A. Schapiro and Company, Inc., "A Look at the Prime Rate," *Bank Stock Quarterly*, June 1961, pp. 11–14.

For example, when credit is scarce, large banks serving the "national" market may deliberately maintain the prime rate above the rates available in the market in the hope that some of their larger borrowers will sell commercial paper or seek acceptance financing and thus relieve the direct pressure of loan demand on the banks themselves. Under similar circumstances, if banks find term loan demand too heavy, they may set higher rates on such loans, thereby persuading some of their potential customers to sell securities in the capital market. Conversely, the posting of lower-than-average rates can serve to attract business which a bank considers especially desirable. Thus, if a bank offers lower rates than do the finance companies on consumer loans which meet specific high standards, it tends to attract the cream of the business in its community. Some banks establish competitively attractive rates for mortgages of shorter-than-average term or above-average protective equity, and most banks, as stated above, will shave normal rates to obtain or hold large and particularly credit-worthy loans.

The rates established by the individual bank on loans in clearly distinguishable categories will play a substantial part in determining the quality and character of that bank's loan portfolio. The very process of defining the categories and setting the rates is an instructive exercise in policy formation. It compels the directors or senior management to consider carefully the bank's long-run portfolio objectives, makes management more keenly aware of the bank's competitive position, both rate-wise and cost-wise, and, if rates are set on the basis of an established policy and impartially administered, there will be little difficulty in convincing customers that they are fair. Borrowers seldom complain about high rates, *per se;* they do complain if they think they have been arbitrarily charged more than someone else for the same kind of loan.

Within the competitive framework described above, and with the "floor" of lending costs always in the background, the spectrum of lending rates ranges from the prime rate on the low side to the "ceiling" established by the usury laws of the various states. The prime rate tends to reflect the shifting balance between the overall supply and demand for bank credit. It changes rather infrequently. It tends to lag behind market rates, and usually signals a general and widespread recognition of a substantial change in the availability of credit.

The usury laws provide an effective ceiling because, even though the laws of many states provide that corporations cannot plead usury, banks hesitate to charge higher rates to their corporate customers than they may charge individuals and partnerships for obvious reasons of public relations. In communities isolated from competition the "usury" rate is often virtually the only rate.

The interest yield of a given loan, however, is influenced not only by the rate but also by the bank's requirement regarding the average balances which borrowers must maintain.[16] As interest rate levels rise toward the effective usury ceiling, requirements for the maintenance of "compensating balances" usually become more stringent and are administered more rigidly. The result of such requirements is to increase the effective rate. Thus if a borrower must maintain a 20 per cent balance in connection with a $10,000 loan on which he is charged 5 per cent interest, he will be paying $500 per annum for the use of only $8,000, or an effective rate of 6¼ per cent. The impact of this arithmetic, of course, will be more severe on borrowers whose businesses require relatively little working cash balances, such as finance companies, and less severe on companies which need to maintain more sizeable cash balances to conduct their normal business.

Some bankers claim that compensating balances also serve to keep in the bank money which can be loaned to others. This is questionable, however, since the customer seldom borrows more money than he intends to use. If he needs $10,000, for example, and the bank requires a 20 per cent compensating balance, he will simply arrange to borrow $12,500, leaving $2,500 on deposit, and the bank will have no more funds to lend than it would if it had loaned the $10,000 without a balance requirement.

However, in addition to being a device by which banks can increase the effective rate of the interest they charge, compensating balances have important significance as a measure of the "relationship" between the bank and its customer. The potential borrower who has maintained good working balances with his bank, year in and year out, whether or not he needed to borrow, will seldom be denied credit up to five or six times his average balance no matter how "tight" money becomes.

---

[16] Federal Reserve Bank of New York, "Compensating Balances," *Monthly Review,* Vol. 43, No. 12 (December 1961), p. 205.

XI

LENDING PRACTICES

It is necessary not only to devise sound lending policies but to put them into practice. This calls for the establishment and supervision of an effective organization and the adoption of appropriate procedures which, in turn, involve additional policy considerations. This chapter will assess the problems involved in granting and servicing loans, and examine the implications, for various kinds of lending, of the general policies discussed in the previous chapter.

GRANTING AND SERVICING LOANS

The manner in which loans are made, reviewed, and collected involves important policy decisions. It is the responsibility of the directors to determine the organizational structure of the lending function, to delegate appropriate authority to the lending officers, and to establish procedures for the review of important loan applications and outstanding loans.

ORGANIZATION

While the basic responsibility for lending policy rests with the entire Board of Directors, it is customary for the board to delegate special responsibility for supervising the lending function to a Directors' Loan Committee or, in smaller banks, to the Executive Committee. The lending officers are required to report to the committee the loans granted, and the committee must assure itself that the loans have been made in accordance with the law and the bank's own lending policies. In larger banks there is usually also a senior officers' loan committee which directly supervises the work of the lending officers and reviews policy matters on a continuing basis. The Officers' Loan Committee serves as the principal liaison between the lending function as a whole and the Board of Directors. In small banks, the chief executive officer is the principal lending officer and exercises the functions of the Officers' Loan Committee.

As banks increase in size the lending function becomes more specialized. The various forms of lending require quite different techniques and each involves a large body of specialized knowledge which is not likely to be found, to an optimum degree at least, in any one individual. In larger banks, therefore, the lending function is usually organized into departments such as the mortgage department, the consumer credit department, etc. The largest banks, serving businesses across the nation, organize their commercial lending officers into area groups or industry groups as well. This specialization enables a bank to render the maximum service to the borrowers whose line of business or area problems are thoroughly familiar to the lending officers serving them. This specialization is one of the principal advantages of larger banking organizations.

One reason why many small banks have not adequately served all the credit needs of their communities is the simple fact that they are not large enough to afford specialists even in such a common field as consumer lending.[1]

LENDING AUTHORITY

It is poor policy under any circumstances for the directors themselves to grant loans, although it is frequently done, especially in smaller banks. In the first place, most bank directors lack the technical knowledge to make loans on any other basis than the amount of the security or their personal knowledge of the character of the applicant. These may be safe enough loans, but they are not likely to be all the loans that the community legitimately needs.

---

[1] Consumer lending officers, more often than not, have been recruited from the ranks of the finance company because the whole philosophy of consumer lending differs so sharply from the commercial lending in which bank officers had been trained.

Secondly, directors are likely to be influenced by subjective considerations which have no rightful place in sound lending whether they be considerations of friendship, the social position of the applicant, or unadulterated self-interest. It is virtually impossible for directors who are active in the business, social, or political life of the community not to be influenced in some degree by their outside affiliations, no matter how diligently they strive to remain impartial and objective.

The directors' task is to determine what kinds of loans the bank should or should not make, and to review the loans the officers have granted to assure themselves that they are consistent with established policy. The authority to lend should be delegated to active officers who, ideally, should not be permitted to engage in outside business activities which might in any way conflict with their banking responsibilities. This, of course, is not to say that lending officers should not be free to consult with directors, particularly where policy may not be entirely clear, or where unusually large amounts are involved. But the executive officer who expects the directors to make his decisions for him is not earning his pay, no matter how little it may be.

The maximum amount that a bank may lend to one borrower is established by law. For national banks it is 10 per cent of capital and surplus on an unsecured basis.[2] Higher percentages are generally allowed for secured loans. At least one officer, or group of officers, therefore, should have authority to grant loans up to the legal limit in every bank. The authority of the other officers is generally expressed in terms of maximum dollar amounts, secured and unsecured. These authorities should be established by the Board of Directors, made a matter of record, and periodically reviewed. Frequently the authority to make large loans is vested in two or more officers acting jointly, or in the Officers' Loan Committee.

If lending policies have been clearly stated and are thoroughly understood, rather liberal lending authority should be granted to the officers. Prospective borrowers like to feel they are dealing with the bank officer who makes the final decision. One of the

---

[2] Section 5200, United States Revised Statutes (U.S.C., Title 12, sec. 84). Most state laws have similar provisions.

common complaints about branch banking is that branch managers must refer loans to the head office which may not only cause a delay, but leaves the borrower whose loan is declined with the feeling that he might have been more persuasive had he, himself, had the opportunity to negotiate directly with the "powers that be." The fact is that in limiting the authority of their junior officers too strictly [3] banks hamper the development of their juniors as well as create poor customer relations.   There is no better way of training loan officers than to permit them to exercise their own judgment and, if they make mistakes, to let them work their way out of the ensuing difficulties.   Certainly every branch manager worthy of his hire should have the authority to grant loans on his sole responsibility at least as large as the legal limit of a unit bank of comparable size.   In well-run, progressive branch organizations, even larger authorities are granted.

CREDIT REVIEW

In order to make sound lending decisions, lending officers must have the benefit of all the pertinent information that may be available about the borrower and his affairs.   The assembly and analysis of this information is the task of the credit department.   In small banks the lending officers themselves usually perform the credit review function but this is far from an ideal arrangement. Even the best lending officers are likely at times to become over-enthusiastic about the prospects of their good customers, or to take for granted facts that should be carefully checked and verified. It is for this reason that larger banks establish credit departments, separate from the lending function, whose job is to investigate actual and potential borrowers, analyze their financial statements, and make objective recommendations with respect to specific lines of credit or loan applications.   In the largest banks the credit department is a sizable organization in itself staffed with experts in the

---

[3] *Bulletin* of the Robert Morris Associates, XXXIV (February 1952).   A special survey of loan administration procedures revealed that "About 70 per cent of the reporting banks declare that the loan officers have limited authority. The remaining banks, in theory at least, permit loan officers to lend the legal limit."

analysis of the various lines of industry to which the bank may cater.

The credit review function needs to be performed even in the smallest banks. One bank president has claimed "that in a bank with more than one million dollars of business loans, the credit department should be important enough to justify the use of an experienced officer as the full-time department head." [4] In Chapter VI it was suggested that in banks too small to require a full-time credit officer, the credit review function be assigned to the comptroller-auditor. It is a vital function, and the directors of even small banks should make certain that it is adequately performed.

At the heart of the credit review function is the credit file. It is the bank's written record of its investigation of and business with each important borrower. Bank supervisors have for years been urging even the smallest of banking institutions to establish and maintain at least simplified forms of credit files. These should contain, as a minimum, a comparative analysis of the borrower's statement and earnings record, a brief history of the borrower's business and his relationship with the bank, together with the loan officer's notations regarding the purpose of each loan granted and the repayment program agreed upon. The file is also the natural place to keep copies of correspondence concerning the borrower, records of credit inquiries and interviews both in the bank and at the customer's place of business.

These are the basic rudiments of credit analysis and review; a broad subject, the technical aspects of which lie beyond the purview of this discussion of policy. The task of policy is to require that the credit review function be effectively performed.

Credit analysis, however, is not a decision-making process. It is consultative or advisory in character. It should contribute a careful and factual analysis of all the available information on the basis of which a lending officer can intelligently make his own decisions. It may be, occasionally, that the latter's more intimate knowledge of the borrower's operations, or his faith in the management of a particular enterprise, may outweigh, in his judgment, the credit analyst's danger signals. If so, the lending officer should

---

[4] Kennedy, *Bank Management*, p. 70.

make the loan on his own responsibility, and the directors and senior management should evaluate his performance accordingly.

Credit review, of course, does not stop with applications for new loans. An effective credit department should also analyze the business of prospective borrowers so that the borrowers may be offered approved lines of credit [5] or their requests for credit, if and when they eventuate, may be promptly taken care of. More importantly, the affairs of borrowers having outstanding loans need careful periodic review and revaluation. It is the responsibility of the credit review function to point out any signs of developing weakness in a borrower's affairs and to warn of danger before the bank is faced with a salvage situation. Few loans are bad when made, but even good credits can deteriorate. Careful watching alone can spare a bank from unnecessary losses.

Bank examiners and outside accountants (if requested) perform a somewhat similar function. Their review and classification of outstanding loans is, in effect, an objective credit analysis designed to point out weaknesses of which the directors and senior management should be cognizant. Their periodic visits, however, may be too infrequent to provide timely warning. Moreover, their analyses can be based solely on the information available in the credit files or on the lending officers' specific knowledge. Examination is not a substitute for a continuing credit review within the bank itself. At best it serves as a check or audit of the credit review process.

Recognizing the value of such a check, some of the largest banks, in recent years, have established loan review sections whose sole function is to conduct a continuous review of outstanding loans from what is essentially the bank examiner's point of view. In effect, this is an audit review of the work of both the lending officers and the credit department.

The directors of a bank have a legal responsibility to approve the loans which the officers have made. They should insist, as a mat-

---

[5] A line of credit is an indication given by a bank to a prospective borrower of the maximum amount it is willing to lend on little or no notice during the ensuing year. The amount of the credit line is determined by the borrower's financial condition, the amount of his deposit balances, and sometimes, competitively, as an indication of the bank's desire to increase its share of the particular customer's business.

ter of policy, that loans be granted only on the basis of adequate credit information, carefully compiled and fully recorded in the files. A summary of the file should accompany each important loan when it is submitted to the directors for approval, whether it be a new loan or a previously granted credit up for review.

A further sound policy, not exercised enough, is to require a review of loan applications of substantial amounts which have been denied by the lending officers. It is particularly important in branch banking organizations operating over fairly extensive areas for senior management and the directors to assure themselves that branch managers or loan department heads are not turning down legitimate requests for credit merely to protect their records of "safe" lending. If directors wish to encourage imaginative lending that is "sound" in the broadest sense, they must encourage their lending officers to make sound loans out of some weak-looking applications, and must expect and be tolerant of occasional mistakes.

LOAN COLLECTION

The essential corollary to an aggressive and forceful lending policy is a vigorous collection policy. No loan should be put on the books without an understanding regarding its repayment. Large loans should not be renewed without review by the Officers Loan Committee in large banks or the directors in smaller institutions. Any failure to comply with original repayment terms should be promptly followed up, the reason for the delinquency ascertained, and corrective or protective action insisted upon.

The directors or the Loan Committee should receive reports of all delinquent borrowers. With respect to small loans, such as those in the consumer credit department, the reports may appropriately be in the form of aggregate amounts. In the case of larger loans the directors should receive a detailed account of the cause of the delinquency and the steps which the lending officers are taking to correct it. Prompt action to protect the bank when borrowers first begin to get into difficulty often makes the difference between success or failure of a progressive lending policy.

In some cases, of course, the inability of the borrower to make a scheduled payment may be readily explainable. The loan may still be perfectly sound. Under such circumstances it is better to revise the payment schedule formally to meet the new circumstances rather than to let the apparent delinquency run on even though the reasons for it are recognized. In other words, sound collection policy requires that any changes made in agreed-upon repayment schedules be also by agreement, and not permitted to be made unilaterally by the borrower.

TYPES OF LOANS

The basic principles discussed above and in the previous chapter apply generally to all types of lending but with different shades of emphasis in each case. It may be useful, therefore, to review very briefly the principal types of loans made by commercial banks in the light of these policy considerations. No attempt will be made to examine separately any of the numerous specialized fields of lending found in banks which serve particular industries. Rather, the discussion will be confined to the three main types of lending found in nearly all commercial banks, *i.e.*, commercial loans, mortgage loans, and consumer credit.

COMMERCIAL LOANS

Traditionally and practically, the foremost obligation of a commercial bank is to supply the credit needs of business enterprises, including farm operations, in its community. Loans which accomplish this general purpose, whatever form they take, are essentially commercial loans. In terms of purpose and payment, they range from short-term self-liquidating loans to finance the manufacture, storage, or shipment of commodities, through loans to supply working capital over varying periods of time, to loans to finance the acquisition of capital assets.[6] Whatever the nature or term of the loan, repayment should be closely related to purpose and, in the light of both, appropriate provisions for protection established.

One relatively small bank, in its formal Statement of Policy, makes an interesting and valid distinction between business loans which

---

[6] Space does not permit more than a cursory discussion of commercial lending. For an exhaustive study of this subject, see *Business Loans of American Commercial Banks* (B. H. Beckhart, Editor), sections of which have been previously cited.

are repayable from gross income and those which are repayable from net profits.[7]   The first category consists of short-term advances for the purpose of furnishing working capital in excess of normal needs.   Such loans can generally be made on an unsecured basis. These are the traditional commercial loans conceived of as eligible paper under the Federal Reserve Act.   Loans to be repaid out of net profits, on the other hand, represent extensions of credit for the purpose of financing more or less continuous needs for working capital as well as term loans for longer-term capital or equipment financing.   Loans of this character usually require some protective arrangement.   Such loans make up the bulk of commercial lending today.

Short-term lending.   Lending for seasonal or short-term working capital purposes presents few serious policy questions beyond the need for careful credit analysis.   Principal emphasis is placed on the borrower's liquidity or excess of current assets over current liabilities.   Ordinarily banks actively seek short-term loans, offering favorable rates and established lines of credit as inducements to prospective seasonal borrowers.

Lines of credit, however, can present some special policy problems. A line of credit is not a legal commitment to lend, but a bank would suffer great embarrassment if it could not supply funds virtually on demand under an established line.   If lines are too freely granted, or granted with too little concern for the borrower's actual needs, they may remain unused until, in a period of credit stringency, their sudden activation may put considerable pressure on the bank's own liquidity position.   It is sound policy, therefore, to grant credit lines realistically.   Lines of credit are usually approved by the Board of Directors, who would be well advised to approve them only on the basis of information obtained from a discussion with the borrower concerning his probable needs.

Longer-term Working Capital Loans.   Many business enterprises have need of working capital over periods longer than a season.   Although the amount of credit needed may fluctuate over seasonal periods, its employment in some amount tends to be prolonged or virtually continuous.   Such credit is sound in the sense used here because the loans are related to a constant flow of transactions each

---

[7] The Sullivan County Trust Company, Monticello, New York.

of which, by itself, is of relatively short duration but which succeed each other so rapidly that no sooner has one been liquidated than another takes its place. Any business which must carry a relatively large and varied inventory throughout the year, or a business which sells in volume on credit, is likely to be a user of longer-term working capital loans.

In reviewing such loans bank directors should be concerned not only with the current asset position of the borrower but also with his net worth and profitability. Unless the borrower shows a substantial equity in a profitable business the bank will usually require additional protection in the form of pledged receivables or inventory.

Lending to small concerns on any but a short-term seasonal basis often presents special problems. Many of these are closely-held corporations, which as a matter of tax policy, show minimum profits and operate with a nominal net worth. Salaries paid to the principal stockholders are often larger than net profits, and the real net worth is represented either by loans made to the company by its principals, or by the net worth of the principals themselves. In such cases sound policy requires that debt to stockholders be subordinated formally to bank debt and that the bank obtain the endorsement or guarantee of the principals (and their wives) as additional protection. Where quality of management is a vital consideration in the extension of credit, banks may require the assignment of life insurance on the lives of the principals as well.

One specialized form of the longer-term working capital loan is called the revolving credit. Under such an arrangement the bank grants a firm commitment to lend up to a stated amount over a period of a year or more. The outstanding loan ordinarily rises and falls within the commitment and the borrower may, in fact, be out of debt for extended periods. Under a revolving credit the borrower pays a small commitment fee on the unused portion of his line in addition to the agreed-upon rate of interest on the amounts availed of. This fee compensates the bank for holding money available and assures the borrower that he may use the funds when he needs them.

Revolving credit agreements, like term loans (below), often contain restrictive provisions requiring the borrower to maintain certain agreed-upon balance sheet ratios or to limit dividend and salary payments. Many lending arrangements now handled on a 90-day renewable note basis would better conform to the principles of "purpose and payment" if they were written as revolving credits. Not only should banks be entitled to a modest fee for holding money available, but the writing of a revolving credit agreement would necessitate a closer look at the borrower's financial condition and thus result in sounder lending generally.

Term Loans. Term loans are usually defined for statistical purposes as loans with an original maturity of more than one year. Functionally, a term loan is one which, regardless of its specific maturity, will be repaid out of the net cash income of the business over a considerable period of time. The proceeds of term loans are typically used to acquire capital assets such as plant and equipment, subsidiary companies, or income-yielding properties such as oil and gas leases.

In considering the granting of loans for purposes such as these, bank officers and directors are concerned not only with the net worth and profitability of the borrower but, primarily, with his "cash flow" projections. Cash flow is a measure of the borrower's ability to repay debt. Depreciation charges, which are deducted from gross income to determine net profits, do not affect cash flow and, in fact, are often the main source of funds for repaying loans made to purchase depreciable assets. On the other hand, scheduled loan repayments, which do not affect net profits, do reduce cash flow.

Term lending has assumed increasing importance in recent years. More than half of the commercial loans of New York City banks, for example, are designated as term loans.[8] Such loans probably account for at least a third of the business loans of the country's larger banks and small banks also commonly make term loans although they may not be specifically designated as such. Loans to business secured by chattel mortgage on equipment (a common form of small bank lending both to business and to farmers) are a form of "term" lending even though they are made on a 90-day renewable note basis. Many commercial mortgage loans are term loans in actuality.

---

[8] Federal Reserve Bank of New York, "Term Lending by New York City Banks," *Monthly Review*, Vol. 43, No. 2 (February 1961), pp. 27–31. The statistics reported here include some revolving credits written for more than one year.

Despite the fact that some doubts have been raised about the appropriateness of commercial bank term lending, the term loan represents a clear case of banks meeting the credit needs of their customers by relating purpose to payment. As for protection, in addition to the collateral usually obtained, and to the provisions for regular amortization, term loans typically contain covenants establishing, among other things, minimum working capital levels and minimum net worth-to-debt ratios, as well as limiting dividends or withdrawals from the business during the term of the loan. Such agreements provide a continuing control over the obligor which is not always possible with respect to the market securities of corporations which term loans have replaced in bank portfolios.

Large enterprises traditionally have financed their capital needs primarily in the capital markets or by direct placement with institutional investors. Many needs for capital financing are still so accommodated. Frequently, however, the amount of a particular acquisition will not be large enough to justify a market flotation, or the cash flow will be sufficiently large to enable the borrower to repay all or part of the obligation in a shorter period of time than would be acceptable to an institutional investor.[9] Rate differentials or anticipated rate changes also play a role in the decision of a large borrower to use his bank or to go to the market.

MORTGAGE LOANS

The true purpose of a mortgage loan is to finance the acquisition or substantial improvement of real property. Liens on real estate are often pledged to secure obligations incurred for other purposes but, in such cases, the real purposes, rather than the form of collateral, should determine the terms of repayment and dictate any other protective features that may be called for.

Mortgage loans in commercial banks are first liens on residential or business properties.[10] Residential mortgages are generally considered more desirable because dwellings, unless of unusual size or

---

[9] Arrangements are often made for a bank to take the early maturities of a term loan and for an insurance company to take the longer-term obligations.

[10] National banks may not lend on unimproved property nor may they directly acquire second mortgages (Section 24, Federal Reserve Act).

design, have a broader market than business properties which are often limited to specialized uses. Commercial mortgages, as noted above, are often term loans in disguise, in which case they should be treated as such.

Residential Mortgage Lending. The basic policies required in residential mortgage lending are (1) to limit the amount of the loan to a reasonable percentage of the true value of the property, and (2) to require repayment at a rate which will maintain or improve the mortgagor's original equity during the life of the loan. Value is established by an appraisal made by a committee of the directors or by a professional appraisor under their direction. The basis for such valuations is a keystone of mortgage policy. Conservatism will call for some discounting of peak prices which may reflect an inflated demand. Values, however, will vary in each community since growth prospects strongly affect them. Past trends as well as future prospects need to be taken into consideration and a concept of "fair value" developed to fit each bank's particular circumstances. Competition in appraisals, sometimes indulged in, is obviously a dangerous practice.

Regardless of real estate values, however, the principal consideration of residential mortgage lending should be the borrower's ability to repay the loan in conformity with the scheduled payments. No mortgage loan should be made without a knowledge of the mortgagor's income and other financial obligations. Obvious as this may appear it is information which is lacking in too many mortgage files. If it appears, as it may, on the mortgage application, there is no follow-up to show that ability to repay is being maintained. The good experience of the past 20 years during which real estate prices have increased steadily is no excuse for carelessness in mortgage lending.

The maximum term for residential mortgage lending is generally established by law. For national banks the maximum term is 20 years. Mortgages insured under the National Housing Act of 1934 (F.H.A.) or guaranteed under the Servicemen's Readjustment Act of 1944 (G.I.) are exempt from these provisions. Recently proposals have been made in Congress to extend mortgage terms under the National Housing Act to 40 years. In theory the life of a mortgage should not exceed the useful life of the property, but condition, not age, is the crucial factor, and the quality of the neighborhood may have more to do with sale values than the durability of the structure.

Even though some houses may be maintained in excellent condition and retain their value long beyond 20 years, both the bank and the borrower should be interested in having the debt reduced. Sound lending policy requires that bank credit flow through the economy and not become stagnant; loan repayments are a principal source of new loans to promote further building and growth. From the mortgagor's viewpoint, the burden of additional interest cost on long-term mortgages is considerable. For most homeowners there is no better or profitable method of regular saving than to increase the monthly payments on his mortgage. Five or six per cent saved is just as much income as five or six per cent earned.

As stated above, the condition of a property is as important as its age. Another vital element in the protective arrangements which should safeguard mortgage lending, therefore, is a policy of requiring adequate maintenance. All mortgaged properties should be periodically reappraised,[11] and if deficiencies in maintenance are revealed, the bank should make every effort, including the offer of financing, to encourage the mortgagor to make necessary repairs. If a bank has been reasonably selective as to the character of its mortgagors, the borrower will recognize that adequate maintenance benefits him as much as the bank.

Construction Mortgage Financing. The origination of mortgage loans through the financing of building construction is a specialized field deserving of comment. All banks occasionally finance the construction of a home or business building for a valued customer with the expectation that they will acquire and hold the mortgage on the completed premises. Such loans require special attention because of the ever-present possibility that construction costs may exceed the original estimates and the bank may find itself more deeply committed than it planned.

The bulk of construction financing, however, is done by banks which sell the permanent mortgages to other institutions. The origination and sale of mortgages is a banking business which has its own risks and specialized techniques for minimizing them.

---

[11] Most authorities suggest reappraisal every three years.

However, either directly or in participation with correspondent banks, it can be a very profitable form of essentially short-term lending.[12] If the originating bank retains the servicing of the mortgages, this type of financing is not only a source of additional revenue but provides valuable customer contacts. The origination and sale of mortgage loans is also one way in which banks in rapidly growing areas can serve their communities beyond the limits of their own resources.

Commercial Mortgage Lending. In true commercial mortgage lending the primary consideration of policy is the relationship of the income derived from the property to the cost of maintaining it, paying taxes, and servicing the loan. In some cases the income may be derived from an operating business although such loans are likely to be true business loans. More often, the income from the property is the product of a lease or leases to tenants with whom the bank does not deal directly (except as they may be customers for other banking services).

A complete description and appraisal of the property should, of course, be on file, but the cost or replacement value of a commercial property is distinctly secondary to its yield as an investment; it is the latter that effectively establishes its resale value. As a matter of policy, therefore, it is important that the bank not only know the amount of the income from the property but assure itself of its continuance and availability for servicing the mortgage during its life. Sound policy dictates that banks not only obtain assignment of the leases but know the credit standing of the lessees as well.

CONSUMER LENDING

As far as commercial banking is concerned, consumer lending has come of age in the past 20 years.[13] Long looked upon with suspicion by bankers, many of whom felt that it was somehow immoral for a person to buy something before he had earned and saved the money, consumer credit has become a way of life for millions of

---

[12] *Cf.* James F. Schneider, *Construction Loans for Your Short-Term Portfolio,* thesis for Graduate School of Banking, Rutgers University (A.B.A. Library).

[13] Commercial banks held, on the average, about $17 billion of installment credit during 1961 (*Federal Reserve Bulletin*).

Americans. Buy now and pay later—with bank credit bridging the gap.

Much has been written about the economic implications of the vast growth of consumer credit.[14] The pros and cons of its effect on the business cycle have been hotly debated. Twice in recent years it has been subjected to Federal regulation and some still advocate at least stand-by authority to regulate it again. This book is not immediately concerned with these issues. It suffices to note that banks have found lending to consumers to be both safe and profitable if sound policies are followed, and it is with such policies that this discussion is primarily concerned. Consumer loans are an important element of the community's total demand for credit, and the bank which does not reasonably meet this need is, to that extent, failing in its obligations.

In broad usage consumer credit includes both installment credit and noninstallment credit. The latter consists of charge accounts granted by merchants, service credit (such as unpaid doctors' bills), and the occasional single payment loans granted by banks to individuals for consumption purposes. Although in recent years a few banks have entered the charge-account field by purchasing accounts from merchants, installment lending is still by far the more important part of consumer lending in point of volume.

Installment credit, in turn, can be subdivided into that group of loans made to meet previously incurred or extraordinary expenses (the typical personal loan) and loans to finance specifically the purchase of goods or services; the "buy now, pay later" concept. In terms of volume the latter is of much greater significance.

Personal installment loans to individuals are almost all made on the basis of direct negotiation between the bank and the borrower. Installment sales credit may be handled either on a direct or indirect basis. In the latter case installment sales contracts are purchased by the bank from the seller of the goods or services. Indirect lending is almost necessarily engaged in by banks which are seeking a large volume of consumer loans. Many banks do both a direct and indirect business, although some bankers find an inherent conflict of interest between direct automobile financing, for example,

---

[14] *Cf.* Board of Governors, *Consumer Installment Credit* (four parts in seven volumes), 1957.

and their relationships with the dealers from whom they purchase paper.[15]

Consumer Credit Principles. Whether a bank lends on a direct or indirect basis, the credit principles of consumer lending are essentially uniform. Unlike commercial lending, the net worth of the borrower is of relatively little importance. The essential ingredients of sound consumer credit are the borrower's ability and willingness to pay. These ingredients are roughly measurable in terms of the borrower's character, his income, and its stability. Character and reputation are usually synonymous and the applicant's previous record for repayment, at the bank or elsewhere, is usually the best credit guide. Volume lending in the consumer credit field is likely to be unduly risky if the bank does not have access to a credit bureau in which all, or most of the local consumer lenders, including merchants, participate and pool their knowledge of the credit records of consumers. Without such a central record duplicate and excess borrowings are an ever-present danger.

Consumer loans are generally made on the basis of a fairly simple application form on which the borrower is asked to state his income, its source, the purpose of the loan, and his other debts. It is essential to verify all such statements because a borrower who misrepresents any of these vital facts is probably a poor risk.

As in any other form of lending the relationship of purpose to payment is of great importance. The purpose should be a reasonable one in the light of the borrower's capacity to repay. While consumer lenders usually take a broader view of capacity than an officer reared in the commercial lending tradition, and while it is not necessary to make a moral judgment as to whether the applicant *ought* to spend the money for a particular purpose, loans to finance extravagances are seldom good risks. In other words, banks err in financing Cadillacs for borrowers who need transportation but can at best afford a second-hand Chevrolet. Loans to refinance outstanding debt, while sometimes appropriate, are also likely to be a sign of overextension.

It can be firmly stated that the longer the terms of the loan the greater the risk. Too often terms are set by competition (espe-

---

[15] Dealers look to the profit from the differential between the finance charges they assess and the lower rates at which banks discount their paper.

cially in indirect lending), but sound policy should stand firm against undue lengthening of terms. If it does not, delinquencies will mount, collection costs will eat up profits, and losses will be substantial.

Direct and Indirect Lending. Whether to confine a bank's consumer lending to direct loans or to purchase loans from dealers is a key matter of bank policy. About the only virtue of indirect lending is the volume it generates. To obtain and keep the business of important dealers a bank usually has to accept the average run of his credit risks even though it formally reserves the right to be selective. It will also have to finance the dealer's inventory which entails its own risks and expensive procedures. As a result, indirect financing is generally more expensive; it may result in higher collection costs; and the rate of net income is generally lower than on direct lending because of the keen competition for dealer business. However, large volume can be generated and the business is profitable if carefully handled; witness the success of the major finance companies which specialize in this field.

In connection with indirect lending, sound policy requires, in the first place, a careful selection of dealers having both moral and financial responsibility. A second vital principle involves making certain that an obligor actually exists on all paper purchased. This can usually be done by mailing forms directly to the obligor and requiring that all payments be made directly to the bank. Finally, the financing arrangement with the dealer should place at least a portion of the credit risk on his shoulders. This can be accomplished either by purchasing the paper with full recourse (the usual procedure in the purchase of service or appliance-sales paper) or by the establishment of dealers' reserves. The latter is the usual procedure with respect to automobile financing. The customers' notes are purchased from the dealer on a nonrecourse basis at a discount less than that charged by the dealer to the obligor. All or part of the differential is held by the bank as a reserve against which delinquent loans may be charged. The collection of delinquent loans, including the repossession of the chattel, is thus the dealer's responsibility. To the extent that the reserve at the end of a stated period exceeds an agreed-upon percentage of outstanding loans, it is returned to the dealer thus giving him a financial stake in the collectibility of the paper.

Where dealers require inventory financing on a "floor plan" basis, the bank's protection is no better than the dealer's moral responsibility and the bank's periodic, thorough, and surprise checking of the chattels. Sales "out of trust" are an all too common occurrence. In used car and appliance financing a bank can find itself pitted against some of the shrewdest and least principled business operators on the modern scene and losses can be sudden and substantial if the bank relaxes for a moment.[16]

Another important policy aspect of floor-plan financing is that with respect to curtailment. This refers to the reduction of the loans against unsold merchandise. Competitive pressures have often caused banks to relax what they know are sound policies: requirements for monthly payments on unsold cars or other chattels.

Lending directly to the bank's own customers is, by contrast, a safer and less expensive form of extending consumer credit. Mistakes involve no more than a single borrower here and there, and most of the applicants for loans will be already known to the bank. Direct lending promotes customer relationships and brings in other business. For these reasons many banks, which can obtain a satisfactory volume of consumer loans without purchasing them from dealers, have learned that they can afford to offer lower rates to selected borrowers on a direct basis and still earn more net on comparable volume.[17]

Consumer Loan Delinquencies. The best meaure of the soundness of the consumer lending policies of an individual bank is the relative volume of loans on which payments are delinquent. Loans are generally considered "delinquent" when a scheduled monthly payment remains unpaid for 30 days or more, although the operating officers will institute special collection procedures when payments are only a few days past due. Notes 90 days or more past due are seriously delinquent and are usually classified as "loss" by bank examiners.

---

[16] An example of the dangers involved was reported in the *New York Times*, February 27, 1960. Losses of $500,000 were estimated for two savings and loan associations and a commercial bank which had failed to investigate sufficiently home improvement loans which proved to be fraudulent.

[17] Figures furnished to the author by a large suburban bank clearly substantiate its own policy decision to withdraw from dealer financing and concentrate heavily on advertising for direct loans which, it concluded, were considerably more profitable.

Delinquencies should be regularly reported to the directors by class of loan and, where indirect financing is involved, by individual dealer account. The American Bankers Association [18] and some state bankers associations and local credit bureaus regularly publish average consumer loan delinquency rates for various localities and different classes of loans. Comparison of the individual bank's figures with these published statistics will give the directors a clear indication of the relative success of their own bank's operations. Any increase in the rate of delinquencies either absolute or in comparison with other banks is a danger signal which may indicate that credit policies or collection techniques need tightening. Individual dealers whose paper shows an abnormally high rate of delinquency should be carefully investigated and perhaps dropped.

On the other hand, if a bank's delinquency rates are consistently below average, its credit policies may be too strict and it could be turning away some acceptable business.

LOAN DEVELOPMENT

A discussion of lending practices would be incomplete without some comment on the spirit with which banks approach lending. To many banks and bankers the negotiation of a loan still appears to represent a situation in which the bank is on the defensive: protecting itself against the onslaughts of potential borrowers behind barricades of minimum ratios and standardized lending procedures. Other banks appear to regard lending as a challenging opportunity and go out seeking loans, some perhaps a little too aggressively. This book's viewpoint concerning bank policy has been that local lending is the primary function of a commercial bank; that a bank should make all the sound local loans it can. If this viewpoint is valid, no well-run bank can take a passive attitude toward lending.

In recent years demands for all kinds of loans have sometimes pressed hard against the funds which many banks have had available for lending. Loan-deposit ratios have been rising steadily and few banks have felt the need to go out and look for loans. Yet now, as in the past, the outstandingly successful banks in all parts

---

[18] American Bankers Association, Instalment Credit Committee, "Delinquency Rates on Bank Instalment Loans" (Monthly Bulletin).

of the country are those which have found the means to make more loans than their neighbors, and to make some loans which their neighbors do not make at all. Even today there are still many banks with relatively low ratios of loans to deposits. This may be the result, at least in part, of their failure to seek out and service all of the potentially worthy users of credit in their communities.

The essence of loan development lies, first, in a willingness to examine carefully every request for credit and to try conscientiously to make it "bankable," and second, to search actively for opportunities to promote the growth of the community and the individual businesses therein with sound credit. The two go hand in hand and the bank which has an established reputation for constructive lending will not have to do as much searching. Nevertheless, a major objective of visits by bank officers to their customers' places of business, be it farm or factory, should be to find new ways or additional productive purposes for the customers' use of credit.

Those banks which have done an outstanding job of loan development are usually managed by outstanding and imaginative men. It is doubtful if directors can establish loan development as a policy objective without full confidence in the high quality of the bank's operating management. But even in the most conservatively managed bank there is room, if not for broad loan promotion, at least for a limited amount of "promotional lending." The directors could well afford to set aside a modest percentage of the bank's capital and surplus as a revolving fund from which loans they consider to be marginal credits might be made. Such lending, if successful, can contribute materially to the growth and welfare of the community. As the president of a relatively small bank which has aggressively followed such a policy points out:

> Every one of our town's industries grew up here from small-scale beginnings. Not one of them was "attracted" from elsewhere. Our bank financed each one through its early stages, sometimes employing considerable ingenuity to find ways of keeping the loans bankable. For example, today's largest local employer started with one assistant in a basement garage. He financed his entire business expansion, above that permitted by plowed-back profits, on credit obtained from this bank.[19]

---

[19] James A. Maurice, President, The Monticello State Bank, Monticello, Iowa, *Burroughs Clearing House,* January 1962, pp. 37, 82.

Opportunities for promotional lending do not present themselves regularly. Each one is different, yet experienced lending officers will recognize promising situations when they arise. They present banks with a challenging opportunity not to deny credit automatically but rather to "use considerable ingenuity," to assess ideas imaginatively, and within reasonable and previously established limits, to take considered risks. Many of an aggressive bank's most valuable and loyal customers will be those who initially were something of a credit gamble, a greater-than-average risk, deliberately taken. Good bank examiners will continue to list such loans in reports of examination, but good bankers will continue to make them.

XII

PORTFOLIO POLICY

The policy approach advanced in this book has stressed the primary obligation of a commercial bank to serve the credit needs of its community. It has emphasized, also, the need for protective liquidity and has advocated the provision of sufficient additional liquid assets to meet any foreseeable local demand for loans. Banks in some areas, however, or at some times, will have provided adequate liquidity, granted all the sound local loans they can, and still have excess funds to invest. Funds so employed represent the bank's "investment portfolio" as distinguished from its liquidity position and its loan account.

The portfolio should consist of funds for which the bank can foresee no local demand during the succeeding five years or longer. If the bank's calculations are reasonably accurate, there should be no need to dispose of portfolio assets in advance of their maturity because of any normal demands made upon the bank by depositors or borrowers.

In communities where the demand for credit is high, banks may have very modest investment portfolios, or even none at all. Where the investment portfolio is substantial the community is likely to be relatively stable with little immediate growth potential. Banks with large portfolios also may have chosen not to make all the local loans they could, or may not have been fully aware of the extent of local demands for credit. In any event, given funds which have not, and in all probability will not be used for lending, the problem of how best to invest them poses policy considerations of notable complexity.

As the term is used here, investment is not necessarily confined

231

to the purchase of investment securities. It includes the acquisition of any earning asset outside the credit market or from others than the customers whom the bank customarily serves. Thus the purchase of F.H.A.—insured mortgages on properties outside the bank's normal territory—is in this sense an investment. Similarly, the acquisition of local municipal securities may be governed by considerations of customer relations and local lending rather than be strictly related to the problem of investing surplus funds.

GENERAL
CONSIDERATIONS OF PORTFOLIO POLICY

The primary aim of bank portfolio policy is to obtain the maximum amount of income with the minimum exposure to risk. Maximizing income, of course, does not mean simply purchasing the highest yields currently available. Income has to be computed over the longer run. Nor can risk ever be entirely eliminated: the taking of reasonable risks is part of the commercial bank's daily routine.

Both the amount of income and the degree of risk [1] in any investment will be directly affected by (1) its quality, (2) the general level of interest rates at the time it is purchased, and (3) the maturity of the obligation being acquired. Each investment decision requires a balancing of income potential against risk in the light of these factors and the particular circumstances existing or foreseen at the time.

Tax considerations also play a vital role in portfolio policy. In putting to use surplus funds with no other aim than to obtain the best return consistent with safety, it is the after-tax income that is of signal importance. For banks in the 52 per cent bracket, tax reduction may well be one of the primary considerations of portfolio management.

Finally, the relationship of earnings from portfolio assets to the amount of capital funds needed to support the intrinsic risks (profitability as contrasted with profit) will also be of concern to manage-

---

[1] For a clear and complete discussion of investment risks see Harry Sauvain, *Investment Management* (2nd Ed.; Englewood Cliffs, N. J.: Prentice-Hall, Inc., 1959), Chapters 5–7.

ment. If higher gross income is derived from "risk" assets requiring relatively greater amounts of capital protection, the return to shareholders may, in some instances, be less than if the funds had been invested at lower yields in assets considered relatively "riskless."

This chapter will discuss these general considerations from a more or less theoretical viewpoint as a background for the determination of portfolio policy.

QUALITY CONSIDERATIONS

Both income and risk are directly affected by the credit standing of the issuers whose obligations a bank acquires. Generally speaking, the lower the credit rating, the higher the yield. At the same time, the risk of market loss is greater on lower-quality bonds since they usually fluctuate more widely in price.

Obligations of the United States Government, of course, enjoy the very highest credit standing. From a credit viewpoint they are virtually riskless and are so considered in several of the "capital adequacy" formulas previously reviewed. Obligations of the various states and of political subdivisions, like those of corporate obligors, vary widely in credit worthiness. Many such obligations, however, enjoy high credit ratings, higher undoubtedly than those of some local borrowers to whom banks lend without question.

The credit standing of municipal and corporate obligors whose securities are actively traded in the market is rated by several well-known "rating services."[2] These ratings receive wide attention. They are referred to by the Comptroller of the Currency in his "Investment Regulations" as being presumptive evidence of investment quality,[3] and they are generally accepted as being a fair measure of quality differences between various securities. They are based, however, on rather rigid statistical formulas and therefore changes in ratings tend to lag behind the circumstances which cause them.[4] Useful as guides, ratings are not a full and valid

---

[2] The best known of these are: Moody's Investors Service, Standard & Poor's Corporation, and Fitch Investors Service.

[3] Comptroller of the Currency, *Digest of Opinions*, Par. 310.

[4] Robinson, *Management of Bank Funds*, p. 307, "But there is one role that statistical and rating services cannot (and do not pretend to) assume; they are not prophets."

substitute for the individual knowledge and judgment of the informed investor who maintains his own credit files and makes his
own careful analyses.

The relationship of the yields on fully-taxable United States Government securities to the yields on corporate securities of high and
medium grade, and to yields on high-grade municipals is shown on
Chart V.

CHART V

BOND YIELDS

Monthly Averages

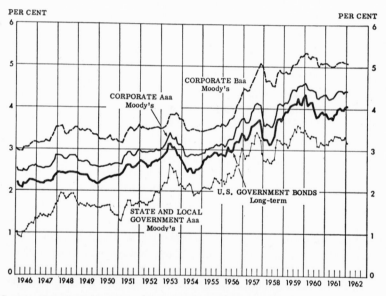

Source: Board of Governors of the Federal Reserve System.

Yields on municipal securities, of course, are lower than those on
obligations of the United States Government and on high-grade
corporate issues because of their exemption from Federal taxes.
Tax considerations aside, Chart V shows graphically the premium
placed by the market on the unquestioned credit of the United
States Government as compared with the best of corporate bonds.
Similarly, the difference between yields on high-grade corporates

and those of medium grade reflects the value the market places on quality or credit worthiness.

Member banks are permitted by law to purchase any readily marketable debt obligation that qualifies as an investment security under regulations promulgated by the Comptroller of the Currency. The Comptroller has defined investment securities, among other things, as securities which are not "distinctly or predominantly speculative," [5] but, as a matter of practice, commercial banks purchase very few corporate bonds even of the highest quality. The reasons for this will become apparent in subsequent discussion. In any event, the maintenance of high quality should be the rule in portfolio policy. A bank's principal source of income, as well as risk exposure, is its loan account.[6] Portfolio income is supplementary. The funds invested in portfolio will not ordinarily turn over as rapidly as loans and liquid assets and, therefore, safety of principal will always be of prime importance.

Closely related to credit considerations are the principles of diversification of risk, both geographic and by industry. These have concerned writers on investment policy in the past. The examination report forms of the Federal supervisory authorities contain elaborate schedules calling for analyses of corporate securities by class and quality distribution, as well as by maturity. In eight cases out of ten these schedules are left blank today because few banks hold any such securities. As a result these concerns have become somewhat academic.

Geographical distribution still has significance, however, with respect to holdings of municipal securities, and some authorities specifically advocate avoidance of local municipals in the portfolio since the loan account (and such municipals as are acquired for reasons of community and customer relations) already represent a concentration in assets subject to adverse developments in the local economy.[7] Some investment in local municipal securities can be justified on the ground of serving community needs, particularly

---

5 Comptroller of the Currency, *Digest of Opinions,* Par. 100, Section 3(c).

6 Robinson, *op. cit.* p. 303. "The primary business of banking is lending. To the extent that banks must assume credit risks, these risks should be accepted in the loan accounts and avoided in investment operations."

7 Robinson, *op. cit.* p. 119, "Possibly the leading principle of diversification that a bank needs to follow is that of not duplicating its loan account."

with respect to issues too small for general distribution. In addition, the advantages of diversification must be balanced against the more complete knowledge that banks often have of local conditions. Geographical diversification, in any case, should be generally sought only in municipal obligations of unquestioned credit standing.

INTEREST RATE LEVELS

A glance at Chart V shows how interest rates for the same quality and maturity of securities have varied over time. Income from portfolio assets will be clearly influenced, therefore, by the level of rates existing in the market at the time they are purchased. Market levels also affect risk since, when prices are abnormally high they are more likely to decline. Conversely, when securities are acquired at relatively low prices (high yields) the chances of market depreciation are greatly lessened.[8]

The rates in the market at any given time reflect, in the first instance, the current equilibrium between the forces of demand and supply. The demand and supply conditions also mirror the expectations of the market in regard to prospective changes in interest rates.[9] Short maturity obligations reflect almost entirely the current strength of the demand for funds; longer term rates are substantially colored by market guesses about the probable course of future events.

Short term securities and marketable paper are part of the floating supply of money and near-money substitutes, while the supply of longer term market instruments is more closely related to the flow of real savings into investment channels. The level of rates, therefore, not only moves up and down, but evidences a constantly shifting relationship between rates for different maturities as changes take place in the supply of money and the flow of savings.

---

[8] William C. Freund and Murray G. Lee, *Investment Fundamentals* (Council on Banking Education, American Bankers Association, New York, undated) Chapter 3, "Bond Prices and Yields." This booklet describes in simple language the technical aspects of price-yield relationships which underlie this discussion.

[9] Lyon, *Investment Portfolio Management in the Commercial Bank*, p. 119, calls this ". . . the psychological make-up of the investing community from the standpoint of its anticipating ability."

The pattern of rates in the market at any given time can be portrayed graphically by plotting the yields of outstanding securities of equal credit standing for different maturities. This is usually done with respect to United States Government obligations, and the resultant yield curve is the visual image of investor preferences and expectations.[10] The shape of the yield curve is closely related to the state of the economy and to the counter-cyclical operations of monetary and fiscal policy. When business activity is high, the demand for money is strong and the Federal Reserve System is likely to be restricting the creation of new credit. Consequently the demand for, and the price of money rise and this rise is reflected in the sharp advance of short-term interest rates. Longer term rates, reflecting expectations of a return to more normal market conditions over a period of time, do not ordinarily increase as rapidly or to as great an extent. When short-term rates are rising the shape of the yield curve tends to become flat, with short-term rates equalling the long. If short rates rise above the long, as they have upon occasion in the past, the curve is said to be descending.

When business conditions are slack, the demand for money tends to decline. At the same time the Federal Reserve attempts to increase the availability of credit through open market purchases of securities, channelling funds directly into the commercial banking system. An over-abundance of funds sharply depresses short-term rates while the decline in longer rates lags behind. In periods of business recession, therefore, the yield curve is usually ascending or upsloping.

Yield curves are shown on Chart VI as of the spring of 1958, a recession period, and as of the fall of 1959, a period of high business activity. They illustrate dramatically how greatly the level of interest rates can shift in a relatively short period of time.

Changes in the level of interest rates are a vital concern of portfolio management. They are of special significance in relation to the considerations of maturity which will be discussed in greater detail below. It would naturally seem desirable for banks to acquire securities when prices are low and rates high, and to sell when the opposite conditions prevail. However, it is usually when rates

---

[10] Such a yield curve is published monthly in the *Treasury Bulletin*.

are high that banks have the least amount of funds available and are experiencing the heaviest demand for loans. When banks have a surplus of funds, rates are always low.[11]

CHART VI

YIELDS OF TAXABLE TREASURY SECURITIES

Fixed Maturity Issues: Based on Closing Bid Quotations

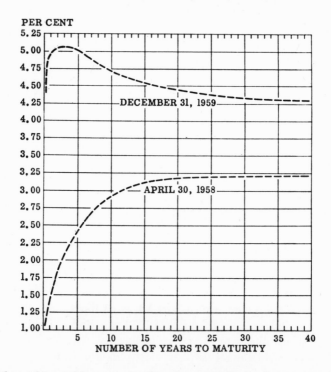

PER CENT

NUMBER OF YEARS TO MATURITY

When the yield curve is sharply ascending, the temptation is strong for commercial banks to confuse their liquidity positions with their portfolios and to lengthen maturities in search of higher re-

[11] C. Richard Youngdahl, "Bank Portfolio Management," *Proceedings,* National Association of Supervisors of State Banks, Fifty-Ninth Annual Meeting, Atlantic City, N.J., September 1960, p. 33. "Basically banks face an investment problem that is loaded against them. Banks typically have surplus funds to invest when interest rates are low and they ordinarily need to raise funds for other purposes when interest rates are high."

turn. In the process they may commit themselves to too low a rate for too long a time. A subsequent rise in rates will cause these purchases to decline in market value, and when the bank needs the funds for lending it is faced with selling securities at a loss. If it cannot afford to absorb these losses, it becomes "locked in" to unnecessarily low yields.

It should be noted that this error of judgment is not a mistake in portfolio policy but in the management of the liquidity position. The poor record [12] of many commercial banks in this regard during the four post-World War II business cycles emphasizes strongly the thesis that the liquidity position, both short- and longer-term, should be kept clearly separated from the portfolio in the minds of bank policy-makers and investment officers.

The portfolio is a more or less permanent revolving fund, the size of which will change only with the slow accretion of stable deposits or with fundamental modifications of the local demand for credit. Its management, to a large extent, consists in making adjustments to changing interest rate levels in ways that will increase after-tax profits without substantially increasing risk.

MATURITY CONSIDERATIONS

If a bank acquires a credit-worthy security for its portfolio with the expectation of holding it to maturity it commits itself, in effect, to receiving a stated yield for a given period of time. This basic concept can hardly be overstressed; true investment is the purchase of income for a fixed period of time. The longer that time period is, the more uncertain will be the conditions not only at the time when the obligation falls due but also during the intervening period as well. This uncertainty is comprised of two factors: a credit factor and an interest rate, or income factor.

With respect to investments involving credit risks, there is always the possibility that the credit standing of the obligor will vary over time. The longer the time, the greater will be the possibility of change. Since banks usually acquire the securities of obligors with high credit standing, the possibility of deterioration is greater than

---

12 *Ibid.* p. 32. "Thus we can see that the aggregate score of bank portfolio management has been on the negative side."

the chance of improvement. Investors were once willing to purchase railroad first mortgage bonds with maturities of 100 years
but subsequent events have amply demonstrated the danger of such
long commitments.

Where credit risk is not an important factor, there is always the
uncertainty over the prospective level of interest rates both at the
time when the obligation falls due and the funds are available for
reinvestment, and (of even greater concern) during the period that
the security is held. The longer the maturity the greater the odds
that income (and market value) over the long run will be affected
(favorably or adversely) by changes in the level of rates. In other
words, an investment in a thirty-year bond yielding 3 per cent is
tantamount to making the decision that the average return on one-
year funds will not exceed 3 per cent over the next thirty years.[13]
The longer the time to maturity the more pellucid must be the investment manager's crystal ball!

There is, however, no fixed relationship between maturity and
either risk or income. There may be occasions when less risk will
be entailed in lengthening maturities than in staying short, as when
yields are abnormally high; on other occasions short maturities are
the instruments of caution despite their abnormally low yields. In
any event, the difference is never simply between short and long; it
is "How short?" or "How long?" that requires the policy-maker's
searching decisions. Nor is maturity a factor that can be measured
in isolation. It must be considered closely in conjunction with the
level of rates at any given time and with the prospects of changes
in that level over the life of the investment being considered.

Full understanding of the implications of maturity for investment
policy requires some knowledge of certain basic technical facts.[14]
The most important of these is the relationship of maturity to the
range of price fluctuation. While short-term rates tend to fluctuate

---

[13] The possibility exists, of course, of selling the bond in the interim, but at
a profit or a loss which will reflect the degree of variance from the expected
yield experience.

[14] Techniques and technical considerations generally have been deliberately
omitted from this discussion where possible. Some knowledge of them, however, is necessary to provide a basic understanding for those involved in
formulating policy. For a more detailed discussion of "The Effects of Maturity
on Price" see Lyon, *op. cit.*, pp. 74–80, or Sauvain, *op. cit.*, pp. 122–130.

more widely than long-term rates (as noted previously) the effect of a given rate change on price increases markedly as maturity is extended. Table 11 illustrates this point.

TABLE 11

Relative Price Changes for
Bonds of Different Maturities
Reflecting a Yield Change from
2½ per cent to 3½ per cent
(3% coupon)

Maturities	Point Change	% Change
One year	.98	.98
Two years	1.93	1.91
Five years	4.62	4.51
Ten years	8.59	8.23
Twenty years	14.98	13.89
Thirty years	19.75	17.87

Source: Lyon, *op. cit.*, Table 4, p. 75 (condensed).

The effect on price is further enhanced if the bonds have optional call dates in advance of final maturity, as is the case with many U. S. Government issues. Such securities trade on a yield-to-maturity basis when current yields exceed the coupon rate, but sell on a yield-to-call basis when current yields are lower than the coupon. The difference in the method of yield computation when the price shifts from below par to above par (or vice versa) magnifies the range of price fluctuation considerably. Thus, when extending maturities at a time when bond prices are relatively low, there can be a definite advantage in purchasing, at a discount from par, bonds with optional call dates.[15]

These technical considerations, for the most part, may be left to the technicians: investment officers, dealers, correspondent banks, and advisory services. What the policy-maker really needs to know is that the prices of securities rise when interest rates fall and decline when rates rise, and that the price swings resulting from any given change in rate will widen as maturity is extended.

---

[15] *Cf.* Harry W. Lussey, "Portfolio Policy Now," *Bankers Monthly*, February 15, 1960, p. 5.

Tax Considerations

The impact of Federal income tax laws and regulations on portfolio policy is another highly technical aspect of investment management with which bank directors can be expected to have little more than general familiarity. Some background knowledge of tax consequences, however, is essential to the broad formulation of portfolio policy.

The Federal income tax laws affect portfolio management in two important ways. In the first place, the income from obligations of states and political subdivisions (including public housing authorities) is entirely exempt from Federal income taxes. This fact naturally makes such securities attractive to investors who, like commercial banks, are subject to the income tax, particularly if they are subject to the surtax. This very attractiveness, however, tends to be reflected in the market where such securities trade at higher prices and lower yields, as was evident in Chart V. The differential, however, seldom reflects the entire tax advantage. The degree by which it does so will vary with market conditions but "As a general rule, tax exempt obligations . . . will sell to provide yields which range from 30 per cent to 52 per cent lower than yields from fully taxable obligations of comparable quality and maturity in the bank investment range, . . ." [16] At those times when the calendar of new municipal offerings is particularly heavy, market prices will reflect an even smaller portion of the differential. To a bank with the major portion of its income in the 52 per cent bracket, there is nearly always some advantage to the purchase of tax-exempt issues. For such banks a rough comparison can be made between tax-exempt yields and the yields on taxable bonds by doubling the quoted yield on a municipal obligation. Thus a 2½ per cent yield on a tax exempt security is roughly equivalent to a 5 per cent yield on a fully taxable Government bond.

For the smaller bank, with all or a major portion of its net income under $25,000, tax-exempt securities will only occasionally be attractive. Such banks, however, should be alert to these occasional market opportunities.

---

[16] *Lyon, op. cit.*, pp. 81–82.

The second feature of the tax law with which bank directors and policy-makers should be familiar is the provision that permits commercial banks to deduct losses on securities sold from current income as an ordinary loss (if there are no offsetting profits in the same year). At the same time, banks, like other taxpayers, are allowed to treat profits on securities sold (if held for over six months and not offset by losses in the same year) as capital gains subject to a tax of only 25 per cent. This tax provision leads to the seemingly anomalous situation in which commercial banks can at times make profits by taking losses.[17] It also leads to the differentiation between "loss years" and "profit years" now common in investment parlance.

The same provision tends to make the low-coupon bonds which sell at substantial discounts in times of high money rates generally more attractive to the high-bracket taxpayer than are the bonds of the same obligor with higher coupons which sell nearer to or above par. The yields on discount bonds are a combination of the coupon rate and the accumulation of the discount to maturity. For tax purposes, however, the coupon income is subject to the 52 per cent tax while the difference between the discount price and par at maturity is a capital gain subject only to a tax of 25 per cent.[18]

Again, the small bank with all or a major portion of its income subject to only the 30 per cent normal tax will find little advantage in this provision. At the times when high-bracket taxpayers are active in the market and no change is expected in the tax laws, the market price tends to reflect this tax advantage rather fully. Dealers usually quote prices on both a taxable and after-tax basis, and it is important that a bank consider each purchase from both aspects.

With respect to tax-exempt securities, on the other hand, it should be noted that deep discount issues are *disadvantageous* to the high-bracket taxpayer unless the market has fully adjusted to the differential. In this case the coupon income is tax-exempt entirely, but the difference between the discount price and par will be a capital gain subject to the tax.

---

[17] *Cf.* Lussey, *op. cit.*, for an "Analysis of Opportunities and Pitfalls" in the technique of taking bond profits and losses.

[18] Lyon, *op. cit.*, pp. 82–3, cites several examples of the effect of this differential on banks of different sizes under varying market conditions.

CAPITAL CONSIDERATIONS

The use by bank supervisors of the various capital adequacy tests previously reviewed has a direct bearing, also, on portfolio policy. Unless a bank has more than enough capital by any measure, the effect of the formulas is to put a premium on assets considered as riskless or minimum risk. In choosing between an issue of corporate securities of the highest credit standing and an investment in United States Government obligations, for example, bank management cannot simply relate the relative yields to the intrinsic risks and choose on the merits. It must first look to the adequacy of its capital to see if an addition to risk assets is likely to bring on a request to sell additional capital. To the extent that these formulas consider municipal securities as risk assets, they also tend to discourage taking full advantage of the tax-exemption feature, for, if a bank's capital is on the borderline between adequate and inadequate, so that any increase in risk assets is likely to result in the need for more capital, a bank may be persuaded to keep its portfolio as riskless as possible.

The reason for this is found in simple arithmetic. When net income after expenses and taxes is related to capital requirements, the relatively greater profitability of riskless or minimum risk assets is readily apparent. Under the risk-asset formula used by the Comptroller no capital is required against Government securities regardless of their maturity. Profitability, in mathematical terms, is infinite. Under the Federal Reserve formulas which require 5 per cent capital protection against longer-term Government securities, the advantage of the latter for the stockholder is still substantial. This fact is made clear in the following example which contrasts the profitability of investing $1 million in long-term Governments as against a similar investment in Aaa municipals and Aaa corporates.[19] The example assumes that the bank's operating costs are 22 per cent of gross income,[20] and that the net income is subject to a tax of 52 per cent. The example does not reflect the "cost of money" which would vary with each bank's demand-time deposit

---

[19] At rates current in December 1960, Federal Reserve Bulletin.

[20] Average cost of overhead, administration and investment processing; Functional Analysis of Bank Income and Expense, Federal Reserve Bank of New York (mimeograph distributed to participants).

mix. The profitability percentages, therefore, are unrealistic but
nevertheless adequately indicate comparative profitability.

TABLE 12

COMPARISON OF PROFITABILITY
OF AN INVESTMENT OF $1,000,000

	Long-Term Governments	Aaa Municipals	Aaa Corporates
Gross Income	38,800	31,200	43,500
Overhead (22%)	8,536	6,864	9,570
Taxable income	30,264	24,336	33,930
Tax (52%)	15,737	exempt	17,644
Net profit	14,527	24,336	16,286
Capital req.	50,000	120,000	120,000
Profitability	29%	20%	13.5%

This table clearly explains one important reason why commercial
banks hold so few corporate securities.[21] It also re-emphasizes the
disadvantages of a strictly "formula" approach to the problem of
capital adequacy. Even when such tests are used only as preliminary screening devices, they tend, perhaps unduly, to influence
portfolio policy in the direction of "staying riskless."

FORMULATING PORTFOLIO POLICY

The considerations which should go into the formulation of sound
portfolio policy, as shown above, are complex and interrelated. Individual actions, taken within any policy that may be established,
require the exercise of sound judgment and an acute awareness of
conditions and expectations in the market. Nevertheless there is a
logical sequence of steps that management, in close consultation
with the directors, can take to establish and operate within a constructive policy.

Before discussing these steps in detail it will be well to repeat
that a bank portfolio, like ancient Rome, is not built in a day. Its
composition is the result of many separate actions taken over considerable periods of time. In most banks the portfolio exists

---

[21] Another reason frequently cited is that the yield differential hardly justifies
the expense of the careful credit analysis which corporate securities require.
Also such securities usually have an early optional call date so that yield for a
known maturity cannot be taken for granted.

whether it was planned or not. Fortunately, however, portfolio planning (which is the essence of what is here at stake) can begin at any time.

Identifying the Portfolio

This presentation has repeatedly stressed the need to separate the portfolio from holdings of securities for liquidity. Common parlance, and many writers, refer to the "investment account" by which they mean all the holdings of securities.[22] Similarly it is common practice for bank management to provide the directors only with a list of the bank's security holdings showing book values and market prices. The list is generally subdivided into Government securities, municipals, and others. The range of maturities is usually shown as well. But seldom is any attempt made to distinguish the liquidity position from the portfolio; to draw a distinct dividing line between what are essentially temporary holdings and those of a more permanent nature.

Length of maturity alone will not be the distinguishing feature because under certain circumstances (in the anticipation of rising rates, for example) a portion of the investment portfolio could well be held temporarily in short-term issues. The real distinction is the purpose for which the securities are held. Liquidity assets are to meet potential demands for funds carefully estimated in a way similar to that discussed in Chapter VIII. The portfolio, by contrast, represents the investment of surplus funds for income. The first step, therefore, in portfolio planning is to consider the two sets of assets separately.

Inventorying Capital

The second step is to ascertain how much of the bank's capital can be allocated to the portfolio and, by the same token, what portion of the risk assets the portfolio may appropriately contain. Us-

---

[22] *Cf.* Robinson, *op. cit.*, p. 279. "According to the conventions of bank accounting, the provision of liquidity by investment (secondary priority) is not distinguished from investment for income (fourth priority). Thus when the investment 'portfolio' or account is spoken of, it is customary to include both these portions. In order to avoid misunderstanding, we shall not depart from that convention." In this author's view the failure to treat the portfolio separately creates more misunderstanding than it avoids.

ing any of the formulas discussed in Chapter IX (preferably that used by the agency which examines the bank), or using an approach to capital adequacy designed by the bank itself, management can determine the amount of capital it should hold against its loan account, as well as for any expected increase in loans for which it has provided liquidity. What is left over will usually be available to support the portfolio.

Most banks have more than the minimum capital required by the supervisor. One way to put this excess capital to work is to increase the bank's net income after taxes either by increasing gross yields through the inclusion, perhaps, of some selected fully-taxable risk obligations, or by seeking to reduce tax liability by increasing the proportion of municipal securities in the portfolio. If capital funds are inadequate to support the risks that might be involved in holding sufficient municipal securities for maximum tax advantage, consideration may well need to be given to the sale of additional stock. In any event, a knowledge of the limitations imposed by the bank's capital position is indispensable to sound portfolio planning.

DETERMINING THE TAX POSITION

The third logical step in portfolio planning is to estimate as nearly as possible the bank's net taxable income and to calculate the amount of additional tax-exempt income, if any, that the bank could profitably use. Since income exempt from taxes is usually obtained at some sacrifice of gross revenue, it is obviously poor planning to have tax-exempt income exceed current operating earnings. In fact, even if a bank had complete flexibility, *i.e.,* a portfolio large enough to provide all the tax-exempt income it could use, it would not ordinarily plan to eliminate all taxable income. Enough margin of taxable income should be left to provide for regular tax-free transfers to the "bad debt reserve" and to absorb actual losses should they develop. In the latter connection, it is important to take into consideration the losses which the bank may wish to take in shifting maturities within the portfolio, a process which will be discussed in greater detail later in this chapter.

The tax considerations for the majority of small banks whose income falls within the $25,000 subject only to the 30 per cent normal tax, as noted above, will be vastly different than those affecting large banks most of whose income is subject to surtax. The latter

are likely to find that tax considerations will outweigh all others in
determining portfolio policy. For the bank in between, with net
operating income ranging from $25,000 to $50,000, a delicate balancing of factors is called for. The objective, in any case, should
be to reduce taxes as much as the law permits consistent with the
bank's obligation to make sound local loans and its ability to support
risk assets with adequate capital funds.

What this will mean as a practical matter to individual banks will
vary widely. Banks have a choice of a variety of lending and investing opportunities. Management must know its own costs to
determine the true net income from alternative uses of funds and
relate the anticipated net income to its own particular tax situation.
To illustrate this concept Table 13 assumes that a bank is considering the investment of $100,000 either in an expansion of its whole-
sale consumer loans or by the purchase of municipal bonds. Management does not consider that the loans represent a demand for
credit which the bank is obliged to meet; the paper is that of a
dealer in a neighboring community now being served by a major
finance company. The decision, therefore, is based solely on relative profitability.

TABLE 13

Comparison of Net Profits After Taxes
From an Investment in Consumer Loans
and in Municipal Bonds

	If $100,000 is Invested In			
	Consumer Loans		*Municipal Bonds*	
Net current operating earnings (before investment) (Includes tax-exempt income)		191,000 (52,000)		191,000 (52,000)
Proceeds of $100,000 investment:				
Gross yield	8,480		2,940	
Less direct expenses	1,980		80	
Net yield	6,500		2,860	
Less overhead allocation	1,345		51	
Net operating income		5,155		2,809
Accumulated net current operating earnings		196,155		193,809
Total tax-exempt income	52,000		54,940	
Total taxable income	144,155		138,869	

TABLE 13—Continued

	If $100,000 is Invested In	
	Consumer Loans	Municipal Bonds
Tax—First $25,000 @30%) Balance @52%)	69,461	66,712
Net income after taxes	126,694	127,097

Note: The figures are derived from the average functional income and expenses shown in the sample analysis contained in Chapter V.

The table, of course, is based on the average experience of a number of banks and the results would vary for each of the banks included in the group. The table simply illustrates the method of calculation and does not attempt to demonstrate the advantage of either hypothetical alternative. Nevertheless it does show the importance of the tax factor in investment considerations and suggests strongly that gross yields can sometimes be deceptive. Bank directors faced with such policy decisions have a right to insist that management supply them with the information necessary to make similar calculations.

In real life, of course, decisions are seldom made on the basis of comparative profitability alone. Customer relationships (deposit balances), the prospect of collateral business, the bank's long-range plans for growth, and competitive considerations may logically form the basis of a policy decision that does not immediately result in the largest profit. Nevertheless the policy-makers should know, as nearly as possible, the dollar and cents results of whichever alternative they choose.

DETERMINING MATURITIES

Maturities present two problems for portfolio policy. The first is the establishment of a maximum maturity limit, if such should be considered sound policy, and the second is the problem of scheduling maturities within the portfolio. The latter is closely related to the bank's appraisal of the economic climate. Arranging and, if occasion warrants, rearranging portfolio maturities also brings the portfolio manager into the area of taking profits and losses which, as noted earlier, have their own special tax connotations. These aspects of the maturity problem are all interrelated but can perhaps be understood more readily if they are examined separately.

Maximum Maturity. Based on the rising trend of interest rates since the Great Depression of the 1930s, it is fairly easy to conclude that there should be some fairly short-term limit to the maturities of commercial bank investments. Bank experience with longer-term bonds has not been favorable; many banks still find themselves with substantial depreciation on holdings of such bonds acquired 25 years ago. Especially if a bank is purchasing securities for income to maturity, one could readily and wisely counsel, "Never buy a yield that you are not willing to live with to maturity." In the light of the uncertainties of a rapidly changing world such counsel might well limit portfolio commitments to no longer than ten years. Even that is a long time to look ahead.

There were few prophets in 1947 who foretold the extent of the demand for bank loans that would exist in 1957. It is equally improbable that policy-makers today can predict with any greater accuracy the state of the market ten years hence. Beyond a certain maturity, moreover, the potential income advantages of lengthening out tend to diminish as the yield curve typically flattens out. "As a rule, there is little to be gained from the standpoint of income by lengthening maturities beyond the fifteen-year range, and the bulk of the bank's investment portfolio might well be kept within this range." [23]

On the other hand one should not lose sight of the full sweep of history and the long periods in the past during which the secular trend of interest rates was downward. Should the policy-maker be convinced that this particular phase of history was in the process of repeating itself, there would be ample justification for extending maturities beyond fifteen years.

Clearly one should not be doctrinaire, but if management expects the demand for bank credit to continue as strong as it has been in the past ten years, or to grow stronger, it will set a fairly short maximum maturity for the bulk of portfolio investments leaving open the

---

[23] Lyon, *op. cit.*, p. 143.

possibility of making exceptions to the rule under unusual circumstances.

Scheduling Maturities. Scheduling maturities within the investment portfolio is undoubtedly the most difficult and exacting task of portfolio management. Other policies can be established, periodically reviewed, and occasionally adapted to new circumstances. Maturity policy, in contrast, requires constant review and decision making as funds become available for investment or as opportunities to improve the maturity or yield position present themselves.

From the previous discussion of the relation of maturity to yield it should be clear that the ideal course of action in portfolio management would be to hold short-term securities when interest rates are likely to rise and to lengthen maturities when rates are expected to decline. Under the flexible monetary policy followed by the Federal Reserve System since 1951 this is tantamount to shortening maturities when business conditions (and the demand for credit) are expected to strengthen and to lengthening maturities when the first signs of a recession appear on the horizon. Portfolio management can be seen to be closely integrated with economic forecasting, considered by some to be a dubious art at best.

Because of the manifest uncertainties involved in such an "ideal" approach, banks have frequently been counselled to solve the problem of maturity distribution by spacing maturities more or less evenly within the maximum range previously established.[24] In this way the bank will assure itself of at least average yields, or a little better. It will not be gambling on changes in the level of rates or the state of the economy. As long as the yield curve is rising, the reinvestment of maturing assets at the longest end of the maturity schedule will assure the bank of maximum income on a portfolio of which the average maturity will be relatively short.

For those who may not have the competence, or who do not wish to take the trouble to frame a more flexible portfolio policy, average results obtained through regularly spaced maturities are undoubt-

---

[24] Robinson, *op. cit.*, p. 335. "Once an account has been put on a spaced basis and as long as there are neither additions or withdrawals from this investment account, the proceeds from the securities which mature each year can be reinvested in securities of the longest maturities admitted to the account. This reinvestment tends to keep the average maturity of the account constant."

edly better than what might result from a purely haphazard or intuitive approach to the problem. Spaced maturities are probably an acceptable solution for the very small bank. But for those who are willing to exercise judgment, it will certainly not make sense, for example, to invest the proceeds of maturing securities in the longest term bonds permitted by the bank's policy at a time when the economy is obviously in a slack condition, when banks hold excess reserves, and when money rates are abnormally low.

Even the most competent investment managers, of course, will not be able to call every turn, nor do they need to.[25] Alert and informed management can take advantage of events that have already occurred; it does not need to gamble on the future. There is a vast difference between recognizing the economic situation as it exists and acting accordingly, as contrasted with a blind following of a rigid spaced maturity policy in all kinds of economic weather.[26]

TAKING COGNIZANCE OF THE BUSINESS CYCLE

It is obviously not to be presumed that every bank director will become his own economist. Nevertheless, bank directors should be expected to be aware of what is happening in the economic world around them. Not only portfolio policy, but lending policy and liquidity considerations demand that the policy-maker be generally aware of the position of the economy in the business cycle.

The business cycle is no new phenomenon in American economic history; it has been the rule from the beginning. Much of our economic legislation, in fact, has been designed to temper the "boom and bust" pattern of the past but the cycle has not yet been eliminated entirely. Since World War II the nation has experienced a

---

[25] Lussey, *op. cit.*, p. 1. "A sound portfolio manager may not make any spectacular moves and may never 'sell at the top' or 'buy at the bottom.' However, he will take advantage of every important opportunity that is presented to improve earnings and he *will never make the big mistake* of being trapped in either an excessively short position when interest rates drop sharply or in a top-heavy long-term position when an 'unexpected' major rise in interest rates takes place."

[26] Daniel M. Kelley, "Bank Investment in a Dynamic Money Market," *Bankers Monthly,* November 1957, p. 24. An experienced investment officer puts it, "It is my conviction that the best interests of neither the bank's depositors nor stockholders are well served by flatly denying the patent reality of market opportunities as they occur."

series of periods of high level business activity followed by lulls or recessions.

These cycles are of great significance to portfolio policy exactly because the monetary and fiscal authorities are charged with the responsibility of alleviating or counteracting them. Since 1951 (the year of the Treasury-Federal Reserve accord) monetary policy has sought to restrain the expansion of credit when the resources of the country were fully employed and to expand credit when resources of plant and manpower were redundant. Monetary restraint limits the supply of funds in the market; monetary ease increases the supply just at those times when demand is already slack.

No two periods of high economic activity or of comparative recession have been (or are likely to be) exactly alike. However, in very brief summary, it can be said that each recent period of boom has been characterized by relatively high levels of employment, rising prices, a strong demand for bank credit, rising interest rates and, as a direct result of monetary restraint, the need for banks to borrow from the Federal Reserve banks in order to maintain their legal reserves.[27]

Periods of recession have been characterized by rising unemployment, relative price stability, a slackening in the demand for bank credit, falling interest rates, and the existence of excess bank reserves. It does not take much of an economist to recognize these signals in broad and general terms. Nor does it require an excess of perspicacity to avoid making long-term portfolio commitments when the economy is in a period of slack and the authorities are pursuing a policy of active ease, or to lengthen maturities when economic activity is at a high level and interest rates are rising.

The real danger is not that the portfolio manager will not recognize the state of the economic climate but that he *will* attempt to forecast or to rely on the forecasts so freely offered by the "experts." Then, in an attempt to hold out to the last basis point, he will probably miss the market entirely.[28]

If portfolio management will accept the fact that timely action

---

[27] Lyon, *op. cit.*, p. 154, suggests that a $200–300M level of either "net borrowed reserves" or of excess reserves is, perhaps, the best single indicator of the "restrictive" and "ease" phases of monetary policy.

[28] Lussey, *op. cit.,* p. 1, says that ". . . probing the future and shaping operations to conform with someone's guess as to what the future holds is hardly portfolio management."

is better than no action, that it cannot really expect to hit the "top of the market," if it will settle for intelligent decision making on the basis of known facts, it can still turn in a commendable performance.

Portfolio Switching. Portfolio policy need not wait until funds are available either as the result of new deposits or the maturity of portfolio assets. Indeed a primary task of portfolio management is to adjust maturities to current economic conditions whenever the opportunity to do so presents itself. If a bank has followed the pattern of investment policy suggested above, stayed short when money rates were low and lengthened out when money rates rose, it will be afforded opportunities to take important profits from the account when the market is high, or to improve yield and eventual profit by taking judicious losses when the market is low. The advantages of portfolio switching are greater for the bank with income subject to surtax, but even the small bank can take advantage of the changing pattern of rates to improve its long-range rate of income.

The switching of maturities and the taking of profits and losses to the best advantage is another technical aspect of portfolio management which must be left in great part to the experts in the field.[29] A few general principles, however, should be familar to those primarily responsible for policy.

In periods of high money rates and monetary restraint the price of securities will be below average levels. Many of the bonds in the portfolio of the average bank will then show market depreciation. This will be the time to extend maturities in anticipation of the next business recession. It will be advantageous, therefore, not only for the bank to reinvest the proceeds of maturing issues at the longer end of its portfolio but to "refund in advance" by selling the issues which will mature in the next year or two and reinvesting the proceeds of such sales in longer-term bonds as well. The losses thus incurred will be more than offset by the higher yields obtainable on the new purchases either in the form of higher coupons or, more importantly because of the tax advantage, by way of the discounts which will represent capital gains at or before maturity.

---

[29] *Cf.* Lussey, *op. cit.*, for an unusually clear discussion of these technicalities.

When securities are selling below average prices, a simple switch from a Government bond of a given maturity into one of comparable maturity will often assure the bank of a profit if it is in the 52 per cent tax bracket. It will not, however, accomplish the major portfolio objective of *lengthening maturities when taking losses* in order to put the portfolio in a position to benefit from the expected easing of rates at a later period. Examples of such switches are shown below. The "Simple Tax Operation" is a switch into comparable maturities solely to take advantage of the lower tax rate on capital gains. The "Combination Tax Operation" combines loss taking with maturity extension and increases income materially as well as guaranteeing a substantial gain to maturity.

TABLE 14

THE "SIMPLE" TAX OPERATION

SELL

Par	Issue	Assumed Book Value	12/31/59 Market Bid	Market Value	Loss	Net Income
$1,000 M	2½'s of 8–15–63	$1,000,000	91.16	$915,000	$85,000	$25,000
	Less 52% recoverable as a tax deduction				44,200	
		Net Loss to Bank			$40,800	
		Less 52% Federal Income Tax				13,000
		Net Income after taxes				$12,000

BUY

Par	Issue	12/31/59 Offer	Cost	Net Income
$985M	2⅝'s of 2–15–63	93	$916,050	$25,856
	Less 52% Federal Income Tax			13,445
	Net Income after taxes			$12,411

SUMMARY

Increase in annual income: $856 gross and $411 net.

Change in maturity is negligible and in the wrong direction.

Guaranteed future profit only $68,950 versus loss taken of $85,000.

The only worthwhile benefit is assurance of a net eventual capital gain of $51,712 versus a net loss of $40,800.

Source: Lussey, *op. cit.*, p. 3.

TABLE 15

THE "COMBINATION" TAX OPERATION

SELL

Par	Issue	Assumed Book Value	12/31/59 Bid	Market Value	Loss	Net Income
$1,000M	2½'s of 8/15/63	$1,000,000	91.16	$915,000	$85,000	$25,000
	Less 52% recoverable as a tax deduction				44,200	
			Net Loss to Bank		$40,800	
			Less 52% Federal Income Tax			13,000
			Net Income after taxes			$12,000

BUY

Par	Issue	12/31/59 Offer	Cost	Net Income
$ 400M	4⅞s of 11/15/63	99.30	$399,750	$19,500
605M	2½s of 6/15/67/62	85.10	516,140	15,125
$1,005M			$915,890	$34,625
		Less 52% Federal Income Tax		18,005
		Net Income after tax		$16,620

SUMMARY

Increase in annual income: $9,625 gross and $4,620 net.

Change in maturity is average lengthening of about 2½ years which is an important objective when taking losses.

Guaranteed future profit of $89,110 (plus probable important appreciation over par on the 4⅞s when money rates ease) versus a loss taken of only $85,000.

Thus there is ample justification for making this revision aside from the 27% tax differential between profit and loss of about $26,033—it accomplishes real banking objectives.

Source: Lussey, *op. cit.*, p. 5.

When the economy is clearly in a recession stage and interest rates are relatively low, bonds will be selling at prices above average levels. Portfolio holdings, especially if acquired at comparatively low prices during the previous period of high interest rates, will show market appreciation. This is the time when banks generally should keep their new investments short. The income which they must sacrifice to do so can be in large measure offset by taking profits in the longer bonds.

Taking profits always seems more desirable than absorbing losses but nothing can be more dangerous than merely taking profits and reinvesting in comparable (or longer) maturities. To do so is to leave the bank even more vulnerable than before to declines in prices which are bound to come, since these declines will affect booked profits rather than unbooked appreciation. The general rule therefore should be: *Never take profits without shortening maturities.* The reasons that should lead a bank to take profits (a conviction that the economy is close to the bottom of a recessionary period) are the same reasons that should convince it to shorten maturities in anticipation of a later rise in rates.

Profits (after taxes) taken in times of low money rates should not be looked upon as permanent additions to the bank's capital funds. They should be carried to reserves against future security losses where they will be available to absorb the losses when the next turn in interest rate levels provides new profit possibilities.

It should be kept in mind that a flexible portfolio policy that takes full advantage of the swings in the business cycle will result in fairly wide variations in portfolio income from year to year. If a bank stays short at times when money rates are low it must make a considerable sacrifice of income to do so. It may anticipate better yields and additional profits but they may not come on the books in time for the annual report to the stockholders. One must remember (and there is no reason not to explain to the stockholders) that sound portfolio management on a flexible basis must be judged by the combination of income and profit over the period of a full business cycle.

In those relatively few cases where income from portfolio assets is a major portion of current operating income, accounting methods may be devised which will carry a legitimate portion of portfolio profits to income.[30] One of these is the practice of "accumulating discount," *i.e.*, adding to earnings each year the proportionate share of the difference between a discount purchase price and par. Member banks are required by regulation of the Comptroller of the Currency to amortize premiums (the price paid above par). Accounting logic would seem to call for the accumulation of discount

---

[30] Lyon, *op. cit.*, p. 157, suggests a quite elaborate system of separating profits from real earnings and separately accounting for them when bonds are sold at a premium.

which is the other side of the same coin but banks have been reluctant to follow this practice for fear of endangering the tax advantage they have in treating this discount as a capital gain rather than income.

A compromise solution, permitted by the authorities, is to take accumulated discount into current earnings "above the line," and to credit it to reserves for taxes and bond losses "below the line." [31]

THE WRITTEN
PORTFOLIO POLICY STATEMENT

Having reviewed the factors and considerations which should enter into the formulation of a sound and flexible portfolio policy, and having examined the ways in which these factors may be applied to the implementation of such a policy, one comes full circle to where many writers on the subject start; the statement of the broad objectives and the policy limitations which will govern portfolio management. The policy-maker, however, needs to know what tools he has to work with before he can plan the broad outlines and the finer details of finished policy.

In the broadest sense the objectives of portfolio policy are the same for all banks: to obtain income, to maintain high quality in the portfolio, to keep the bank's capital funds fully employed, and to reduce tax liability to a practical minimum. It is useful, however, to state these objectives clearly in writing, preferably by resolution of the Board of Directors. It cannot be emphasized too often that policy becomes clear only when the people concerned in its formulation and execution have agreed on the exact words in which policy is framed.

The management and directors of each bank must put their own variety of flesh and blood on the bare bones of policy outlined in this discussion. What level or range of income? How high a degree of quality as a minimum or as a range? What relationship of capital to what kind of "risk assets"? These are questions which

---

[31] What is referred to here are the Reports of Income and Dividends required to be filed by all banks. Income and expense "above the line" affects net current earnings, while "below the line" adjustments determine final net profits. *Cf.* Comptroller of the Currency, *Digest of Opinions*, Par. 620.

the policy-maker needs to grapple with and solve for each individual bank. The making and recording of such decisions is the essence of portfolio planning. The broad objectives and the narrower, specific limitations will serve as guiding stars in navigating the often perilous waters of the marketplace.

XIII

PERSONNEL POLICIES

The emphasis of previous chapters has been on the management of bank assets through the formulation and implementation of constructive policies. The present chapter invades a field which lies outside the usual concepts of banking theory but is nonetheless vital to successful bank operations. It is trite, but true, to say that people are the most important asset any organization has; and probably the most difficult to manage. Perhaps this is because the managers themselves are subject to all the vagaries and instabilities of human nature.

What follows is far from a complete treatise on personnel management. That is a field in its own right and its literature is extensive indeed. All that will be attempted here is a brief summary of personal observations on personnel policy at work in commercial banks, with special emphasis on the deficiencies most frequently found in actual banking situations.

Personnel administration, like other policy matters, should be directed to well-defined objectives and guided by clearly understood principles. Those responsible for policy should at least know of the various tools and organizational arrangements available to implement policy. The bank director need not be a personnel expert, but he should be acutely aware of the fact that the human relationships which in the aggregate produce a high level of morale seldom simply take care of themselves. They require direction, encouragement, and understanding. To see that these are provided is the role of the policy-maker.

MANAGEMENT OBJECTIVES

The primary objective of personnel policy is to get jobs done effectively, economically, and with as little friction as possible. In commercial banks, the job, broadly speaking, is to render banking services to the community and to manage the bank's assets in the best interests of the stockholders. To accomplish these objectives a number of people, at different levels of skill and talent, must work together under effective leadership.

One should never lose sight of the fact that people are the instruments, not the objects of policy. Desired results—the long-range objectives of policy—are produced through people, not upon them. In other words, the aim of personnel policy is not to make people happy (or anything else) but to get the job accomplished by getting people to "do what you want, the way you want, because *they* want to do it." [1] Job satisfaction is a fine thing for the individual, but, from management's viewpoint, it is only a means to an end: the most effective performance of the bank as a whole.

A second and closely related objective is to develop better ways of performing banking operations and to devise new and better services to render to the community. To accomplish this aim, the inventiveness and imagination of people must be stimulated. Personnel policies, therefore, should encourage rather than stifle initiative.

A third major objective is to train and develop successor management, a task which many small banks have woefully neglected and which even large banks find difficult to accomplish.

To bring these broad and generally recognized aims to fruition requires an awareness of some fundamental principles of personnel management, an organization to apply them effectively, and a knowledge of some of the tools or instruments which will help attain the desired goals.

---

[1] The stated objective of "Job Relations Training," Training Within Industry Division, War Manpower Commission, 1941.

MANAGEMENT PRINCIPLES

A few basic concepts underlie effective personnel administration. The leader in banking, as elsewhere, follows them almost intuitively. It will be useful, nevertheless, to make them explicit—to understand how and why they are effective.

The first of these principles is the need to provide a clear definition of duties and responsibilities throughout the organization. Such definition, in effect, constitutes the organizational structure of the bank itself (Chapter III). Each officer's responsibilities should be clearly defined. Even the lowliest clerk is entitled to know as exactly as possible what is expected of him. Job description and job evaluation are the tools which put this principle into operation.

Somewhat more elusive is the principle of good communications. The willingness, the ability, in fact the determination to maintain mutual understanding throughout the organization is a basic prerequisite of success. Failure to communicate adequately and the inability of officers to issue clear, concise instructions defining objectives in ways that all can understand probably lead to more wasted effort and individual frustration than any other factor in bank operations. The lack of adequate channels of communication upward can stifle initiative, keep new ideas long buried, and produce pressures of discontent that are completely destructive of morale.

A third general principle involves the quality of leadership itself. In judging and selecting people for promotion, the man himself is more important than his knowledge or skill. The ability to inspire others to do their best is the essential talent of management at all levels. It is a function of the true leader's whole personality, often characterized by an objective awareness of his own limitations coupled with a compassionate knowledge of the strengths and weaknesses of others.

The need to find this talent in top management underlies the modern emphasis on a broad and, at least partly, nontechnical training for executives: the growing insistence on a liberal arts education. It is not by accident that the most successful bankers have so often been men with a broad grasp of history, an acute awareness of their community responsibilities, and diversified interests in the fields of art, politics, or community planning. They are men who have a philosophy of banking as well as the necessary technical knowledge. Often they have been men who came into banking from other fields to out-perform men who had spent all their lives in banks. By bringing imagination and a broad approach to banking problems, the nontechnical outsider can sometimes strip away the moss of routine and custom to uncover new and vital possibilities.

PERSONNEL ORGANIZATION

The organizational structure needed to put these principles into effective operation starts with the Board of Directors. It is customary in banks of all sizes for the directors to appoint or approve the appointment of officers and to establish levels of compensation for both officers and employees. Directors also authorize pension plans, bonuses, and other so-called "fringe" benefits. Too often, regrettably, directors do not follow personnel administration closely enough. They make little formal effort to satisfy themselves that sound and effective personnel programs are being carried out if, indeed, they are even aware of such policies as may exist. It was for this reason that the designation of a directors' personnel committee was urged in Chapter III. At least a few specially interested directors should be aware of the ways in which the bank's policies are being implemented, and of the progress being made in developing future officer potential. It is the directors' task to state the aims of personnel policy, and it is their obligation to raise serious questions if sound policies are not being followed and progressive programs are not being utilized to full advantage.

The responsibility for the execution of policy rests with the bank's executive officers. It is the duty of the chief executive officer to keep the board informed and interested on the one hand, and to set the example of effective leadership on the other. The "boss" sets the pattern, good or bad. No matter how great his talents as a credit analyst or a new business getter, the bank's operations will suffer if the chief executive officer cannot provide effective, sympathetic, and dynamic leadership to his entire staff.

In larger banks the executive officer will have the assistance of a Personnel Officer and his staff. Many of the day-to-day responsibilities of policy execution and record-keeping can be readily delegated to staff officers. But true leadership can never be delegated. It can be inspired in others and thereby passed on down through the ranks of the largest organization, but it is always personal. It is a matter of spirit rather than program or policy and, as such, permeates every echelon of a well-run organization.

Effective leadership, of course, will seek the widest practical participation of others in formulating and carrying out constructive policies and practices. Delegation of authority, the effective use of committees, and the assignment of responsibility for directing and evaluating the work of others will be parts of an effective personnel administration.

THE TOOLS OF PERSONNEL MANAGEMENT

To the professional personnel officer there will be little that is new in this discussion of the techniques of personnel administration. The ideas expressed here are widely current in progressive banks and other industries; have been discussed in hundreds of articles in personnel journals; and are stressed in all of the various banking schools. Nevertheless, they are still too seldom found in actual use, particularly in the small and medium-sized banks which have not developed a professional approach to personnel problems.

It is the junior officer who goes to school but it is the policy-maker who needs to know at least enough to encourage, if not insist upon, the application of this knowledge. Repeatedly, in lecturing to bank officers, one is told, "All that you say is true, but you should tell it to my directors."

It does not require a professional personnel officer to put most of the proven tools of sound personnel administration into effect. It does require policy-makers to recognize that people are a vital ingredient of a smoothly-functioning organization. It is from that viewpoint that the remainder of this chapter considers some of the basic instruments of personnel administration.

Recruiting

Policy begins when a bank first selects its employees. The standards set at that time will largely determine the caliber of the staff in the future. Bankers have too frequently said, "We cannot afford to compete for the best people in the community." If banks are to be successful, they cannot afford to do less.

Recently the president of a sizeable bank related his difficulty in bringing potential officers into the bank. He had urged the recruitment of several young college graduates at competitive salaries. The most influential director, a substantial stockholder and owner of a local manufacturing business, adamantly took the position that, "We can hire plenty of good young boys at the mill for $1.75 an hour."

This director, like many others, is unaware of the first rule of good recruiting, *i.e.*, to know what one is hiring the person for. There is obviously no point in hiring mathematical geniuses to be tellers and bookkeepers when one is simply looking for reasonably intelligent and personable people who will be content to work, for a while at least, in routine positions. On the other hand, if there is a known need for officer replacement in five or ten, or even twenty years, it behooves management to look for prospective employees who, at the outset are believed to have officer potential because of their education, aptitude, interest, or previous experience. At every level, from bookkeepers to officer candidate, it is important to take the time to select the best prospects available. A poor selection is always a waste of time and money.

The most desirable people rarely come to the bank of their own accord. Successful banks seek out the more talented employees. For clerical personnel, they maintain close relationships with guidance directors of local high schools; they encourage employees to bring in their friends; they see to it that school children have opportunities to visit the bank and hear about some of the advantages of working there. In recruiting for more responsible posts they carefully adjudge the bank examiners who visit them; they follow the college careers of local boys who are interested in banking or finance and employ them for summer work whether they need them or not. Good recruiting requires a policy of actively seeking the people with the specific qualities which the bank needs without counting the cost too closely. It is difficult to pay too much for quality personnel.

TRAINING

The newly hired employee generally starts as a "clean slate" on which nothing has yet been written. His attitudes toward the bank and the job will be shaped by his first few weeks of experience.

How quickly will he be made to feel a part of the organization? In the process of learning the first few simple tasks, will the new employee get some grasp of the relationship between what he is doing and the work of the department or the bank as a whole? "Orientation" is the name that personnel people give to the fundamental need to give new employees a broader idea of their jobs.

Many bankers complain that the young people they hire seem not to be interested in learning about banking; and they probably won't be unless an opportunity to learn is provided for them; unless someone is eager, in fact, to instruct them. A few will insist on learning, but most need patient teaching. It occurs too frequently that the person who is selected to train new employees is a person whom the bank plans or expects to replace, perhaps a girl who is leaving to get married and is no longer interested in the bank. Too often it is a junior clerk who isn't very sure himself about the job to which he has been assigned. Good training is an art, if not a science, and should be entrusted only to those within an organization who have an aptitude for it or who have received special training in instructing others.

Nor should training cease just because a person has learned a job, no matter how well. Whether it be a clerical position or an assignment of considerable responsibility, training should be a continuing process. The most valuable people in banks are those who can take over any one of a number of tasks or responsibilities and do them well. The author has frequently asked groups of bank officers which they would consider the more valuable, tellers or bookkeepers. Ninety per cent will answer "tellers." This appears to be an established hierarchy in banking. Traditionally, bank clerks start in the bookkeeping department and graduate to the tellers' line. However, a good case can be made for the bookkeeper's task as the more exacting and one which involves the greater responsibility. The question is designed, not to prove that point, but to bring out the fact to which all will eventually agree, that the person who can and is willing to serve as either, as the occasion demands, is twice as valuable as the person who can or is willing to act in only one capacity.

Unfortunately it frequently occurs in banks that the better a person knows and does one job the less is the likelihood he will have an opportunity to learn another. After a time he becomes either routinized and incapable of change, or will have long since left to seek change (and new knowledge) which was not offered him. Training in new areas of work is a challenge to the individual and provides a flexibility of staff that is an essential ingredient of an efficient organization. Belief in this principle, which can be readily demonstrated in practice, calls for job rotation and continued training. The smaller of the two very profitable banks referred to in Chapter V, with aggregate salary costs of less than 15 per cent of gross income, has just such a program of rotational training. Each clerk is taught every job in the bank within the first eighteen months of his (or mostly her) employment and all are regularly rotated so that they spend no more than three weeks in any one particular assignment. Knowledge and usefulness are thus enhanced, boredom is reduced, and the result is a job better done with fewer people at substantially less cost in the long run.

JOB DESCRIPTION AND EVALUATION

Job description and job evaluation are standard concepts of personnel administration. They are widely used by large banks and can be adapted to even the smallest.[2] A detailed written description of each job serves as a basis for what is expected of each person in his particular capacity. The evaluation of that position in relation to other jobs in the bank assures each individual of fair and comparable treatment. The job descriptions and the evaluations thereof are most likely to be accepted and effective if they are participated in by the people involved. A job evaluation committee on which responsible employees serve in rotation will not only assure acceptance of the program but provide valuable management training to the participants as well. A constant review of position descriptions and their evaluation will assure flexibility and prompt adjustment to changing circumstances.

Care should be taken that a job evaluation program does not result in unnecessary rigidities. Few such programs, for example, give adequate credit for the ability of an individual to perform more than one task when called upon to do so. A job description

---

[2] American Bankers Association, Country Bank Operations Committee, *How to Set Up a Salary Program in the Smaller Bank,* New York, 1950.

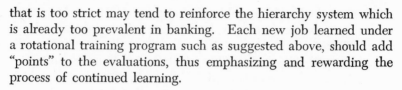

that is too strict may tend to reinforce the hierarchy system which is already too prevalent in banking. Each new job learned under a rotational training program such as suggested above, should add "points" to the evaluations, thus emphasizing and rewarding the process of continued learning.

PERFORMANCE REVIEW

The primary value of a job description and evaluation, however, is to serve as the basis for a review of the individual's performance in the job. Each employee must have a clear understanding of what is expected of him if an appraisal of his performance is to have any validity. To work in a bank or any other organization and not have one's work periodically evaluated and one's progress made a matter of record, is like playing a game without keeping the score. This obvious fact, attested to by all who have worked intelligently in the field of personnel administration, is nevertheless frequently neglected in daily banking practice. It is neglected because other things seem more important at the moment; because no one really likes to point out other people's shortcomings; it is neglected, in short, because it is not made a matter of definite policy. Too few bank officers even take the time to point out the good points of their assistants' perfomance! Yet nothing will do more to strengthen an organization or to improve the performance of the people in it than a periodic full and frank discussion of objectives and accomplishments with respect to each individual in each and every job.

To be effective, performance review must start at the top, with the chief executive officer setting the example by periodically reviewing the performance of the other officers with them. Only then can top management expect that the junior officers will do the same with the department heads, and that the latter will conscientiously review the performance of the employees working under their direction.

The program needs to be a fairly formal one. Appraisals should be written on standard forms or along standardized patterns. Off-the-cuff evaluations are generally carelessly phrased and frequently evoke emotional responses which tend to defeat the purposes of a careful and objective appraisal. Both the appraisal and its discussion with the individual should be made a matter of record and each employee who is not satisfied with his appraisal should have easy and regular access to a higher authority for further review. The objective in all such procedures is to help the individual employee help himself.

SALARY ADMINISTRATION

The principal elements of a well-considered salary policy are, first, the relationship of the bank's salary scale to salaries paid for comparable jobs in the community and, second, the relationship of the salary paid to one person to that paid to others for jobs of comparable difficulty within the bank. Both elements are affected by the fact (often lost sight of) that salaries, in the long run, are set in a competitive market for talent. The bank that consistently pays its people less than the competitive market rate will end up with a lower caliber of officers and employees at every level of responsibility.

Compensation, of course, encompasses more than salary. Working conditions, job security, prestige, and opportunity for advancement all enter into the competitive package. Many fine employees stay in banks despite the opportunity of earning higher wages elsewhere because of shorter hours, better working conditions, or simply because the job is interesting. However, banks cannot rely too blindly or heavily on these or other "fringe benefits." The only sure test of the adequacy of a bank's scale of compensation is the caliber of officers and employees it keeps. The objective of salary policy is to insure that, at whatever cost, the bank maintains a competent and enthusiastic staff.

It has been repeatedly demonstrated by those who pursue such a policy that competent people at almost any price are less costly in the long run than the incompetent (or even the mediocre), because they produce more. It is just that simple. Much as a harassed bank supervisor may need two hands to get a job done, he will waste the bank's time and money unless a "head" comes with the hands. In short, the ancient maxim that one gets pretty much what one pays for applies aptly to the policy decisions regarding a bank's salary scale. The converse applies just as aptly to salary decisions within the bank. One should pay for what he has! This means simply that a bank should pay well for merit, withhold increases in the case of mediocrity, and dispose as quickly as practical of those who do not measure up to standard. Even within the framework of a job evaluation plan, salary should be related to performance—not to length of service nor to what someone else may earn.

Logical and simple as this may sound, salary administration of this variety is too seldom found. Some sort of paralysis seems to grip management at the thought of giving an unusually large increase to a truly outstanding employee and a comparable fear makes management reluctant to "pass by" the well-meaning but inept. The result is likely to be a program of regular increments which makes too little distinction between the star performer and the hack. Carried on long enough, such a policy results in a preponderance of hacks, and higher aggregate costs for salaries of too large a number of low-paid and inefficient people. The star performer, meanwhile, will have attained his proper level by finding a job in another bank.

In general, banks provide greater "fringe benefits" than do most other industries. Except for the smallest banks, pension plans, hospitalization, and group life insurance are the rule. These plans effectively contribute to the "security" of bank employees and, as pointed out in Chapter VI, serve to an appreciable extent to reduce the temptation to "borrow" illegally. Many banks, in addition, pay cash bonuses of a flat percentage of salary. This is a somewhat self-deluding process whereby bank directors manage to compensate their officers and employees more adequately without taking the "desperate" step of increasing their salaries. In theory the bonus can be discontinued should the bank's earnings decline. In practice the employee measures his total compensation, including bonus and fringe benefits, against what he might earn elsewhere. The discontinuance of a bonus has no less depressing an effect than a general cut in salaries.

A more effective incentive is a well-designed profit-sharing plan with benefits that vary from year to year in direct proportion to the financial success of the bank's operations. Given adequate salaries for clerical personnel, profit-sharing is probably most effective if the participants are limited to those persons in positions of supervisory responsibility who make a true management contribution to the bank's success.

Stock options have from time to time been advocated for banks. They are legal in only a few states but not for national banks. Aside from general questioning of the equity and ethics of stock options in any company, some bankers, and most bank supervisors, believe that they would lead to a "swapping" of loans for the purpose of exercising the options and, as a consequence, would bring back some of the evils attendant upon unregulated borrowing of bank officers, from their own and other banks, to which the Banking Act of 1933 put an end.[3]

COMMUNICATIONS

A good deal of verbal interchange takes place in every bank each day but all of it is not necessarily effective communication. Orders are given and requests made which are not clearly understood because the person giving them does not take the small amount of extra time to find out if he has made himself clear, or whether the person to whom a task has been assigned understands the objectives being sought. Misunderstanding, resulting from faulty communication, is without doubt one of the major sources of wasted time and effort in banks.

Communication is a two-way street. The competent officer *discusses* rather than directs; he *listens* in addition to instructing. The importance of this basic concept can perhaps best be illustrated by the true story of a bank president who had been listening to a discussion of communications. He suddenly got the point and exclaimed, "You know, I've been in this business for thirty years, and I have just realized that every time I call my cashier into my office I say 'Joe, do this,' 'Joe, this is what I want,' and then I wonder why the stupid dolt doesn't have any initiative."

It cannot be too often stressed that teamwork—the essential ingredient of success in banking as in any other business—depends on mutual understanding; on letting people know what the bank's

---

[3] Board of Governors, Regulation O (12 C.F.R. 215), Loans to Executive Officers of Member Banks (amended to July 1, 1939).

objectives are and in seeking and listening to their suggestions. Good communication starts with the written policies adopted by the directors and should run all the way down the line in the form of clear and understandable instructions related to known and agreed-upon objectives.

The major portion of the communications necessary to accomplish the day-to-day operations of a bank consists of simple man-to-man conversations. More complex ideas, however, gain clarity if they are reduced to writing. The ability to write clearly, as well as speak succinctly, is an invaluable management talent in need of constant practice and development.

One of the most effective of all communications media is the staff meeting. Essentially it is an extension of the conversational or discussion technique embracing a larger segment of the organization. Such meetings are regular features of efficiently operated banks and take a wide variety of forms, ranging from daily or weekly officers' meetings to annual week-end conferences. The size of the bank and the number of people involved, of course, tend to shape the specific program. In very small banks the entire day's operations are virtually a continuous staff meeting. It is the need to maintain the same kind of group effort that makes a more formal program essential for larger organizations.

Many large banks have employees' handbooks and publish "house organs" which aim to keep employees informed of the bank's (and fellow employees') activities. These are only a few among the wide variety of communications media available.

EXECUTIVE TRAINING AND DEVELOPMENT

The shortage of successor management in banks, particularly the smaller ones, has been pointed out over and over again in hundreds of speeches, articles, and pamphlets.[4] At least a dozen banking

---

[4] A 1956 study of Indiana banks found that within a fifteen year period new officers equal in number to 87.4 per cent of present officers would be necessary as replacements and to provide for the expected expansion of banking facilities. This finding is probably typical of the entire country.

Harry C. Sauvain and J. B. Black, Jr., "Future Officer Requirements of Indiana Banks," *Business Information Bulletin No. 26*, Bureau of Business Research, School of Business, Indiana University, 1956.

schools throughout the country are attempting to remedy the situation through banker education, but the problem still exists.[5]

It is a problem not only of replacing present bank officers and of increasing the number of officers to staff a growing banking system, but of improving the quality of all bank officers as well. Banking itself is becoming increasingly complex. New forms of lending, the changing banking structure, electronic data-processing, national and international problems unknown to the "country banker" of yesterday, all require a higher degree of talent and knowledge than the simple "common sense" which largely sufficed in the past.

In the light of all the available literature on this vital subject, it can only be suggested here that perhaps too much emphasis has been placed on training and too little on development. Training may increase the knowledge and skills of an individual but it seldom turns him into a true executive: a person with high qualities of leadership, constructive imagination, and a desire to assume responsibility. An executive is one who can make effective decisions and get tasks accomplished through the organized efforts of others. Training can improve management techniques; it can help people make better decisions, but training alone will seldom result in a person *wanting* to make decisions.

Development, on the other hand, has a different connotation; it is involved with the inner man and his growth. Some understanding of the nature of this growth, and a conscientious effort to foster it in each individual, are necessary if the tremendous amount of training to which well-meaning bank directors have subjected their junior officers is to be productive. The bank director interested in this problem and, especially, the senior officer seeking to develop his successor, need to know something of psychology as well as the techniques of banking.

The late Karen Horney, one of the more imaginative of modern psychologists, believed that "inherent in man are evolutionary constructive forces which urge him to realize his given potentialities." Horney called this the "struggle toward self-realization" of which she said:

---

[5] The American Bankers Association has developed an excellent manual on the subject. American Bankers Association, *Executive Development in Banking* (New York, 1955).

Man by his very nature and of his own accord strives toward self-realization, and his set of values evolves from such striving. Apparently he cannot, for example, develop his full human potentialities unless he is truthful to himself; unless he relates himself to others in the spirit of mutuality. Apparently he cannot grow if he indulges in a 'dark idolatry of self' (Shelley) and consistently attributes all his own shortcomings to the deficiencies of others. He can grow, in the true sense, only if he assumes responsibility for himself.[6]

The same essential concept is presented by an industrial psychologist and personnel officer in the following terms:

First, we believe that we must have a basic philosophy of personal improvement, a philosophy which says, by developing the people who comprise our organization we develop our organization. Secondly, we believe that all development is *man* development. That is, each man submits a separate and unique development problem. Three, we believe that development or growth must come from within each individual, that he must want to change and, of course, change or develop purposefully. Four, we believe that each man's boss creates a climate which either fosters or hampers personal development. Finally, we believe that action is the thing, not specifically placement charts, not lists of promising young men, not detailed psychological procedures. By action, we mean developmental action and planning with each individual concerned.[7]

What both these statements mean is that bank directors and senior officers seeking to develop successor management cannot rely on banking schools and other training devices alone. At the best they can only provide opportunity and encouragement to the individual; opportunity to use and develop his talents, and encouragement to assume responsibility for himself. In its most effective form the kind of counselling between senior and junior that is required to encourage growth results in what is essentially a parental relationship in which the senior takes personal pride in the accomplishments of the junior.[8]

---

[6] Karen Horney, *Neurosis and Human Growth* (New York: W. W. Norton and Company, 1955).

[7] Joseph Trickett, *Journal of American Society of Training Directors*, Vol. 12, No. 8, August 1958.

[8] The time required to train an assistant bank examiner in the Federal Reserve Bank of New York was effectively halved when each new trainee was assigned to a senior examiner who was made personally responsible for his training. No examiner wanted "his boy" to progress any less rapidly than some one else's trainee.

The directors of a bank have a duty to see to it that the climate of the bank is favorable for the growth and development of potential executives. They can insist, for example, that junior officers occasionally attend board meetings or make reports to the directors. They can insist on being apprised regularly of the progress of the bank's executive development program. In smaller banks they can personally explore the minds and talents of the junior officers and lend encouragement to their assumption of responsibility. At the very least they can assure themselves that senior management is not arrogating all decision-making to itself and thus effectively stifling the exercise of initiative.

XIV

COMMUNITY RELATIONS

In recent years banks have been almost excessively self-conscious about their public image. Public relations has become a veritable fetish. Few banks of any size are without their public relations officers or membership in the Financial Public Relations Association. Speeches and magazine articles by the score and specialized banking schools have drummed into bankers' consciousness the necessity of putting their best foot forward to redeem a reputation supposedly besmirched by past bank failures and a tradition of glassy-eyed hard-heartedness that was always more "amusing" than true.

The result has been a feverish and sometimes misguided effort in the field of public relations. There has been, perhaps, too much emphasis on promotional activities and too little attention paid to the fundamental purposes of a bank or to the appropriate means of accomplishing such purposes in the community. The latter is community relations, a warmer and more neighborly concept than the "sales" approach of many public relations programs. It is the aim of this chapter to sketch in briefly some of the basic concepts of a sound and constructive approach to this important area of bank policy.

BASIC CONSIDERATIONS

The relationship between a bank and the community it serves is a vital and dynamic one. It is concerned with the needs of the community for banking services and the ability and willingness of

276

the bank to supply them. A bank is an integral part of the community's economic life, and in this respect it functions either poorly or well. The object of a bank's community relations, therefore, is not directly sales and promotion but the effective functioning of the bank as a vital organ in the community's economic life and growth.

In this conception, community relations is not specifically a program, although a bank may have need for a program for making its community relations meaningful. "Service," even with a smile, is a superficial word for what banks provide: they offer the means of satisfying human wants and business needs to the extent that constructive credit and banking safety can supply them. Service is the way a bank sells, not what it sells.

The key to a bank's community relations, therefore, lies in the manner in which it plays its role of financial leadership; how it fulfills its responsibilities as the holder of the community's liquid resources and the supplier of its essential credit needs. In this sense, all that has gone before, liquidity, capital adequacy, and sound lending and investing policies, are the first requisite of a community relations program. And, in truth, no amount of high-pressure advertising or promotion will long disguise a bank's failure to make the loans or to supply the other banking services its community requires. Dissatisfied customers, if they have the choice, will simply go elsewhere.

This, however, is not the whole story. Unprogressive banks can actually retard the growth of their communities just as a weak heart will curtail the activities of the human body. Progressive banks, on the other hand, can stimulate growth and, at the same time, spur their own progress and augment their long-range profits. The over-all objective of a bank's community relations program should be the growth of the community itself. A bank's fundamental contribution to this growth is productive credit. Beyond this lies the opportunity to advance community welfare through a wider range of activities, including economic education and direct participation in community affairs, as well as promotion of the bank's services. All these together constitute a full-scale community relations program.

KNOWLEDGE OF THE COMMUNITY

To contribute effectively to its community a bank must know its customers, their needs, and prospects. This seems to be such an obvious truism that one may well wonder why it needs to be mentioned. But it is only in comparatively recent years that a few banks have systematically attempted to find out something about the people they serve and, in the process, learned how little they previously knew.

Bank officers and directors, of course, have always known a great deal about their communities. If the directors are representative business and professional people they will be in close touch with the community's economic, political, and social life. Daily contacts with the bank's customers, in themselves, can yield a fruitful harvest of knowledge if those relationships are sympathetic and designed to serve the customer. Nevertheless, a more formal and systematic program of market research will develop facts about present customers and potential market opportunities of which many banks are only partially aware.

The American Bankers Association has recently undertaken the preparation of a series of booklets on the technical aspects of market research. The first of these, "Customer Analysis," sets forth the following objectives of a market research program: [1]

> This first phase (customer analysis) involving the analysis of internal records, will place management in a position to take succeeding steps toward the full utilization of market research.
>
> When an internal research program is coupled with an economic analysis of the trade area, management can chart the future of the bank, thus avoiding the nonproductive effort which often results when operations are on a day-to-day basis.
>
> To supplement the facts gathered from internal records and trade area analysis, the bank can study the attitudes of its customers and then plan the most effective advertising, customer and community relations program.

While there is not space here to discuss the techniques of market research, the kind of information a progressive bank needs to have

---

[1] American Bankers Association, Country Bank Operations Committee and Research Committee, *Customer Analysis,* ABA Market Research Series Number One, New York, 1961.

may be indicated by some of the questions market research can answer:

Who uses the bank's various services? What is their age, sex, and economic status?

To what extent do large or small accounts dominate the bank's business?

From which geographical, ethnic, or occupational segments of the bank's trade area do its customers come? Are there sections or groups which are not presently making use of the bank's facilities?

What are the community's land resources? How are they zoned? Are there prospects for greater utilization?

What is the volume and composition of the labor force? To what extent is it fully employed?

Who are the suppliers of competing services? How has the bank been faring in competition with them?

How do the bank's customers evaluate its services? What are *their* reasons for using them?

This list of questions, of course, is only a sample. But they are questions which any intelligent new director might ask. Relatively few banks, however, could supply accurate or definitive answers. The value of being able to answer questions of this kind seems self-evident. Only such knowledge can provide an effective guide to a productive community relations program.

Market research, incidentally, is a tool that can be used just as effectively by small banks as by larger ones. In some respects, the smaller the trade area served the easier it is to know it well. Market research can also be a vital factor in helping smaller banks to do a more efficient job of community relations and, in the process, become larger.[2]

EDUCATIONAL ASPECTS
OF COMMUNITY RELATIONS

An important part of a bank's community relations is educational in nature. The community looks to the bank for financial guidance of all kinds and it is the bank's responsibility to make certain that the community understands the role of money and banking in the

---

[2] Thomas O. Cooper, President, Jefferson State Bank, Jefferson, Iowa (Resources $7 million) stated: "If we had all of the business of our present customers we would be twice our present size." "Guinea Pig Bank Tests Customer Research Program," *Burroughs Clearing House,* February 1961, p. 122.

economy. The nation's battle against inflation and its striving for sound economic growth can be successful only if bankers are in the forefront of a continuing educational campaign. Banks have a vested interest in sound money and a growing and prosperous economy. Inflation steals away the value of their customers' savings as quickly as does unsound lending, and the sharp decline of inflated values has been the principal cause of bank losses and bank failures in the past.

Once a bank consciously assumes the role of financial and economic leadership in its community, many avenues of activity immediately open up. First among these is the necessity of seeing that the bank's own officers are well-informed. Does the bank subscribe to a variety of banking periodicals, economic analyses, important market letters—and are they read? Here, perhaps, is grist for the staff meeting. Herein lies justification for a rather wide attendance at bankers' schools, meetings, and conventions followed by reports to the board or the staff on what was learned or discussed. Education, like charity, begins at home.

Much of a bank's educational effort will take place naturally across the officers' desks or in the midst of social or business contacts away from the bank. At cocktail parties, for example, bankers are invariably a target for quizzes about current financial headlines. And the banker who takes his community relations seriously will be prepared to answer such questions intelligently.

More formal educational programs range from showing the bank to school children to adult business forums where selected customers are invited to listen to experts in various fields of business, investment, or finance. A number of banks have established "speakers bureaus" consisting of their own officers and senior personnel who are willing and able to discuss the banking activities with which they are most familiar at service clubs and meetings of other interested groups. The community's demand for this kind of educational endeavor is virtually insatiable and, in meeting this need, banks often discover unsuspected talents in their own officers and employees.

The range of possibilities for educational activities is restricted only by the imagination of the bank's officers and directors. What is essential is that a bank recognize clearly its opportunities in this field.

PARTICIPATION IN COMMUNITY ACTIVITIES

Another phase of a bank's community relations is the degree to which its officers and directors participate in and foster community activities. The encouragement of such participation should be an explicit matter of policy. In general, banks have a good record in this regard. Progressive banks not only pay their officers' membership dues in service clubs and the chamber of commerce, but provide the time for active participation in charitable drives and other civic efforts. It goes almost without saying that a person who works in a bank will be asked to serve as treasurer of whatever organization he is active in. The bank should at least inventory and give formal recognition and encouragement to this important kind of community relations. An annual report of all such participations to the Board of Directors and the circulation of the report to officers and employees is a simple means of accomplishing this recognition.

Outstanding bankers are frequently found in the forefront of the more significant community efforts. Many of them have taken leading parts in community redevelopment, urban renewal, campaigns for better farm management; whatever activity will lead to the fullest possible use of the community's resources. Directorships with important local industries, as well as civic organizations, offer opportunities for putting the banker's specialized financial knowledge to work for the healthy growth of the community. Hundreds of examples of this kind of civic leadership could be cited. Unfortunately, there are still too many banks—and particularly the smaller ones—to which such a concept would be foreign.

Directors as well as officers can play an important role in this phase of community relations; in small banks theirs will be the major role. In fact, in choosing new directors, the community-mindedness of prospective candidates should be a key factor of selection.

Where facilities are available or can be built into new construction, banks often provide meeting rooms for civic and social groups. This, too, is a form of community participation. In the same general category is the provision of space in the bank's lobby for displays of local products or the wares of merchants. Exhibitions of the work of local artists or the collections of hobbyists can partake of both education and community activity. The specific programs which may be developed are varied indeed. They will constitute sound community relations if their guiding principle is the concept of meaningful participation in the economic and educational life of the community.

PROMOTIONAL ACTIVITIES

A third major aspect of community relations may be called "promotional." It deals with formulating and putting into effect specific programs and engaging in definite activities designed to enlarge the individual bank's share of its market.[3] It is important that a bank's promotional activities be based on the sound and basic precepts of community relations discussed above, but the fact that each bank competes with other banks and other financial institutions cannot be lost sight of. The promotional aspect of a community relations program will encompass most of the area of direct competition with other institutions for a share of the banking business and the profits which may be derived therefrom. In the competitive world it is not enough to be a good fellow; one must aggressively seek business. Promotional activities include, among other things, the bank's advertising, its program of customer calls, and its training of employees in the customer relations aspects of their jobs.

ADVERTISING

Commercial banks spend relatively less on advertising than mutual savings banks and savings and loan associations, their main competitors for "deposits." It seems strange that the mutual institutions, without the spur of the profit motive, should outdo commercial banks in this major area of promotional activity. Perhaps commercial bank directors have been penny wise and pound foolish in their approach to advertising, falsely feeling themselves secure in a comparative monopoly of banking services which, in recent years, the mutuals have so aggressively challenged.

The amount of money spent, however, is less important than the

---

[3] For a valuable handbook on public relations principles and techniques, see Robert Lindquist, *The Bank and Its Publics* (New York: Harper and Brothers, 1956).

effectiveness of the advertising for which it is expended. Bank directors would do well to give at least as much consideration to the impact of a bank's advertising on the public as to its impact on the budget. Even for the smaller bank which may not be able to afford professional assistance, a good deal of sound guidance is readily available. There is ample literature on productive advertising techniques, and various bankers associations have prepared effective material in the form of advertising "kits" for banks which want to use it. Despite this, however, too large a proportion of bank advertising is still purely institutional in nature, or lacks imagination or motivational content.

Bank directors are not likely to be advertising experts and they should not hesitate to call in the best professional talent available. Directors are, however, human beings and should be able to judge the effectiveness of the bank's major advertising efforts on no more complicated a basis than that of putting themselves in the place of the prospective audience and asking themselves what impact the bank's advertising would have upon them. If they did so, thousands of dollars now spent on such nonproductive aims as reminding the public that the First National Bank was established in 1898, and that it accepts deposits, would be put to more effective use.

At the beginning of this chapter it was stated that community relations is primarily a question of relating the community's needs for banking services to the ability and willingness of a bank to supply them. This simple statement is an excellent guide to advertising policy. The most effective advertising copy, whatever its form, will be that which clearly relates a potential customer's needs or desires to specific services which a bank is able and anxious to provide. Backed up by the bank's generous participation in community affairs and its patient educational efforts, productive advertising will meaningfully stress the bank's sincere desire to fill legitimate banking needs.[4]

It is important, therefore, at the policy-making level, to determine not only how much the bank will spend for advertising (and perhaps to spend more) but to evaluate and constantly reevaluate the effectiveness of the bank's program in terms of community relations.

---

[4] For example, the effective advertising of a large New York City bank stresses that, whatever your banking problem, "You have a *friend* at Chase-Manhattan."

DIRECT CUSTOMER SOLICITATION

Advertising is aimed at a wide-spread and largely unseen audience. By contrast, conversations with actual and potential customers can be brought to focus directly on specific objectives and, for obtaining particularized goals, can be far more effective. Nothing illustrates this better than the experience of a relatively small bank which found itself with some two dozen unrented safe deposit boxes. A fairly prominent advertisement in the local weekly newspaper for four successive weeks resulted in renting two boxes. The bank's cashier then called a meeting of the entire staff (some 15 people) and urged them to try to sell safe deposit boxes to their friends and neighbors. The remaining boxes were rented in a week!

This experience does not prove that advertising is relatively useless; it demonstrates, rather, that for specific purposes, direct personal contacts produce more spectacular results. In truth, advertising and direct solicitation go hand in hand. Effective advertising, over a period of time, will create the receptivity to banking services and to a particular bank which is required to make direct solicitation effective. Imaginative advertising causes the fruit of potential customer relationships to grow and ripen; some may fall to the ground of its own accord, but the best fruit requires individual picking.

Implicit in this illustration, also, is the principle that customer calls (whether the person called on is already a customer or only potentially one) are most useful if they are made with a specific purpose in mind. Purely social calls may build a certain amount of good will; on the other hand, they may backfire if the customer finds them to be a waste of *his* time as well as that of the bank representative.[5] The most effective call is one that is related to a specific offer of service. This principle cannot be overemphasized.

Calling on the bank's larger commercial customers (whether they are currently borrowing or not) should be a regular part of the lending officers' duties. The rendering of effective credit service re-

---

[5] Country bankers themselves have often complained about the purely "social" visits of some of the representatives of city correspondents. The solicitation of an account is *never* as effective as the offer of a service.

quires first-hand knowledge of the customer's operations and financial problems. Many banks require their officers to make a certain number of such calls each month and to render brief reports of these visits. In addition to providing the basis for a complete credit service to the customer, such calls will provide the bank with essential information about the borrowers' future credit needs and the probable ebb and flow of their deposit balances. They will also enable the calling officer to discuss some of the bank's other services such as time deposit facilities, trust services, in-plant banking, etc. In calling on potential customers (most of whom are already banking elsewhere) the offer of some new and valuable service is, obviously, an essential incentive.

In areas where industrial and commercial activity is expanding, the opportunity to visit first with the management of new enterprises is obviously a competitive advantage which alert bank managements avidly seek. They look to their correspondent banks for "leads" and to their directors for "inside knowledge" and make every effort to offer their services as soon as possible. Some banks make similar efforts with respect to new residents in the community. They may either join with other businesses in the community to use the services of professional solicitors [6] or use their own personnel to represent the bank in the community. The offer of a free book of checks, for example, to a new resident of the community is both a good reason for making the call and a potent inducement to opening a "convenience" checking account. A modest prize or premium, similarly offered, will often result in the transfer of savings balances from the customer's previous place of residence.

An elaboration upon the customer calling program is the new business "contest" which has become increasingly popular. In such contests points are assigned for various types of new accounts and valuable prizes offered to the employees who obtain the highest number of points within a stated time period. Such campaigns have been outstandingly successful not only in increasing business but in building employee enthusiasm and morale as well. Even without formal contests, it is important that all officers and employees of a bank be encouraged to, and rewarded for obtaining

---

[6] *E.g.,* "The Welcome Wagon," whose representatives offer gifts and introductory free services to new residents on behalf of a number of local merchants providing a wide variety of services.

new business at all times. In fact, such solicitation should start
with the directors themselves. Some banks divide the directorate
into teams to which "points" are awarded for new business obtained.
Competition, thus engendered, not only brings in new accounts but
supplies a lively source of conversation and interest at directors'
meetings. The losing team, of course, buys the dinner!

In short, if the bank's interest in the community has been demonstrated over the years by a policy of active participation and educational effort, and if its advertising has imaginatively portrayed the
value of the services it is prepared to render, the groundwork will
have been laid for an effective program of personal business solicitation. Such a program should use all the talents of everyone in the
bank from the directors themselves to the newest bookkeeper.

DIRECT CUSTOMER CONTACTS

The keystone to the arch of community relations and business
development is what the customer finds when he comes into the
bank. Is it *really* the warm and friendly place which the advertise-
ments have told about? Having actively advertised for mortgage
loans, what does the bank do with mortgage applications? [7] In the
long run community relations stand or fall across the tellers' windows and the platform officers' desks.

Banks have spent sizable sums in recent years to improve their
facilities and to make them more attractive. This is certainly the
first step in making the actual and potential customer feel welcome.
Drive-in facilities and adequate parking for his convenience; off-
hour and evening banking hours to suit his needs; the substitution
of low, accessible counters for the forbidding cages of yesteryear;
carpeted lobbies, attractively decorated; all are part of good community relations. They represent a substantial change from the
picture of towering and forbidding strength which banks sought to
create in the past to the modern banking image of friendliness and
community participation.

Even more than physical facilities, however, the human equation
plays the vital role at this direct point of contact between a bank

---

[7] One large bank hired professional "shoppers" to find the answer to this and
similar questions. What they learned led to an intensive educational program
and to the decision to "shop" its offices on a continuous basis.

and its public. This key fact makes a continuing program of customer-relations education imperative for bank officers and employees. Nor can bank management ever take for granted that its admonitions of politeness and patience will be uniformly followed. It must be ever alert to customer reactions and, in this regard, attitude surveys (a part of market research previously discussed) can play a valuable part. Without repeated checking on this vital phase of community relations, the directors will never know how much business the bank may have lost because of the manner in which a bank guard approached a stranger in the lobby, because of a teller's impatience or inattention, or because of a bank officer's unconscious but erroneous assumption that a shabbily-dressed or odd-appearing person could not possibly be a good potential customer. Customers switch from one bank to another most frequently not because another bank offers them better service, but because they feel they have been in some way slighted or neglected. It is such a slight, real or imagined, that usually brings to fruition the competitor's solicitation.

A special facet of direct customer relations lies in the art of loan declination. Competent lending officers who are acutely aware of the importance of community relations will spend twice as much time turning down a loan as in granting it. If the loan cannot be made bankable, he will attempt to suggest alternatives or patiently explain the reasons for the bank's decisions while trying to demonstrate that an unsound extension of credit often harms the borrower as much as the lender. In addition to being sound customer relations, such explanations represent an important phase of the bank's educational effort; instruction in sound credit principles. A surprisingly large number of customers thus treated will in time come to appreciate the bank's counselling.

SPECIAL GROUPS IN THE COMMUNITY

So far the discussion has been largely in terms of the community and bank customers in general. Actually, of course, the community is not a homogenous whole but is made up of a number of overlapping segments and special groups to which specific community relations activities should be directed. The approach to potential trust department customers will differ widely from a campaign to increase the bank's consumer credit outstandings. Specialized programs can be developed, for example, with respect to schools, ethnic groups, the savings market, the farm community, or the other groupings into which market research will indicate that the bank's trade area is roughly subdivided. The larger the bank, and the more extensive the markets it serves, the more numerous will be such groupings.[8]

A few of these groups deserve special comment because, even in the light of modern banking's acute awareness of its public relations obligations, these groups have received perhaps less attention than they deserve. Among them are the bank's own stockholders, the legislative representatives of the bank's trade area, and (strangely enough) the bank examiner and his "boss" the bank supervisor.

Relations with Stockholders

Stockholders in commercial banks have a direct financial interest in the success and growth of the institutions whose shares they own. They are partners in the business and, as previously noted, wide distribution of a bank's stock is, of itself, a foundation stone of good community relations. Banks which pride themselves on being truly community institutions will be constantly seeking ways to increase the number of their shareholders.

Despite his vital role as the supplier of capital, and in spite of his potential value as a representative of the bank in the community, the stockholder is too often neglected. He has sometimes been called the "forgotten man of banking" because so many banks still fail to inform stockholders adequately concerning the progress of their business. Annual reports to shareholders have improved noticeably in recent years but even in many large banks, as well as in the vast majority of small ones, the stockholder is still left in the dark regarding the true value of his shares and the amount earned thereon.

It is difficult to see why bank shareholders are not entitled to such information; yet bankers strongly (and successfully) opposed the

---

[8] Educational and promotional programs may be devised even for rather narrow groupings; *e.g.*, automobile dealers, accountants, teachers, association executives, etc. *Cf.*, Lindquist, *op. cit.*, pp. 87–88.

inclusion in the Financial Institutions Act of a provision which would have required the publication of bank earnings. Why bankers cling to this aura of secrecy is difficult to understand. It has been repeatedly demonstrated that informed shareholders are a powerful force in strengthening a bank's community relations. Those banks which publish their earnings in detail and have done so for many years suffer no ill consequences. On the contrary, they have found increased acceptance for their stock in the market at higher price levels and greater community support from a wider circle of informed shareholders.

Aside from adequate reporting, the most important contact with the stockholder is the annual meeting. Seldom, however, is the small stockholder directly encouraged to attend such meetings. Too often management faces the annual meeting with trepidation lest some unexpected stockholder show up to ask embarrassing questions. The few banks which have made a definite effort to broaden stockholder participation have been delighted with the results. But something more than a dry reading of the minutes and the election of directors is needed: a buffet lunch, a tour of the bank, a review of local economic conditions, a frank discussion of the bank's plans and prospects are examples. The possibilities of attracting stockholders to the annual meeting are legion and should be energetically explored. Interim reports to the shareholders and personal letters suggesting that they call the bank's services to the attention of their friends and business associates are also productive. No other group in the community is as interested in hearing about (and promoting) the bank's business as those who, collectively, own it.

RELATIONS WITH LEGISLATORS

Bankers, generally, have long considered themselves the forgotten men of politics. It is difficult to determine whether their attitude is one of "holier than thou" or simply abject defeatism. Over and over again bankers talk to each other about needed legislation or importune the bank supervisor to seek constructive changes in the law, but at the first suggestion that they approach their representatives in the legislature directly (or even write them a letter) they shy away as if the suggestion were somehow immoral. If banks are to play their rightful role as financial leaders in the community they have a duty to be at least on speaking terms with the political leaders of that same community. It is not that they should seek favored legislation, although at times bankers have received less than equal treatment from the lawmakers. It is, rather, that sound legislation in the long run benefits both the community and the bank, and the most constructive laws will be enacted only by legislators who have been adequately informed about the economic consequences of legislative proposals. Members of the Congress and of state legislatures have, themselves, complained that they seldom hear from bankers and have stated they would welcome closer contacts.

A bank's obligation to be in the educational forefront of its community where financial and economic matters are concerned has already been highlighted. Its educational efforts can hardly be better directed than to make its views and its sound supporting arguments known to those who pass the laws which will shape the directions and conditions of the community's economic growth. And this can best be done through personal acquaintanceship and face-to-face discussion.

RELATIONS WITH THE SUPERVISOR

Bank supervision in the United States has developed in response to our unique banking structure which is composed of thousands of banks many of which are still quite small. The bank examiner, originally something of a policeman, and still concerned with enforcing an elaborate set of banking laws, has become in recent years more like a family doctor. His primary concern is the healthy functioning of his bank "patients." His annual physical examination of bank assets and management policies is directed to helping banks function more effectively as well as safely in their respective communities.

Bank managements have become increasingly aware of the potential helpfulness of supervisory examinations. Many bank officers have learned to welcome the examiner and willingly subject themselves and their thinking to the challenge of his objective review and occasional criticism. They have gradually become aware of the fact that the examiner has no other interest than the soundness of the bank and its ability to serve the community needs safely and constructively. They look to him for that cross-fertilization of ideas which stimulates growth and innovation. They have all too seldom, however, introduced him to their directors.

When difficulties develop in a particular bank, the examiner or the bank supervisor calls a meeting of the directors. Such meetings are apt to be awkward and painful at best. The directors are generally on the defensive. Criticism by the examiner, though warranted, is seldom conducive to good understanding and good feeling. On the other hand, if the directors were to invite the examiner to meet with *them* to seek to learn from him all they can about sound banking practices and the trends which may be developing in the banking field, the atmosphere would be quite different. In a free and voluntary exchange of questions and answers, the examiner may be able to shed a good deal of light on the very problems of policy with which the directors have been struggling. To be most effective the initiative for such meetings must come from the directors themselves, or from management, rather than from the examiner and the supervisor.

In the absence of a formal meeting, the bank director who takes his position seriously should at least stop in and visit with the examiners when they are in his bank. It is a rare opportunity for the director to ask searching questions about banking policies and practices, to get the "feel" of what other banks are doing, and to obtain an objective viewpoint as to the adequacy of his own bank's practices. Too few directors avail themselves of this opportunity.

The value of closer relations with the bank supervisor will depend, of course, on the competence of the bank examiners and the supervisory organizations which they represent. This, too, is a matter with which banks and bank directors should concern themselves. Banks have a great deal to gain from effective and enlightened supervision. Bankers themselves, therefore, should insist, as a matter of public policy, that bank examining staffs be maintained at a high level of competence.

THE ROLE OF THE
DIRECTOR IN COMMUNITY RELATIONS

The role of the bank director in shaping and guiding his bank's community relations is one of the most vital roles he plays. In a sense the directors represent the community as well as the stockholders. In the long run the interests of the stockholders and those of the community are identical because a bank will prosper only if its community thrives. In establishing policy in the area of public relations the director is, in effect, setting the long-range objectives of the bank, determining what kind of a bank he wants it to be, and how full a part it should play in community life.

As in other banking activities, the execution of policy should be left to the active management, but the broad objectives of the bank's community relations program should be stated by the board. A special committee of the board may well be charged with the responsibility of seeing that the established policy is competently carried out and that it is adequate to the needs of the community. The day-to-day decisions, however, the decisions as to specific programs and the nature of advertising copy, should be left to duly designated and competent officers. In large banks the public relations program is generally the responsibility of specially designated officers versed in the best and latest techniques. In smaller banks, where community relations is not a full-time job, some authorities point out the advantage of combining the responsibility for community relations with that for personnel management, since employee training and employee attitudes with respect to customer contacts are such a vital part of community relations.[9]

Furthermore, the directors directly and personally represent the bank in the community. They can, and should seek business for the bank. Their participation in the life of the community, as well as the effectiveness of their over-all direction, will determine the esteem in which the bank is held. And, finally, directors are in a position to be alert to community opinion concerning the bank, its services, and the attitudes of its employees. Directors should be ever on the alert to get to the root of legitimate community complaints.

To serve as a bank director is a challenge as well as a unique opportunity to serve the welfare of the community. No other duty of bank directors is more important than insisting that their banks know and serve community needs to the fullest possible extent consistent with the ultimate safety of their deposits.

---

[9] *Cf.*, Lindquist, *op. cit.*, p. 21.

SELECTED BIBLIOGRAPHY

GENERAL

Kennedy, Walter, *Bank Management*. Boston: Bankers Publishing Company, 1958. A practical handbook of management techniques written by a successful bank president.

Robinson, Roland I., *The Management of Bank Funds*. New York: McGraw-Hill Book Company, Inc., 1962. A standard work on bank lending and investing policies recently extensively revised and brought up to date.

Bank Management. New York: The American Bankers Association, American Institute of Banking Section, 1960. A textbook on bank management principles and practices written for aspiring managers from the viewpoint of the responsibilities of executive management and their relation to the fundamental banking functions.

BANKING STRUCTURE

Butt, Paul D., *Branch Banking and Economic Growth in Arizona and New Mexico*. Albuquerque: University of New Mexico, Bureau of Business Research, New Mexico Studies in Business and Economics No. 7, 1960. A comparison of economic growth in Arizona where banking is highly concentrated in statewide branch banking systems with that of New Mexico where only very limited branch banking is permitted.

Fischer, Gerald C., *Bank Holding Companies*. New York: Columbia University Press, 1961. A history of group banking and of the legislation which governs it together with an evaluation of the role which holding companies can play in the banking structure.

Nadler, Marcus, *The Banking Situation in New York State*. New York: New York State Bankers Association, 1956. A comprehensive analysis of banking problems in New York State with particular emphasis on the impact of structural changes on the scope and efficacy of banking services.

Nadler, Marcus and Jules I. Bogen, *The Bank Holding Company*. New York: New York University, Graduate School of Business Administration, 1959. A study of how bank holding companies operate and an evaluation of their service to the public.

Schweiger, Irving and John S. McGee, *Chicago Banking*. Chicago:

University of Chicago, Graduate School of Business, 1961. A comparison of unit banks with branch institutions in Illinois and elsewhere from the viewpoint of their service to the public.

STRUCTURE OF A BANK

Drucker, Peter F., *The Practice of Management.* New York: Harper and Brothers, Publishers, 1954. A dynamic statement of management concepts and practices.

McDavitt, Clarence G., Jr. *If You're a Bank Director.* Cambridge, Mass.: Bankers Publishing Company, 1950. A witty commentary on the duties and responsibilities of bank directors.

Newman, William H., *Administrative Action.* Englewood Cliffs, N. J.: Prentice-Hall, Inc., 1951. A comprehensive analysis of the techniques of organization and management in general; basic theory that has wide application in banking.

Duties and Liabilities of Directors of National Banks. Washington, D. C.: Office of the Comptroller of the Currency, Treasury Department, Form 1417 (Revised), 1956. An authoritative statement emphasizing the legal responsibilities and potential liability of bank directors.

EARNINGS AND COST CONTROL

Bogen, Jules I., *The Adequacy of Bank Earnings.* New York: New York University Graduate School of Business Administration, 1957. An analysis of the record of bank earnings and the factors which contribute to them.

Bank Cost Accounting Principles and Procedures. New York: The New York Clearing House Association, 1961. Principles and practice of cost accounting developed by a committee of the controllers of New York City banks but which has wide general application.

Bank Costs. Chicago: National Association of Bank Auditors and Controllers, 1951. The basic handbook of bank cost accounting.

AUDIT AND CONTROL

Corns, Marshall C., *Bank Auditing.* Cambridge, Mass.: Bankers Publishing Company, 1955. A comprehensive study of the principles and procedures of bank control and audit.

Rankin, Russell G., *Safeguarding the Bank's Assets.* New York: The New York State Bankers Association, 1953. A simplified handbook of audit procedures written especially for the directors' examining committee and the accountant new to bank auditing.

Audit Program for the Smaller Bank. Chicago: National Association of Bank Auditors and Controllers, 1951. The minimum audit program with which directors of small and medium-sized banks should be familiar.

Direct Verification for Smaller Banks. New York: The American Bankers Association, 1961. Describes the techniques involved in this essential audit procedure too infrequently followed in smaller banks.

LIQUIDITY

Gurley, John G., *Liquidity and Financial Institutions in the Post-War Period.* Washington, D. C.: Joint Economic Committee Study Paper No. 14, 86th Congress, 1st Session. A study of the growth in the volume of liquidity instruments or near-money in the financial system.

Roosa, Robert V., *Federal Reserve Operations in the Money and Securities Market.* New York: Federal Reserve Bank of New York, 1956. Includes an easy-to-understand description of the liquidity instruments used by commercial banks and the market in which they are traded.

The Problems of Commercial Bank Liquidity. New York: The American Bankers Association, Economic Policy Commission, 1957. A complete, but concise statement of the principles and considerations involved in maintaining adequate liquidity in the individual bank.

A Report of the Committee on Asset Allocation. New York: The New York State Bankers Association, 1960. A discussion of the techniques for measuring liquidity needs closely related to the method outlined in this book.

CAPITAL ADEQUACY

Freeman, Gaylord A., *The Problem of Adequate Bank Capital.* Chicago: The First National Bank of Chicago, Analysis Prepared for the Illinois Bankers Association, 1952. One of the first post-war attempts to grapple comprehensibly with the resurgent problem of capital adequacy for commercial banks.

The Adequacy of a Bank's Capital. New York: The American Bankers Association, Research Council, 1954. A statement of principles based on the belief that the responsibility for determining the adequacy of capital rests with bank management. This booklet contains a check list of the questions management should ask and answer to determine its individual capital needs.

Lending Policies and Practices

Beckhart, Benjamin Haggott, ed., *Business Loans of American Commercial Banks*. New York: The Ronald Press Company, 1959. A comprehensive survey of the many aspects of business lending policies and practices.

Chapin, Albert F. and George E. Hassett, Jr., *Credit and Collections Principles and Practice*, Seventh edition. New York: McGraw-Hill Book Company, Inc., 1960. A comprehensive textbook on credit principles and credit instruments.

Ettinger, Richard P. and David E. Golieb, *Credits and Collections*, Fourth edition. Englewood Cliffs, N. J.: Prentice-Hall, Inc., 1956. A comprehensive handbook for the credit analyst and lending officer on the principles and practices of credit extension.

Investment Policies

Freund, Irving and Murray G. Lee, *Investment Fundamentals*. New York: The American Bankers Association, Council on Banking Education. A basic primer for the student of bank investments which defines the terms and details the procedures followed by commercial banks in dealing for their own accounts and advising their customers.

Lyon, Roger A., *Investment Portfolio Management in the Commercial Bank*. New Brunswick, N. J.: Rutgers University Press, 1960. A comprehensive study of bank investment policies including the related problems of liquidity and capital adequacy.

Nadler, Marcus, Sipa Heller and Samuel S. Shipman, *The Money Market and Its Institutions*. New York: The Ronald Press, 1955. Basic knowledge of the money and securities markets, their structure, instruments and operations.

Sauvain, Harry, *Investment Management*, Second edition. Englewood Cliffs, N. J.: Prentice-Hall, Inc., 1959. A basic study of investment principles and their relationship to varying investment purposes.

Personnel Policies

Dubin, Robert, *Human Relations in Administration*, Second edition. New York: Prentice-Hall, Inc., 1961. Management organization studied from the viewpoint of the people involved therein.

Executive Development in Banking. New York: The American Bankers Association, 1955. A practical discussion of field-tested techniques in this all-important area of bank management.

How to Set Up a Salary Program in the Smaller Bank. New York: The American Bankers Association, Country Bank Operations Committee, 1950. A well conceived plan for a simplified job-evaluation and salary progression program in the small bank.

COMMUNITY RELATIONS

Lindquist, Robert, *The Bank and Its Publics.* New York: Harper and Brothers, 1956. A thorough discussion of the principles and practice of public relations, advertising, and sales promotion in the commercial bank.

Customer Analysis. New York: The American Bankers Association, Country Bank Operations Committee and Research Committee, 1961. The first of a planned series of booklets on how to conduct a market research program in banks of moderate size. This first booklet concentrates on the information that is available in a bank's files and its significance for business expansion.

INDEX